Praise for

Teaching Students with Dyslexia and Dysgraphia

"An extraordinarily valuable resource that fills a critical void in our ability to successfully address reading difficulties and dysgraphia ... a must-read for researchers and practitioners!"

—**G. Reid Lyon, Ph.D.**
Distinguished Professor
Southern Methodist University

"A gift to both teachers and the children they teach. Berninger and Wolf bring the latest scientific information on dyslexia and dysgraphia right into the classroom."

—**Sally E. Shaywitz, M.D.**
The Audrey G. Ratner Professor in Learning Development
Co-Director, Yale Center for Dyslexia & Creativity
Author, *Overcoming Dyslexia*

"An invaluable resource ... required reading for anyone interested in making students in elementary schools lifelong learners."

—**R. Malatesha Joshi, Ph.D.**
Editor, *Reading and Writing*
Professor, Texas A & M University

"Written as a dialogue between a gifted teacher and an accomplished researcher, this book juxtaposes two perspectives that enrich one another. It offers an unusually detailed rationale and description of multimodal language instruction within an intellectually engaging curriculum."

—**Louisa Moats, Ed.D.**
Sopris West Educational Services

"Scholarly and practical ... I intend to make the book required reading for our staff of teachers, psychologists, and researchers."

—**Jeffrey L. Black, M.D.**
Medical Director
Luke Waites Center for Dyslexia and Learning Disorders
Texas Scottish Rite Hospital for Children

Teaching Students with Dyslexia and Dysgraphia

Teaching Students with Dyslexia and Dysgraphia

Lessons from Teaching and Science

Virginia W. Berninger, Ph.D.

University of Washington
Seattle

and

Beverly Wolf, M.Ed.

Slingerland Institute for Literacy
Bellevue, Washington

·PAUL·H·
BROOKES
PUBLISHING C^o.®

Baltimore • London • Sydney

Paul H. Brookes Publishing Co.
Post Office Box 10624
Baltimore, Maryland 21285-0624
USA

www.brookespublishing.com

Typeset by Integrated Publishing Solutions, Grand Rapids, Michigan.
Manufactured in the United States of America by Sheridan Books, Inc.,
Chelsea, Michigan.

The individuals described in this book are composites or real people
whose situations are masked and are based on the authors' experiences.
In all instances, names and identifying details have been changed to protect
confidentiality.

Library of Congress Cataloging-in-Publication Data

Berninger, Virginia Wise.
  Teaching students with dyslexia and dysgraphia : lessons from teaching and science /
  Virginia W. Berninger, Beverly Wolf.
      p.   cm.
  Includes bibliographical references and index.
  ISBN-13: 978-1-55766-934-6 (pbk.)
  ISBN-10: 1-55766-934-1
  1. Dyslexic children—Education.   2. Language arts—Remedial teaching.   3. Dyslexia.
  4. Agraphia.   I. Wolf, Beverly, M.Ed.   II. Title.
  LC4708.B47   2009
  371.91'44–dc22   2009004896

British Library Cataloguing in Publication data are available from the British Library.

2013   2012   2011   2010   2009

10   9   8   7   6   5   4   3   2   1

Contents

About the Authors ix
Introduction x
Acknowledgments xiv

I Beginnings: From the Past to the Present

1 Historical and Contemporary Contexts 3

**II Classroom Environment: What Works in Teaching Students
with Dyslexia, OWL LD, or Dysgraphia?**

2 Organizational Issues and Instructional Approaches 15
   Appendix   Information for Obtaining Instructional Programs
Listed in Table 2.1 29

3 Teaching Oral Language. 31
   Appendix A   Questions of the Day. 44
   Appendix B   Children's Books that Help with Language
Learning 46

4 Teaching Reading 49
   Appendix A   Concept Words that Reinforce Comprehension 75
   Appendix B   Small, Important Words that May Require
Special Instruction. 76

5 Teaching Writing 79

6 Teaching Across the Language Systems with Intellectual
Engagement 105

III Blending Science and Educational Practice

7 Contributions from Science Disciplines 115

8 Contributions from Clinical Disciplines 127

9 Contributions from Instructional Disciplines 141

10 Creating Building-Level Plans for Teaching All Students
Effectively and Efficiently 159

IV Professional Development for Blending Science and Educational Practice

11 Preservice Teacher Education 173
    Appendix   Recommended Readings and/or Instructional
    Resources for Supervised Practica for Preservice Teacher
    Education 178

12 In-Service Teacher Education and Models for Teacher
    Mentoring. 181
    Appendix   Representative Syllabi for Professional
    Development of Educators. 191

V Commencement: From Book Endings to New Beginnings in Teaching Students with Dyslexia, OWL LD, and Dysgraphia

13 Commencement: From Book Endings to New Beginnings. 201

References 215

Index 233

About the Authors

Virginia W. Berninger, Ph.D., Professor and Director, Multidisciplinary Learning Disabilities Center, University of Washington, 322 Miller Box 363600, Seattle, WA 98195

Virginia Berninger is a professor in the Educational Psychology Department at the University of Washington. She has been director and principal investigator of the The Eunice Kennedy Shriver National Institute of Child Health and Human Development (NICHD)-funded Literacy Trek and Multidisciplinary Learning Disabilities Center at the university. A former general and special educator and reading specialist, Dr. Berninger is also a licensed clinical psychologist. Dr. Berninger's research focuses on nature–nurture interactions in learning to read and write. She studies the phenotypes of the functional reading and writing systems and related aural/oral language and nonlanguage processes in children with dyslexia, dysgraphia, or language learning disability and in typically developing readers and writers. With a team of brain imagers, Berninger also studies related brain processes and how they change as a result of specific instructional treatments.

Beverly J. Wolf, M.Ed., Director, Slingerland Institute for Literacy, One Bellevue Center, 411 108th Avenue N.E., Bellevue, WA 98004

Beverly Wolf is a trainer of teachers and President of the Board of Directors of the Slingerland Institute for Literacy in Washington State. She has worked with children and adults with language learning disabilities for more than 30 years in her positions as Dean of Faculty at the Slingerland Institute and Director Emeritus of the Hamlin Robinson School for Dyslexics, and through contributions to local and national organizations. She has served on both local and national boards of The International Dyslexia Association and is also an author of independent activity and language materials for classroom use.

Introduction

Definitions of Dyslexia, OWL LD, and Dysgraphia

Developmental disorders affecting written language acquisition are considered specific kinds of learning disabilities and may affect 10%–15% of students. *Dyslexia* is a word of Greek origin. *Dys* is a prefix that means "impaired." *Lexia* is a base word that is derived from the word *lexicon* (the mental dictionary of word meanings, spellings, and pronunciations) and means "word." Thus, students with dyslexia are impaired in word-level skills such as decoding, word reading, and spelling. Both accuracy and rate may be impaired, or only rate.

Decoding problems are usually assessed by asking children to read pseudo-words (i.e., pronounceable words that do not have conventional meaning but sound like English words, such as in the "Jabberwocky" poem in *Alice in Wonderland*). Word reading problems may be assessed by asking a child to pronounce real words that do have meaning on a list without context clues or in a passage with context clues. Some children do better when context clues are available.

Dyslexia is not just a reading problem. Invariably, students with dyslexia also have problems spelling (Berninger, Nielsen, Abbott, Wijsman, & Raskind, 2008). However, except for impaired phonological awareness interfering with learning to decode, read, and spell words, their oral language listening comprehension and verbal reasoning are spared. Once children with dyslexia learn to recognize words at a grade-appropriate level, their reading comprehension tends to be grade-appropriate (Berninger, 2000).

Some children, however, do have significant oral language problems, including listening comprehension and reading comprehension problems, in addition to the word decoding, word reading, and spelling problems that affect their learning to read and write. These children have oral and written language learning disability (OWL LD) rather than dyslexia per se. Chapter 4 provides more information about the nature of these oral language problems (e.g., phonological awareness as well as other aspects of oral language).

Dysgraphia is also of Greek origin. As noted previously, *dys* is a prefix that means "impaired." *Graphia* is a base word that means "letter form," "hand," or "making letter forms by hand." Students with dysgraphia, therefore, are impaired in letter writing skills. Their handwriting may be impaired in 1) legibility—how easily others can recognize their letters out of word context, 2) automaticity—how many legible letters they can write in 15 seconds, and 3) speed—how much time it takes them to complete a writing task. Students with handwriting disabilities may also have more difficulty in learning to spell written words. In one form of dysgraphia, which does not occur as often as typical dysgraphia, the child's handwriting is adequate, but written spelling problems occur in the absence of reading problems. Fayol, Zorman, and Lété (in press) showed that about 4% of French-speaking children have significant spelling problems despite their being able to read at developmentally appropriate levels. Some English-speaking children also have spelling problems but adequate handwriting and reading skills.

Students with dyslexia or OWL LD always have spelling problems but may also have dysgraphia. The learning problems resulting from dyslexia, OWL LD, and/or dysgraphia are not related to lack of cognitive or thinking ability, which is always at least in the normal range.

Even though students with dyslexia, OWL LD, and/or dysgraphia have a biologically based disorder with a genetic and brain basis, research has shown that they do respond to reading and writing instruction tailored to their learning profiles (e.g., Berninger, 2000; Berninger, Winn, et al., 2008).

It is important to remember that not all reading and writing problems are the result of dyslexia, OWL LD, and/or dysgraphia. Other disorders also cause reading and writing problems. Cognitive or thinking ability may not be within the normal range in these disorders. Some children fall outside the normal range in all areas of development (i.e., cognitive, language, motor, attention and executive function, and social emotional) or in one or more of these areas of development; or they have a neurogenetic developmental disorder (e.g., fragile X) or a brain disease or injury that affects their learning of written language. These children also are likely to have reading and writing problems—but the biological bases for their written language problems are different from those of children with dyslexia, OWL LD, and/or dysgraphia. The nature of effective instruction may also be different. Although all students may respond to some of the same reading and writing instructional components, overall instructional programs may need to be tailored for students with specific kinds of developmental or learning disorders other than the three specific learning disabilities discussed in the current book. Also, children with even more severe developmental disabilities or neurogenetic disorders, whose thinking ability falls outside the normal range, cannot be expected to reach the same levels of reading and writing achievement that children with dyslexia, OWL LD, and/or dysgraphia might reach in response to instructional intervention.

Teachers should be able to refer all students with significant and persisting reading and writing problems, many of whom are from families with a history of significant reading and writing problems (Berninger, Abbott, Thomson, & Raskind, 2001; Pennington & Lefly, 2001), to the multidisciplinary team in the school for comprehensive assessment to make an accurate diagnosis of the nature of the reading or writing problem and design an appropriate individualized education program (IEP). This book will focus only on teaching students with dyslexia, OWL LD, and/or dysgraphia whose cognitive ability is within the normal range.

An appropriate IEP for students with dyslexia, OWL LD, and/or dysgraphia can often be implemented in the general education program using the instructional approaches described in this book and the accompanying book, *Helping Students with Dyslexia and Dysgraphia Make Connections: Differentiated Instruction Lesson Plans in Reading and Writing,* also coauthored by Berninger and Wolf (2009). Many students may need differentiated instruction to meet their individual learning needs. Both authors have had experience in differentiated instruction and offer many practical suggestions for adapting the nature of reading and writing instruction to individual differences in learners—and organizing the learning environment to do so. On the one hand, all children may benefit from common components of literacy instruction. As a former Washington State governor, Dan Evans, remarked, in response to a presentation in April 2000 by the first author at the Science and Technology Roundtable, Ranier Club, Seattle, WA, about effective instruction for students with dyslexia, "that kind of instruction should be beneficial for all students—not just those with reading disabilities!" On the other hand, when students at the same grade level are at different stages of reading and writing development, instruction does have to be adapted in some ways to meet all students' instructional needs, including reasonable challenges and sufficient success in daily learning. General educational teachers can organize the learning environment to meet those needs for all students in the classroom through differentiated instruction that is explained in this book.

OVERVIEW OF THE BOOK

Section I, which includes Chapter 1, provides an overview of the historical and contemporary contexts for a book on teaching students with dyslexia, OWL LD, and/or dysgraphia in general education. Although federal legislation recognizes the need for appropriate education for students with learning disabilities and requires special eligibility procedures for qualifying students for special education, the federal legislation does not deal adequately with how to apply research-supported definitions for students with dyslexia, OWL LD, or dysgraphia of specific learning disabilities to diagnosis and instruction provided in the general education program, often referred to as "mainstream."

Section II focuses on what works in teaching students with dyslexia and related disorders to read and write in terms of feasible, effective practices in the classroom. As explained in the Preface, a unique aspect of this book is including the contributions of two professions—teachers and researchers. Chapters 2 through 6 present teacher contributions followed by researcher contributions to introduce general education teachers, as well as special education and other support teachers, to the following: 1) organizational issues in differentiated instruction to address individual instructional needs (Chapter 2); 2) effective oral language instruction for learning written language (Chapter 3); 3) effective reading instruction (Chapter 4); 4) effective writing instruction (Chapter 5); and 5) instruction geared to all language systems (listening, speaking, reading, and writing), language learning across the curriculum, and intellectual engagement (Chapter 6). Both the teacher, based on successful experience in teaching students with dyslexia and/or dysgraphia to read and write, and the researcher, based on scientific studies, reach similar conclusions.

Section III, in contrast, first provides the contributions of researchers to increasing scientific knowledge of the biological causes of, behavioral indicators of, and effective treatment for specific reading and writing disabilities and then presents the contributions of a teacher who has kept up to date with new research developments in applying research to practice for children with oral and written language learning disabilities. Chapter 7 synthesizes basic research findings from genetics, neuroscience, cognitive science, and linguistics that are relevant to understanding the nature of dyslexia, OWL LD, and dysgraphia and differential diagnosis of these specific disabilities in written language acquisition. (See http://www.brookespublishing .com/Berninger for links to functional MRI images in color.) Chapter 8 reviews research relevant to instructional treatment for these written language disabilities. Chapter 9 introduces a theoretical framework called "grammar of teaching," which guides teachers in adapting their conceptual frameworks for learning and instruction to teach ALL students effectively. This theory of teaching reading and writing is illustrated with references to the accompanying book, *Helping Students with Dyslexia and Dysgraphia Make Connections: Differentiated Instruction Lesson Plans in Reading and Writing* (Berninger & Wolf, 2009). Chapter 10 discusses alternative building-level plans for teaching students with specific written language disabilities within and across grade levels.

Section IV covers professional development issues for practitioners who desire to base their educational practice on science. Chapter 11 focuses on science-based preservice teacher education and features the interdisciplinary Ph.D. program in literacy at Middle Tennessee State University. This program prepares future university professionals to train preservice teachers in science-based practices in literacy instruction for students in general education and for those with dyslexia. Chapter 12 focuses on science-based in-service professional development and showcases Tennessee's innovative, state-funded model for in-service education of teachers of students with dyslexia in hopes that it serves as an inspiration for other states to follow suit. This program provides assessment and treatment services for students throughout the state and also offers workshop and professional development services for practitioners in the schools.

Section V, which includes Chapter 13, summarizes all of the main points in Chapters 1–12 and highlights principles that general educators should keep in mind in applying evidence-based practices to teaching students with dyslexia, OWL LD, and/or dysgraphia. These general principles are illustrated in the lesson sets in the accompanying book, *Helping Students with Dyslexia and Dysgraphia Make Connections: Differentiated Instruction Lesson Plans in Reading and Writing* (Berninger & Wolf, 2009).

REFERENCES

Berninger, V.W. (2000). Dyslexia an invisible, treatable disorder: The story of Einstein's ninja turtles. *Learning Disability Quarterly, 23,* 175–195.

Berninger, V.W., Abbott, R., Thomson, J., & Raskind, W. (2001). Language phenotype for reading and writing disability: A family approach. *Scientific Studies in Reading, 5,* 59–105.

Berninger, V.W., Nielsen, K., Abbott, R., Wijsman, E., & Raskind, W. (2008). Gender differences in severity of writing and reading disabilities. *Journal of School Psychology, 46,* 151–172.

Berninger, V.W., Winn, W., Stock, P., Abbott, R., Eschen, K., Lin, C., et al. (2008). Tier 3 specialized writing instruction for students with dyslexia. *Reading and Writing: An Interdisciplinary Journal, 21,* 95–129.

Berninger, V.W., & Wolf, B. (2009). *Helping students with dyslexia and dysgraphia make connections: Differentiated instruction lesson plans in reading and writing.* Baltimore: Paul H. Brookes Publishing Co.

Fayol, M., Zorman, M., & Lété, B. (in press). Associations and dissociations in reading and spelling French: Unexpectedly poor and good spellers. *British Journal of Educational Psychology Monograph.*

Pennington, B., & Lefly, D. (2001). Early reading development in children at family risk for dyslexia. *Child Development, 72,* 816–833.

Acknowledgments

In writing this book we acknowledge the many who have worked diligently before us to assess and teach children who struggle in reading and writing and to conduct research to understand why and how to help them learn to read and write. We also acknowledge the many and varied contributions of our contemporaries and pay tribute to the many who will follow as they continue the efforts to optimize the learning outcomes for students whose development is typical except for specific aspects of their reading and writing acquisition and related processes. We also acknowledge the many families with multigenerational histories of affected individuals who struggle with reading and writing and often with related oral language skills. These families—children, adolescents, and adults—as well as siblings, parents, grandparents, great-grandparents, aunts, uncles—have also contributed to the efforts through their participation in the genetic, brain imaging, assessment (phenotyping), and instructional treatment studies.

This book would not have been conceived or birthed without the able staff of Paul H. Brookes Publishing Co. Jessica Allan, former Acquisitions Editor, invited the first author to write a book on the applications of her research for educational practice. She agreed only if a teacher leader was involved because she is deeply committed to the perspective that effective instructional practices are based on two kinds of knowledge—that generated by master teachers from successful experience in teaching students to achieve in academic domains and that validated in research (proof of a concept). The second author has contributed many ideas for teaching oral as well as written language based on practical experience that are consistent with research validation of the concept. When Jessica left Brookes Publishing, Acquisitions Editor Sarah Shepke provided the highly capable editorial contributions that enabled the authors to bring the book to fruition. It was her idea to transform the original single book into a set of two related books, with one including the four sets of lesson plans validated in research at the University of Washington. She was assisted by the sustained and valuable contributions of Production Editor Janet Krejci. Thanks also go to Amanda Donaldson, Acquisitions Assistant.

In addition, each of the authors offers personal acknowledgments to their family members who learned to read by engaging in reading with an experienced reader (the "lap method") and well as those who required and benefited from a knowledgeable teacher's explicit reading instruction.

Virginia Berninger thanks the professor who welcomed a curious psychology undergraduate student into her classes in teaching reading and related language arts in general education classrooms; the Masonic Children's Home in Elizabethtown, Pennsylvania, which facilitated tutoring a boy with dyslexia for her undergraduate honors project in psychology; and the psychology of reading program at Temple University where she took courses in how to "assess for reading instruction" students with reading problems including but not restricted to dyslexia. These early experiences in how to assess and teach both students who show typical variation in reading and those who show atypical variation provided a unique perspective from which to approach both the general and special education teaching experience and the training in experimental psychology (developmental psycholinguistics, cognitive, and neuropsychology) and clinical psychology (applied developmental and learning disabilities) that followed. Throughout the many years her instructional, assessment, and research has been in progress, she has been sustained by the support of her husband, Dr. Ronald Berninger, and her family of origin including her brother, Dr. Douglas Wise.

She thanks project officers at National Institutes of Health, including David Gray, Ph.D., who was instrumental in her initial funding for research on writing; G. Reid Lyon, Ph.D., who facilitated continued funding for that research and the multidisciplinary learning disabilities center from 1995 to 2006; and Brett Miller, Ph.D., who facilitated the completion of the writing research aims from 1989 to 2008 and the continued genetics research.

She also acknowledges the contributions of Wendy Raskind, M.D., Ph.D., who heads the family genetics research; Ellen Wijsman, Ph.D., who encouraged the identification of behavioral markers (phenotypes) associated with the variation in expression of written language disorders; Todd Richards, Ph.D., who heads the brain imaging research; neuroscientists Christiana Leonard, Ph.D., and Mark Eckert, Ph.D., whose collaborations helped develop a unifying theoretical framework based on structural, chemical, functional magnetic resonance imaging regional activation and temporal connectivity imaging, family genetics, and behavioral assessment and intervention for diagnosing and treating specific learning disabilities; and Robert Abbott, Ph.D., the statistician who has contributed data analysis expertise since 1990. Many colleagues at other universities also provided valuable contributions to the research, including but not restricted to H. Lee Swanson, Stephen Hooper, Richard L. Venezky, William Nagy, Joanne Carlisle, Richard Wagner, Mary Anne Wolf, Michel Fayol, and Dick Hayes. In addition to many graduate students at the University of Washington, many schools and educational professionals in the community contributed to the research efforts. Psychological Corporation (now Pearson Assessment) personnel were instrumental in translating assessment and intervention procedures validated in concept in our research into tests and lesson plans for practitioners to apply to practice.

Beverly Wolf thanks the early pioneers, such as Samuel T. Orton and Anna Gillingham, in the field of language disability and learning disability and past and contemporary leaders of the International Dyslexia Association who have carried the word of this debilitating disorder across the world. She also acknowledges the efforts of families with affected individuals who have wandered through the mysterious world of learning to read and write. Their support of us and our work with persons with dyslexia and related language disorders made this book possible. Among the many individuals who have locally strengthened our understanding of ways to identify and provide help for those with oral and written language needs are Linda Azure, speech-language practitioner extraordinaire; Bonnie Meyer; Jan Gill; Nan Lynes; Dian Burrows; and others locally and nationally who have connected creative teaching to structured language instruction.

Bev would like to give special thanks to her mentors, Eldra O'Neal, Regina Cicci, and Beth Slingerland. Their knowledge, support, and guidance provided the schooling in how to listen to what students' performance tells us about their difficulties and how to teach each individual child even in a group. She is also grateful for the ongoing support and appreciation of her efforts by her husband, children, and extended family.

In Native American culture, the lowest person on the totem pole is the one who is most important because that person is closest to the ground, where the action is.

We dedicate this book to classroom teachers who, because they are closest to the ground—that is, the day-to-day instructional and learning environment of children with learning disabilities—are the most important for bringing about change to improve the instructional environments and learning outcomes for these students. The world is changed not only from the top down but also from the bottom up.

Beginnings: From the Past to the Present

If ye don't know the past, then
ye will not have a future. If ye don't
know where your people have been, then
ye won't know where your people are going.

The Education of Little Tree (Carter, 1990, p. 40)

CHAPTER 1

Historical and Contemporary Contexts

Written symbol systems for representing visible speech have existed for more than 5,000 years and have been used for many purposes ranging from sacred religious texts to everyday business transactions. Only recently in the history of human civilization, however, did societies attempt to teach all of their citizens to read and write and in the process discover that some struggle more than others in learning written language.

In the late 19th and early 20th centuries, two emerging fields—psychology and neurology—provided clues as to why some children struggle to acquire literacy. Psychologists used the experimental method to identify the mental processes involved in reading (e.g., Huey, 1968), and neurologists learned about brain function and behavior by observing individuals who had lost a language function before death and performing autopsies on their brain after death or by observing children who struggled in acquiring a function.

Together, psychologists and neurologists introduced the idea that individual differences in the mind or brain might make it difficult for some students to learn from reading and writing instruction that is adequate for most students. Many professionals now recognize that reading and writing disabilities are educational problems that are treatable even though they have biological bases. However, because most children with specific learning disabilities respond to developmentally appropriate reading and writing instruction, others still question whether these disorders really have a biological basis.

In this book, we take the perspective of nature–nurture interactions and explain how learning disorders can be biologically based and how individuals with such disorders can still respond to appropriate instruction. We also explain why the biological basis should not be minimized because of its possible influences across the life span. (For further discussion of these issues, see Berninger & Richards, 2002.)

THE EARLY YEARS

In this section of the chapter we discuss the pioneering contributions from both the medical and educational professionals to understanding and teaching children with dyslexia and specific language disorder. Their early contributions continue to influence the field today.

Contributions from Medical Professionals

Groundwork for studies in oral language disorders began in the 19th century when Paul Broca, a French surgeon and neuroanatomist, examined the brain of an individual who lost the power of speech with apparently no other impairments. When the individual died, an autopsy showed that a lesion in the left side of the brain was the cause of that speech disability—this section of the brain is now named *Broca's area* in his honor. At the time, Broca assumed that the area of the brain that controlled speech output was located on the left side in the front of the brain and that injury to that area caused expressive aphasia; however, contemporary research has shown that this region is involved in more than speech and may indeed house the executive functions for all language systems—listening, speaking, reading, and writing (see Chapter 7). Following Broca's research, German neurologist Paul Wernicke studied an individual who could speak but who had lost the ability to understand oral language. During the autopsy, Wernicke found a lesion in the left side of the brain near the back, which is now understood to be the area of the brain that controls language comprehension—this section of the brain is now named *Wernicke's area* in his honor. Contemporary brain imaging research has found structural and functional differences between typical readers and writers and individuals with dyslexia in both of these regions (see Berninger & Richards, 2002).

Modern understanding of learning disabilities such as dyslexia began at the end of the 19th century. The first report of "word blindness" in a child came from W. Pringle Morgan, an English doctor. In an 1896 article in the *British Medical Journal*, Morgan described a bright student who knew his letters but was unable to read and spelled bizarrely: "His visual memory for words is defective or absent, which is the equivalent of saying that he is what Kussmaul has termed 'word blind'" (Morgan, 1896; Henry, 1999, p. 10). Morgan believed that the problem was congenital because the student's father had similar problems and had learned to read with great difficulty.

In 1917, James Hinshelwood, a Scottish ophthalmologist, summarized 13 cases of word blindness and concluded that it was not as rare as once thought. He pointed out how symptoms of word blindness were similar to those of adults with brain injuries who lost the ability to read. He was the first to advocate a specific mode of instruction for children with written language disorders who were unable to learn to read by sight alone: an alphabetic method that involved "as many cerebral centers as possible" (Richardson, 1989, p. 8).

In 1925, Samuel T. Orton, an American psychiatrist and neuropathologist, began to expand the early work on dyslexia. As chair of the University of Iowa's Department of Psychiatry, he created the Mobile Mental Hygiene Clinic to provide multidisciplinary services to communities in rural Greene County, Iowa. He studied a 16-year-old boy who could not learn to read even though he seemed bright. Orton discovered a number of other students with similar difficulties and was impressed by the "serious effect upon the personality development of children with this unrecognized and untreated handicap" (1937/1989, p. xvi). Based on clinical observation, Orton noted five different kinds of learning disorders:

1. Developmental alexia (without word reading) or word blindness—the inability to read in a way consistent with mental age or other academic skills that was not due to visual disturbance in seeing or copying letters or words

2. Developmental word deafness—the inability to identify sounds correctly and understand spoken language despite adequate hearing

3. Special disability in writing

4. Motor speech delay

5. Stuttering

Orton conducted experimental work on basic cerebral anatomy and physiology and on reading, spelling, handwriting, auditory comprehension, stuttering, and language disabilities associated with brain damage. He made important neurological inferences about differences between children whose language problems were and were not related to brain injury. In this work he collaborated with Lauretta Bender, an associate at Iowa who investigated the physiology of animal brain anatomy.

Orton, like Hinshelwood, recognized that dyslexia was neurologically based but that its treatment must be educational (Richardson, 1989). Orton contributed by proposing instructional procedures for reading, handwriting, and spelling that were informed by the neurological organization of the brain; for example, the multiple primary zones for sensory input that include somatosensory (touch) and kinesthetic (movement) as well as visual and auditory. He advocated for an approach in which the strong neurological channels strengthen the weak. For example, the kinesthetic sensory channel could be used to strengthen the association between the auditory and visual channels. Orton stressed both the oral and written components of language and recognized the importance of teaching phoneme–grapheme correspondences.

Norman Geschwind's (1982) study of individuals with aphasia, a disorder of oral language, led to the recognition that lesions (actual brain damage) or brain anomalies (brain differences of genetic origin) may be localized in the brain. His findings had a profound effect on behavioral neurology, particularly those regarding brain asymmetries that occur more often in children with specific learning disabilities than without such disabilities.

Additional information on the pioneering work of medical professionals in studying dyslexia can be found in Shaywitz (2003) and Richardson (1989).

Contributions from Educators

At the time the existence of developmental dyslexia was first being documented by medical professionals, a handful of educators were developing teaching methods for treating this written language disorder. While chief of psychiatric social services in the University of Iowa's Department of Psychology, June Lyday worked in Orton's mobile clinic with Lauretta Bender and other pioneers. After her marriage to Orton in 1928, June Lyday Orton remained active in her husband's private practice. She made her husband's work her own, and after his death she continued to see children, write, lecture, and work with teachers and students at Bowman Gray School of Medicine in Winston Salem, North Carolina. She established a clinic for reading and speech disorders, and she worked on the diagnosis and educational treatments of individuals while she trained remedial teachers and taught students in medicine and psychology. She published details of her training approach in *A Guide to Teaching Phonics* (1964).

Devotion to her husband's work led June Orton to gather a group of friends and colleagues on the first anniversary of his death. From that meeting came the founding of the Orton Society (now called The International Dyslexia Association), which was dedicated to disseminating Samuel Orton's work and encouraging and promoting research, diagnosis and treatment, and training of practitioners (Columbia University Health Sciences Library, n.d.).

Anna Gillingham was one of the first educational psychologists at a time when women were just emerging as educational leaders. While associated with the Ethical Culture School, she had become interested in reading problems and corresponded with Samuel Orton regarding remedial cases. In 1932 she joined him in the Language Research Project of the New York Neurological Institute to take charge of organizing teaching procedures based on Orton's findings (Childs, 1968). He set forth the neurological principles for intervention while Gillingham and her colleague Bessie Stillman established the educational basis for the development of teaching techniques and materials. Orton also encouraged her to explore early identification and preventive programs.

The Orton-Gillingham Approach emphasized the structure of language and understanding its principles. The instruction was direct but always involved a teacher–student interaction to learn a concept. Phonology, sound–symbol association, syllables, morphology, syntax and semantics, and comprehension of written language were taught using techniques that were diagnostic, structured, sequential, systematic, and cumulative and that provided the simultaneous association of auditory, visual, and kinesthetic sensory channels. This intersensory association may be automatic in typical readers but not in individuals with dyslexia. Many editions of the Gillingham-Stillman manual, *Remedial Training for Children with Specific Disability in Reading, Spelling, and Penmanship,* were published, including the most well known editions in 1956 and 1960. Gillingham was a rigorous taskmaster, expecting teachers to understand and defend their rationales for instruction (Slingerland, 1980). The Orton-Gillingham Approach continues to influence the various other approaches used to teach students with dyslexia.

Gillingham's colleague, Bessie Stillman, was a master teacher whose understanding of dyslexia was based on her own teaching experience. Her instructional approach provided the foundation for many of the techniques used in the Orton-Gillingham Approach. From Stillman, teachers learned how to use the techniques for which Gillingham provided rationale. Stillman taught them to plan a succeeding lesson at the same time one was tutoring a pupil (Slingerland, 1980).

Sally Childs was a student of Gillingham's at the Ethical Culture School. When her twin daughters showed evidence of a specific language disability, she turned to her former teacher. In 1941 she received her first training from Gillingham and Stillman at Massachusetts General Hospital. She went on to train teachers, assisted in the revisions of the Gillingham-Stillman manuals, and published her own teaching materials, including a systematic program of phonics for the classroom (Childs, 1962).

Marion Monroe, psychologist and educator, was also a member of Samuel Orton's mobile clinic. She conducted a lab school and was responsible for the examination of errors in oral and silent reading in experimental and control groups. She developed the *Reading Aptitude Tests* (Monroe, 1936). The version of this test used in Virginia Berninger's master's program in reading at the University of Pittsburgh influenced much of the research that culminated in the handwriting and silent reading fluency subtests in the second edition of *Process Assessment of the Learner* (PAL II; Berninger, 2007). Monroe's influence also extended beyond teachers of children with reading problems to all classroom teachers and their students, as she was the primary author of many of the *Dick and Jane* reading books. These books were widely used at a time when mainstream education tended to use whole-word rather than alphabetic methods.

Grace M. Fernald pioneered one of the first multisensory teaching approaches (visual, auditory, kinesthetic, tactile [VAKT]) for teaching sight words using all four modalities of input. Using this approach, students would see a word, trace it with their finger, and say each word as they traced it. Progress with this approach was slow because only three or four words were presented at a time. This look-say-do method is described in Fernald's (1943) *Remedial Techniques in Basic School Subjects.* Although described as multisensory, Fernald's VAKT method also included a motoric output component (see Chapters 7 and 9 for why that is important).

Katrina de Hirsch applied much of Orton's information to children with developmental speech problems and contributed to a greater understanding of the interrelationships between reading disabilities and speech and language problems. With Jeanette Jansky and William Langford, she published *Predicting Reading Failure* (1966). She and Jansky also published *Preventing Reading Failure* (1972), which included The Predictive Index, a valuable diagnostic instrument in early identification and intervention for early learning problems. That work inspired Berninger's early intervention research beginning in 1989.

While at Punahou School in Honolulu, Beth H. Slingerland was assigned a group of children who, despite social, economic, and cultural advantages, had not responded to reading instruction (Slingerland, 1980). She was unsuccessful with many methods until she began working with Gillingham and Stillman on neurological principles, basic instructional components, and identification of reading disability. Slingerland worked with Gillingham and Stillman full time and gained practical experience in identifying language disability, planning lessons, and developing appropriate teaching programs. At the end of 2 years, Slingerland was convinced that preventive measures were to be her contribution to working with children with specific language disabilities, in particular, dyslexia.

After working with Gillingham and Stillman in Honolulu, Slingerland moved to Washington State and was encouraged by the Renton, Washington, superintendent of schools to continue her work with children with dyslexia. Each day after her regular morning class, Slingerland worked with individual children in need of intervention and before long concluded that "one-to-one teaching never could reach all of those who were not learning. . . therefore I must concentrate on a classroom approach that used the same Orton-Gillingham basic principles" (Slingerland, 1980, p. 5).

To train classroom teachers as quickly as possible, Slingerland departed from the one-to-one training Gillingham advocated and worked with a group of 12 teachers. The graduate-level class included lectures on background, rationale, phonics, and language structure, as well as daily demonstrations and a practicum in which the teachers in training tutored individual students using the approaches modeled for them each morning. Interest in the Slingerland teaching approach spread to public school districts in Texas and California and then throughout the country.

Slingerland's adaptation for the classroom of the Orton-Gillingham Approach is structured, sequential, and systematic. The total language arts program included daily work with handwriting, practicing automatic intersensory association of sounds and symbols, encoding (sounds to written symbols), decoding (written symbols to sound), and writing (expressive) and reading (receptive). Additional contributions included strategies for developing sight recognition of words and a unique way of teaching reading comprehension by teaching the structure of language in a reading context. This allowed teachers to begin reading instruction with conventional reading materials before children had decoding skills.

Beverly Wolf was trained by Slingerland in the methods for teaching the structure of oral language while teaching reading (written language) and has applied these methods successfully for more than 40 years. (See Chapter 3 for a discussion of these methods.) Berninger heard Slingerland speak at a presentation in Baltimore and used the Slingerland Screening tests (Slingerland, 1977) in her resource room work in the 1970s. This test influenced much of Berninger's research on orthographic coding processes—results of this research during the past 20 years are described in the chapters in Section III. PAL II has subtests that assess orthographic coding processes.

Aylett Cox had such success in tutoring students with the Orton-Gillingham Approach that she was asked to work with children at the Hockaday School in Dallas. Grateful and enthusiastic parents raised funds to establish a program and teacher training there. In 1965 the program was moved to the Texas Scottish Rite Hospital for Children in Dallas. Like Slingerland, Cox found that the need for teacher training was too great for a one-to-one approach, so she, too, worked with groups of teachers. She gradually refined and added to the Orton-Gillingham Approach, eventually publishing a textbook (1992), materials, and criterion-referenced evaluations. Her *Alphabetic Phonics* training program is still in use in many clinics and schools across the country.

Many other contemporary teachers have continued to carry on the work of the educational pioneers just discussed. Wilson Anderson, Judith Birsh, Sandra Dillon, Helene Durbrow, Mary Lee Enfield, Tori Greene, Marcia Henry, Lucia Karnes, Arlene Sonday, Nancy Cushen White, Barbara Wilson, and many more use Samuel Orton's work as a basis for their own efforts to train teachers and to help students with dyslexia. See Birsh (2005) for examples of this work. The goal for these researchers and teachers is to provide the instruction defined by another pioneer, Margaret Rawson:

> If we give him a therapeutic climate and a skilled, flexible teacher, and present the language in a way which is, multisensory, structured, systematic, sequential, cumulative, and thorough we can teach him skills adequate to his intellectual and social needs whatever their level, and help him taste the joy of mastery and the enthusiasm that goes with using human language. (1973, p. 144)

THE DEVELOPING YEARS: EMERGENCE OF THE FIELDS OF PSYCHOLOGY OF READING AND LEARNING DISABILITIES

In this section we discuss how two fields—psychology of reading and learning disabilities—emerged as the result of growing interest in understanding and teaching children who struggled to learn written language.

Emergence of the Psychology of Reading Field

By the middle of the 20th century, psychology of reading had generated considerable basic and applied knowledge about teaching children to read and assessing their reading achievement. This knowledge was shared with teachers in classics such as *The Improvement of Reading* (Gates, 1947), *The Teaching of Reading and Writing* (Gray, 1956), and *Reading Difficulties: Their Diagnosis and Correction* (Bond & Tinker, 1967), which were used in preservice teacher education and graduate-level courses on reading. Many states had requirements for teacher certification to teach in the public schools that required a course or two in the teaching of reading at the preservice level to obtain initial certification and additional courses at the graduate level to obtain permanent teaching certification.

Some schools had reading specialists with 60–90 graduate credits in reading who were available for assessment, consultation, and small-group instruction in local buildings. In schools with reading specialists, decisions about whom to test and teach and about how to work with teachers were left to these specially trained professionals who were allowed to function in a flexible manner without burdensome regulations and paperwork. However, not all schools had access to such professionals. Many parents became frustrated because they could not get help within the public schools for their children who were struggling with reading.

Emergence of the Field of Learning Disabilities

During this same time period, parents often turned to professionals outside of public schools if their child had a specific learning disability in reading or writing—for example, to a neurologist and tutor trained in multisensory or structured language teaching methods, as discussed earlier, or to a special school that used these methods. As a result, much of the pioneers' work had a greater influence outside of rather than inside the public schools, few of which adopted these methods on a widespread scale.

Mainstream reading educators did not interact much with medically oriented educators. They had different professional training backgrounds and attended different professional organizations. Mainstream reading educators often participated in the International Reading Association, whereas the medically oriented, multisensory, structured-language educators were more likely to belong to The International Dyslexia Association (discussed later in this chapter). Special educators who were interested in reading education may have participated in the Council for Exceptional Children, the National Center for Learning Disabilities, and/or the Learning Disabilities Association of America. Moreover, there was little interaction among many educational professionals and the speech and language and medical professionals.

By the early 1960s, a national political movement led by parents who were increasingly frustrated because they could not get educational services for their children with a variety of disabling conditions—ranging from intellectual and developmental disabilities to specific learning disabilities (development within the normal range except for oral and/or written language)—was gaining momentum. Parents did not understand why schools would not enroll many children with intellectual and developmental disabilities and why schools could not teach children with specific learning disabilities to read and write. Many parents came together and organized a landmark conference in 1963 in Chicago where Samuel Kirk gave a keynote address. To cover the range of educationally disabling conditions with which parents were concerned, he proposed the generic label *learning disabilities.* The parents took a strong position that a multidisciplinary team approach was needed to meet all of their children's educational needs.

After the conference, parents of children with learning disabilities partnered with parents of children with intellectual disabilities to mount a national political movement to gain services and rights for students in the United States with these and other educationally disabling conditions. That parent-initiated effort culminated in the Education for All Handicapped Children Act of 1975 (PL 94-142), which guarantees a free appropriate public education for all students with educationally disabling conditions. Given the wide range of educational disabilities covered, it is not surprising that professionals could not agree on how to define a learning disability. They ended up with a definition that is based on exclusionary criteria—what a learning disability is not. They determined that a learning disability is not due to intellectual disabilities, sensory acuity or motor impairments, a lack of opportunities to learn, or cultural differences. They could not, however, agree on a definition based on inclusionary criteria (but see Chapter 8 for recent developments on this issue).

Unfortunately, the categories in the special education law are not diagnostic criteria for the nature of a specific learning disability but rather for the eligibility of a student for special education services. The federal special education laws do not require that children who struggle with learning to read and write be 1) assessed for research-supported diagnoses that explain why they struggle with written language or 2) given instruction that research has shown is effective at specific developmental stages of written language acquisition for specific kinds of written language disabilities. It is no wonder, therefore, that the eligibility criteria for qualifying for special education services under the category of learning disabilities vary widely from state to state, and many parents and educational professionals find the system confusing. See Torgesen (2004), Johnson and Myklebust (1967), and Kirk and Kirk (1971) for further discussion of these issues and more information on the history of the field of special education.

To support the field of special education, the U.S. Department of Education provided funding for training programs for special educators, model demonstration projects, and research on teaching special populations with educationally disabling conditions. McCardle and Chhabra (2004) noted, however, that the increasing knowledge of research-supported instructional practices seemed to influence general education initiatives more than special education policies.

And, because *appropriate* instruction in special education legislation was not defined on the basis of evidence from developmental and educational science, the ambiguity in the legislation has resulted in legal disputes between parents and schools. These legal disputes are costly and create adversarial relationships without necessarily resulting in better reading and writing achievement for students with written language learning disabilities. For example, meta-analyses show that special education for students with learning disabilities has not been effective (e.g., Bradley, Danielson, & Hallahan, 2002), especially in reading (Vaughn, Moody, & Schumm, 1998). Simply legislating special education services may not be sufficient. Special education services may not have been effective for many reasons, including lack of teacher knowledge of effective practices for designing, implementing, and evaluating differentiated instruction in the general education classroom.

THE CONTEMPORARY SCENE

Special education is the main mechanism for teaching children with dyslexia in public schools whether or not the dyslexia is diagnosed. Because dyslexia is not a diagnostic category in the special education laws, many school professionals continue to tell parents that dyslexia does not exist. As reported to the University of Washington Multidisciplinary Learning Disabilities Center (see Preface) by many families whose children are struggling and who have multigenerational histories of struggles with reading and writing, such a claim is puzzling and painful. Dyslexia can be defined and diagnosed (Lyon, Shaywitz, & Shaywitz, 2003); however, not all reading problems indicate dyslexia (see Chapter 3). As the Assistant Secretary of Special Education stated in a presentation by U.S. Department of Education officials on the 2004 reauthorization of IDEA to the University of Washington in 2007, much work remains to bridge the gap between general education and special education in meeting the needs of all students with learning differences.

Teaching children with biologically based reading and writing disabilities probably requires educating the educators as well as teaching the affected individuals. Some learning problems may be related to ineffective or inappropriate instruction for the specific learning profile. Through the years, the pendulum of educational thought has swung back and forth between phonics and whole language methods, with little consideration for the individual differences among diverse learners and the need for most students to be taught skills in an intellectually engaging way that includes meaning but also explicit instruction to bring the structures of oral language (by ear and mouth) and of written language (by eye and hand) into conscious awareness at all levels of language (subword, word, and text). Teaching skills in this way allows children to decode unfamiliar written words, understand what they read, write legible letters, produce conventional word spellings, and create developmentally appropriate written compositions. All children with dyslexia, oral and written language learning disability (OWL LD), and/or dysgraphia need specific, intense, structured, sequential, language-based instruction that is provided in an intellectually engaging way to reach these literacy goals.

Even if students with dyslexia, OWL LD, and/or dysgraphia receive pullout special education services, they will still require some kind of specialized, differentiated instruction in the general education classroom—usually from kindergarten through 12th grade. The nature of the particular special education services, however, will change as curriculum and assignments change across the grades. Teaching students with dyslexia to read and write is the responsibility of both general and special educators. And, according to PL 94-142 and every modification thereafter, including the IDEA 2004 reauthorization (PL 108-446), specialized instruction should be available to any student in the public schools, and parents should not have to pay for special services outside of the public schools or have to pay for special schools to obtain specialized instruction for their children with dyslexia, OWL LD, and/or dysgraphia.

EDUCATORS AND SCIENTISTS ARE CONNECTED

In this chapter we honor many early pioneers who contributed to understanding the nature of specific learning disabilities and effective instructional practices for helping children with such disabilities overcome their learning problems. Each new generation builds on past contributions and extends them. We hope this book will inspire a new generation of educational professionals in making their own contributions. We also emphasize the added value of scientists and teachers partnering in this effort. Both scientists from many disciplines and teachers have contributed to the progress that is being made in serving students who struggle with learning written language.

Classroom Environment

What Works in Teaching Students with Dyslexia, OWL LD, and/or Dysgraphia?

Mr. Winn, Mr. Winn,
you need to teach teachers
how to teach, you have to organize
a bake sale, I mean a really, really,
really big bake sale so you can bring the
teachers here and show them how we learn.

Nine-year-old girl attending the
University of Washington Multidisciplinary
Learning Disabilities Center summer intervention program
for students with dyslexia that emphasized hands-on
learning and intellectual engagement

Organizational Issues and Instructional Approaches

E ach chapter in this section begins with teacher contributions followed by researcher contributions. We are pleased that conclusions about effective instructional practices based on teaching and research experience converge.

TEACHER CONTRIBUTIONS

This chapter offers practical suggestions for the following: 1) organizing the learning environment; 2) differentiating instruction for individual students; 3) choosing instructional components; 4) creating a positive learning environment; 5) aiming instruction at students' instructional levels; 6) planning, implementing, and evaluating lessons; and 7) designing independent work. Individualizing instruction for students with dyslexia, oral and written language learning disability (OWL LD), and dysgraphia in a general education classroom may initially seem like a challenge, but chances are that other children (10%–15%) with intellectual abilities at least in the normal range in the general education classroom are also at risk for reading and/or writing problems. Even though reasons may vary as to why children are at risk (e.g., the parents have little formal education and provide few literacy or related activities in the home, the student is not fully proficient with English, the student has inherited biological risk factors for dyslexia or another learning disability affecting written language acquisition), these children are likely to benefit from many of the specialized instructional approaches to which many students with dyslexia, OWL LD, and/or dysgraphia respond.

Organizing the Learning Environment

Teachers can help students with specific learning disabilities by individualizing instruction and by attempting to understand learning from these students' perspectives. Teachers can build each student's confidence in his or her ability to learn and succeed by structuring the learning environment so that each student succeeds each day in some way, even if he or she is functioning below classmates at the same grade level.

To help motivate students with specific learning disabilities and create success, teachers need to carefully observe and interpret student behavior, remain flexible when planning and organizing the school day differently for individual students, and become knowledgeable of appropriate teaching approaches for students whose skill levels are below the average for the class. The following seven general principles have helped many teachers create such successful learning experiences.

Principle 1: Children Are Motivated to Learn Do not assume that lack of motivation is the cause of a child's struggles in learning to read and write. Most children want desperately to learn, even though they may camouflage their fear of failure with reluctance (avoiding or not completing assignments), aggressive displays (acting out), or humor (assuming role of class clown). With the correct learning tools, students with dyslexia, OWL LD, and/or dysgraphia can succeed and gain confidence in their own abilities to learn, even if they need to work harder than others. Teachers should provide encouragement so that these students do not give up on themselves. Linking instruction in basic reading, writing, and oral language skills to their interests and to intellectually engaging content helps students with dyslexia, OWL LD, and/or dysgraphia sustain hard work over time.

Principle 2: Oral Language Is Related to Written Language Development and Remains Important During All Schooling Teaching reading and writing requires more than written language instruction. Daily instruction should be organized to include instruction in oral language as well because developing both can be mutually facilitative. Children need to develop awareness of sounds, meaning word parts, and syntax in oral language in order to learn to decode unfamiliar words and comprehend text. They also need to process teacher's instructional language in order to learn academic subject matter and to produce oral language in order to answer questions and participate in class discussions.

Principle 3: Never Assume That What Was Taught Is Necessarily What Was Learned The goal for teachers is to bring teaching and learning together. Simply covering the required material is not enough. Teachers need time to plan their teaching, implement those plans, assess student response to the implementation of the plans, and reflect on implementation of those plans and student progress. Teachers need to allocate time on a daily and weekly basis to assess whether students have learned what teachers intended for them to learn. The assessment might include daily probes of accuracy or time; unit tests that accompany textbooks; teacher-designed tests that assess skills or content taught; building-wide curriculum-based assessment at the beginning, middle, or end of school year; building-wide group-administered standardized, normed achievement tests or high-stakes tests; or portfolios with work samples across the school year (see Berninger, 1998b).

Principle 4: Teach Children Based on What Level They Can Appropriately Learn, Not on What Level Their Peers Are Being Taught The writers of curriculum materials follow grade-level guidelines, which often do not reflect the normal variation of learning in most classrooms; however, observant teachers know their own students best and know where they are functioning along the path to reading and writing development. The teacher's goal is to pace instruction to student needs and reteach, restructure, and review as needed. This kind of developmentally tailored instruction is best accomplished using three to four instructional groupings, based on instructional level, for reading and writing within the general education classroom.

Principle 5: One Exposure Is Not Enough for Many Kinds of Learning and Learners
Although sometimes students learn some skills through one exposure (lesson), students with reading and writing problems tend to require even more exposures (lessons) and practice than other students. Repeated practice over time often is needed to acquire mastery and confidence to apply learning to a variety of situations.

Principle 6: Teach How to Learn
Remembering letters and words is not the same skill as thinking. Teachers should acknowledge and celebrate students with dyslexia, OWL LD, and/or dysgraphia for their ability to think and engage in problem solving in order to maintain their self-esteem and create self-concepts that they are bright learners even if they have trouble with handwriting, word decoding, word reading, and/or spelling. Instructional strategies may aid in recall when memory for letters and words fails and may facilitate transfer of knowledge to new situations. An example of a letter strategy is checking that the circular part of lower case *b* faces in same direction as the circular parts of a capital *B*. An example of a word strategy for words not identified automatically is phonological decoding of spelling–sound correspondences in left-to-right direction. "We cannot teach them everything they need to know, but we can teach them how to learn" (B. Slingerland, 1980, personal communication).

Principle 7: Flexibility Is the Key to Master Teaching and Effective Learning
A wise teacher knows when to let go, try another strategy, let it rest, or change direction to take advantage of teachable moments. For example, if a child does not readily grasp what is being taught that day, do not push him or her to do so. Reintroduce the concepts or procedures on another day and with a fresh start the child may grasp what is being taught.

Differentiating Instruction for Individual Students

When the general education classroom teacher is aware of the needs of students with dyslexia and/or related disorders and provides structured, sequential, systematic instruction for these students while meeting the needs of other students in the class, fewer students are likely to be referred for special education. To meet the needs of all students, teachers need to couple carefully planned lessons with daily and weekly monitoring of students' responses to instruction. The observant teacher seeks a balance between challenging and overloading students. When tasks do not demand much intellectual energy, students may become bored; however, when tasks are too difficult, students may become discouraged and frustrated and may misbehave. For example, when teachers observe a student misbehaving, they should ask how the instructional and learning environment might be structured differently so that the student is successful rather than discouraged and frustrated, rather than jump to the conclusion that the student has an emotional or behavioral problem or that the parents are not providing support in the home. Misbehavior may be a signal that learning is not occurring rather than a reflection of moral character or what is happening at home.

After initial instruction in any new concept, a skilled teacher individualizes instruction by adjusting the difficulty of the task for each student so that each student finds success while continuing to move forward. For example, the teacher might form a small instructional group for those students who need reteaching of a concept and form another group for the students who mastered the concept very quickly and need enrichment learning opportunities to extend and elaborate the initial learning (see Delisle, 1984). When students have sufficient time to practice and review concepts, they often become firmly fixed in long-term memory. All students can learn but some need more instruction and practice, even further enrichment, than others. A few simple adjustments to the daily plan, such as selection of words with a range of difficulty for the daily reading and spelling lessons, are typically all that is necessary to allow the teacher to keep the stronger students challenged while providing appropriate input, modeling, and practice for those with weaker skills. Teachers can also adjust classroom and homework assignments to reflect individual needs, whether or not a student has a 504 Accommodation Plan.

Classroom Grouping   Providing small-group or one-to-one instruction for every student in need of individualization is not always feasible; however, it is possible for the teacher to organize the class to provide instruction tailored to the range of instructional levels in most general education classrooms. Several informal reading inventories are available commercially (e.g., Leslie & Caldwell, 2005) or can be designed for the specific textbook(s) used in a school. These inventories can be administered at the beginning of the school year to identify the instructional levels of students and then to form three to four small instructional groups. The teacher can meet daily with each of these groups for 20–30 minutes of teacher-guided instruction while other students do independent work designed for their group (e.g., practicing and applying skills learned from instructional time with the teacher, reading new stories, rereading stories to develop fluency).

The informal inventory can be readministered in the middle of the year to assess whether any children need to be moved to a different group. This kind of assessment of response to instruction increases the probability that instruction remains differentiated throughout the school year. When students are grouped by instructional level, the teacher can pace instruction to the students' rates of learning and adapt students' response to instruction as needed. The most common classroom groupings are discussed in Chapter 10, along with options for differentiated instruction that involve a building-level grouping plan with other teachers at the same grade level and possibly different grade levels.

Individualization within Group Instruction   Even within groups formed on the basis of similar instructional levels, teachers may have to provide additional individualization because instructional levels are rarely identical. Variation in levels of learning, profiles of learning skills and achievement, and strategies for learning are normal. Normal variation in reading and writing acquisition is the rule rather than the exception. Teachers must flexibly adapt to these individual differences within the larger and smaller instructional groups in the classroom.

Choosing Instructional Components

Many federal initiatives have specified the components of science-supported reading instruction (see McCardle & Miller, in press). Major textbooks for reading and instructional materials for writing are incorporating these elements in their materials, and many school districts adopt a particular text book or program for all teachers to use at a specific grade level to implement science-supported reading instruction. For example, the National Reading Panel (National Institute of Child Health and Human Development, 2000) identified five critical areas for early reading skills: 1) phonemic awareness, 2) phonics, 3) oral reading fluency, 4) reading comprehension, and 5) vocabulary. Based on other research on oral language (Silliman & Scott, in press) and writing (Hooper, Knuth, Yerby, Anderson, & Moore, in press), a complete language program for all children, and especially those with dyslexia and/or dysgraphia, should include instruction and practice in oral language, including morphological and syntactic awareness, and orthographic awareness, including handwriting, spelling, and written composition. The programs in Table 2.1, which include some or all of these components, have been developed specifically for students with dyslexia and may be used effectively in small instructional groups as a supplement to the school adopted textbooks. (Note that not all approaches that have been developed for and used successfully with students with dyslexia have been listed.) See Henry (2005) for a conceptual framework to apply in choosing supplementary instructional material for students with dyslexia, OWL LD, and/or dysgraphia.

Creating a Positive Learning Environment

Emotional climate is defined by teacher attitudes toward students and student attitudes toward one another. Teachers provide the emotional safety that encourages students to take risks and allows students to make mistakes. Freedom to make mistakes is necessary for learning. Teachers should praise good performances judiciously—students know when praise is false—and commend hard work as well as the accuracy of performance. Students with dyslexia, OWL LD, and/or dysgraphia appreciate teachers understanding how much effort it may take for them to learn to process, pronounce, and spell written words compared with their classmates. Teachers can build the concept that an error is not failure by helping students to self-correct and discover the correct response rather than turning immediately to another student to answer. Students should be guided through the steps to success, given clues if necessary, and given information in order to perform accurately and feel the satisfaction that comes as a result of their efforts. If a child misspells a word, for example, the teacher can repeat the word clearly and ask the child to repeat it as well. "What sounds do you hear? How do you spell that sound?" Teachers should discourage guessing and teach strategies for cues to figuring out an unknown word. Children who have more difficulty spelling than the majority of students in the class may simply need reteaching and more guided practice.

Teachers can also build the concept that an error is not failure by using a team approach to decoding unknown words, which minimizes the stigma of not knowing a word instantly and calls attention to the fact that the student is not alone—

Table 2.1. Some instructional programs developed for students with dyslexia

Program (also see Chapter 2 appendix)	Use	Levels	Size	Time	Multisensory	Handwriting
Alphabetic Phonics A diagnostic O-G adaptation for remedial use with materials, and criterion-referenced benchmark measure	Remedial	Ungraded Elementary	Individual Group	45–60 minutes 4–5 times per week	Yes	Cursive
Association Method A method using a slower speech rate, precise articulation of phonemes, extensive auditory training, and delays teaching rules. Color differentiation rules taught in upper levels.	Remedial	N/A	Individual Group Class	2–35 hours per week	Yes	Cursive
Language! A comprehensive literacy curriculum. Provides an integrated approach to instruction. Includes an ESL component.	Preventive Remedial General	Grades 3–12 ESL ELL	1–20 per group	1–2 hours daily	Yes	Manuscript and cursive
Lindamood-Bell A method developed to teach auditory conceptualization skills and designed to complement any reading program. Includes an emphasis on speech processes.	Preventive Remedial General	All	Individual Group Class	20 minutes to 6 hours daily	No	Manuscript and cursive
Orton-Gillingham Approach The basis for most structured, sequential, multisensory language programs	Preventive Remedial	Kindergarten to adult	Individual Group	2 hours 2–5 times per week	Yes	Cursive

Program (also see Chapter 2 appendix)	Use	Levels	Size	Time	Multisensory	Handwriting
Project Read A program developed for the public school classroom. Includes detailed guides that provide systematic sequence of skills.	Preventive Remedial General	Kindergarten to adult	1–10 per group	Variable session length 2–5 times per week	Yes	Manuscript and cursive
Slingerland Classroom Approach O-G based, systematic, structured, interactive approach. Includes special techniques for developing reading comprehension and fluency. Can be used with any text materials.	Preventive Remedial General	Kindergarten to adult ELL	Individual Group Class	1–2 hours daily during reading, language arts	Yes	Manuscript and cursive
Sonday System Originally used with older students, this system emphasizes the structure of the English language as well as phonology and morphology. Includes prepared lesson plans.	Preventive Remedial General	Kindergarten to adult ELL	Individual Group Class	Variable session length 2–5 times per week	Yes	Manuscript and cursive
Spalding Method A method in which all sounds are taught before reading begins. Heavy emphasis on phonics, rules, and generalizations.	Preventive Remedial General	Primary	Individual Group Class	2 hours 5 times per week	Yes	Manuscript and cursive
Wilson Reading Systematic, interactive, thorough instruction with emphasis on encoding and decoding. Can be used with Grades 3 and above or with Grades 1 and 2.	Preventive Remedial General	Kindergarten to adult	1–15 per class	30–90 minutes 5 times per week	Yes	Manuscript and cursive

Key: O-G, Orton-Gillingham Approach; ESL, English as a Second Language; ELL, English language learner.

other students may also face challenges in decoding words. Using such a team approach helps to create an atmosphere of support and acceptance. Few things are as gratifying as the applause of fellow classmates when a student, alone or through teamwork, is finally able to read or spell a word. The inner satisfaction of the successful student who has finally mastered a new skill is a powerful motivator. Teachers can help build a spirit of support and cooperation by helping students to help one another. Taking responsibility for one's own learning, recognizing one's own efforts, and helping others all contribute to building self-esteem. In addition, teachers need to recognize that what is a good performance for one student may be less acceptable for another. Although teachers set the standards of students' expected, appropriate level of performance, levels may need to be adjusted for certain students so that their levels are within reach.

Physical Climate and Classroom Organization   Teachers can provide a more positive environment for students with a variety of learning requirements when both physical needs and learning needs are considered. Some children may be easily distracted, confused, or disorganized. They may need order to work effectively. Their classroom should be well organized, neat, and clutter free. Neuhaus (2002) found that some students were still learning the alphabet in fourth grade. A readily accessed alphabet with manuscript and/or cursive letters provides reinforcement for those with insecure recall. As such, the alphabet should be posted in a space clearly visible to all students or at each student's desk to provide ready reference. Prefix and suffix charts and vowel pattern charts should be clearly visible as well, as these will help students with encoding and decoding. Teachers should encourage students to refer to these learning aids whenever they do not have immediate recall.

Display areas in the classroom should reflect the interests and ideas of the students. Such areas are a valuable tool for building self-esteem and motivation when they are used to display student work.

Desks and aisles must be spaced to allow the teacher easy access to all students. On occasions when the whole class is reading content area materials, the teacher must circulate throughout the classroom to ensure that all students are keeping their places and are on task, providing assistance as needed. Having easy access to every student allows teachers to circulate and check writing during practice times and to help prevent errors before performance.

Student desks should be oriented to the front of the room during written language instruction to allow ready reference to wall displays and the teacher's nonverbal and verbal instructional cues. Teachers should ensure that students have access to visual displays without distortions due to distractions in the classroom.

During small-group reading sessions, students in the group should be seated so that they all have a clear view of the board or charts. For example, seating students in an arc or semicircle allows students to see and allows the teacher to easily assist all students, helping them with keeping their places and following along in the story. While working with a small group, the teacher should also have a clear view of the whole class, and the whole class a clear view of the teacher. In this way, without speaking, the teacher can manage the students who are working independently and provide guidance with just a smile, a nod, a shake of the head, or a gesture. Teachers should establish a rule that no one should interrupt while the teacher is with a reading group—instead, teachers can take a few minutes between groups to reinforce independent standards and to give extra help.

Left-handed students might be grouped together so that they have space to move their writing arms comfortably without bumping others. Such grouping may also reduce confusion for students who are uncertain about which is their dominant hand. (Teachers can determine hand preference by asking the child to perform the series of tasks described in Chapter 5.)

Provide Preferential Classroom Seating   Preferential seating may not always mean "front row" seating. Students are often the best judges of what works best for them. Some need to be in front or near the teacher. Others work best when seated off to the side or in the back, away from distractions. Children as young as first grade come to understand that as much as they would like to sit by their friends, they may not be able to manage their behavior if they do. It is the teacher's responsibility, however, to help students recognize their own classroom needs.

Provide a Consistent Routine   Following a consistent routine often helps reassure students with difficulties organizing time and space and helps build organizational awareness. Teachers should post the class schedule daily and take time at the beginning of the day to discuss any changes. Following a schedule helps students know what to expect, reduces anxiety for students who do not manage change well, and helps students move through the day with assurance. The support of an orderly teacher can increase confidence and pattern behavior and can help students understand when and how assignments are expected.

Students of all ages can use a calendar or weekly planner. Teachers can encourage students to use such tools by allowing time for them to copy assignments, if of an age to do so, and to check each morning to see what is due. Some teachers eliminate the need for copying assignments by publishing a weekly calendar with a schedule, special events, assignments, and deadlines printed on it for students' notebooks. Teachers should also educate parents about the importance of learning organization. Organizational patterns can be established if parents and teachers consistently use a calendar and help students to use their own as management tools. Students should follow timelines for outline, rough draft, and final written reports, with specific due dates for each. Teachers should monitor student work completion for long-term projects and assignments to help students follow the timelines.

Aiming Instruction at Students' Instructional Levels

In the next section we discuss the implications of assessed instructional levels for selection of reading materials and pacing of lessons.

Reading Materials   The grade level of the reading material should be matched with the assessed instructional level; for example, through an informal reading inventory that takes into account ability to identify words on a list without context clues, ability to identify words in passages with context information, and comprehension based on answering factual and inferential questions. Basal readers and literature readers are designed to provide a variety of experiences that will allow students to read library materials. They differ in the difficulty of the material in terms of decoding requirements for unfamiliar words, vocabulary level, sentence syntax structures, and other factors that affect readability for ease of reading the materials. Although many students can handle the decoding requirements of grade-level textbooks, students with dyslexia typically have difficulty with decoding unfamiliar words or with automatic recognition of familiar words. They may benefit from extra practice in decoding. For a modest fee (about $60), grade-level books can be downloaded from http://www.readinga-z.com and used to provide extra practice with decoding at a student's instructional level. Another site, http://www.starfall.com, offers free phonological awareness lessons and other instructional materials. At the same time, however, grade-level reading materials may be a better match with a student's vocabulary development or thinking ability.

Content Area Materials Students should work with reading materials that are as close to their instructional level as possible in all content areas of the curriculum. Science, social studies, and other content area materials are written at a reading level appropriate for the grade level that will be using them; therefore, students reading below grade level will have difficulty accessing information in the texts. Some textbook publishers are now providing textbooks with the same content written at a reading level below the grade level for which the textbook is designed. Many textbook publishers are now also providing electronic versions of textbooks in the content areas that can be accessed through special computer programs that read the text orally to students reading below grade level while they follow along reading the text displayed on the monitor. Computer programs also exist that scan in pages in whatever text is being used so that students who are reading below grade level can have the text read orally to them while they follow along with the visual display on the monitor.

Pacing Lessons

Pacing is the key to success in specialized instruction. Teachers should plan lessons in detail and be fully prepared to move through the lesson with no wasted time. For example, when the class follows a routine passing out papers, heading their papers, and preparing to listen, the teacher is relieved of constant redirection that wastes time. Successful pacing requires knowledge of the group, understanding of the material, and careful planning for both longitudinal and horizontal needs. Longitudinal planning is the sequential progression through curriculum materials— the recognition of where the students are in relation to the goals for the year. Horizontal planning addresses the movement from instruction to guided practice and functional use of material within a given lesson. Students are not ready to make longitudinal steps until they are able to apply skills independently.

Teachers should plan thorough horizontal learning lessons as they look ahead to the next curriculum goal. The teacher must be a manager who recognizes each student's strengths, weaknesses, and needs, while knowing the curriculum; responding to school or district requirements, expectations, and schedules; and managing time for the planned and unexpected needs of the students. Knowledge of each student's needs allows the teacher to guide the class as a whole through new learning. An 11-year-old boy wrote of unprepared teachers, saying that his teachers could have ridden with Jesse James because of all the time they stole from him while he waited for them to prepare (Delisle, 1984).

A well-planned lesson will protect both teachers and students from stolen time. Some elements for well-planned decoding, handwriting, or spelling instruction include the following:

- Work on a first-taught skill until it is automatic and functional before introducing a second skill, work on the second skill until it is automatic and functional before a third is introduced, and so forth.

- Integrate new learning with the old. With thorough teaching and practice, students will build patterns for success and synthesize learning to allow them to move forward longitudinally at ever-increasing rates.

- Over teach because one exposure in only one lesson is seldom enough for all students. Presenting the same material in a variety of ways helps build success before introducing additional new concepts.

Designing Independent Work

Independent activities can provide valuable reinforcement for students with dyslexia, OWL LD, and/or dysgraphia and can help strengthen skills. Art or work stations that have taped materials, games, and skill-building activities create a stimulating learning environment. Such stations, however, should be considered a supplement to independent work that provides practice in handwriting and independent reading and writing skills.

Reading and writing activities aid in the development of thought processes for independent functional use of skills.

> Use of (duplicated) worksheet forms...is strongly discouraged because such sheets make the children's task too simple. Children need the practice in copying, and in organizing and placing their own work on the page—something they do not get if all they are required to do is fill in the blanks. (Slingerland, 1976, p. 235)

See Chapter 2 appendix for further resources on independent work.

Providing opportunities for students to apply language skills in content areas such as social studies and science can improve motivation through high-interest activities, which can stimulate creativity. Any independent work should be interesting and meaningful. It will allow students at various levels to practice skills and can turn the classroom into a creative space where structured learning takes place.

Completed independent activities provide teachers with an additional tool for evaluating response to intervention and with documentation of performance while requiring less time for testing. Intervention can be immediately provided as the teacher plans for subsequent lessons for students' small instructional groups. These lessons may involve reteaching or reviewing skills, individualizing instruction, and adjusting the amount or kind of performance expected from an individual student.

Children should be given some open-ended assignments that allow them to work within the limits of their time, interests, and abilities. Teachers should begin independent work by setting clear standards of behavior and performance and by teaching proper use of materials, expectations, and rules. Each activity—whether it is art, writing, or use of the computer or listening station—should be carefully structured. At the beginning of the year, teachers may provide only a few choices for the students; however, as the year progresses teachers should gradually add new activities and build expectations.

It is also important for teachers to provide written directions in addition to oral directions. Written directions (e.g., on the board, on a worksheet) provide a sequence that aids recall. Students who may have difficulty with assignments can be asked to repeat directions so it is clear that they understand an assignment. In addition, providing alternatives to written assignments may give students who do not write well alternate avenues to success. Teachers should always remember to give credit for content as well as for written performance.

Because students work at different rates, some will complete assignments and need enriching or stretching activities, while others may not complete the work at all. A few well-done examples may be all that some students can produce. If a student has been on task throughout the independent tutoring work period, the teacher should accept the parts of the assignment that are completed even if the whole assignment is not complete. At the same time, the teacher should continue to raise standards for the child who is careless or hurries through an assignment. When evaluation takes place with the student, the teacher can clarify expectations and make suggestions. Some teachers, recognizing that correction is most valuable with a child present, may take time to correct before the independent period is over. Other teachers may offer brief daily conferences. More detailed evaluation can occur at the teacher's discretion.

Having peers correct other students' work should be a method that is used judiciously. Children who are learning new skills can be frustrated or intimidated when peers question, criticize, or even make inappropriate comments about their work. For example, one student with whom Beverly Wolf worked said that he discontinued using his clear, readable cursive writing when a fellow student said, "I can't read cursive, and no one writes that way." At some stages of learning when students have more confidence, using peer checkers and peer tutors may be helpful.

RESEARCHER CONTRIBUTIONS

The many practical recommendations teachers have offered are supported by many accumulating research findings demonstrating that students with dyslexia, OWL LD, and/or dysgraphia often have difficulty with *executive functions*—the mental self-government that helps organize the learning process (Altemeier, Abbott, & Berninger, 2008; Berninger, Abbott, Thomson, et al., 2006; Berninger, Nielsen, Abbott, Wijsman, & Raskind, 2008b; Berninger, Raskind, Richards, Abbott, & Stock, 2008; Lyon & Krasnegor, 1996, especially chapter by Denckla; Swanson, 1999b, 2006). For example, they may have difficulty focusing on what is relevant, ignoring what is irrelevant, switching between tasks, or staying on task. To overcome weaknesses in executive functions, teachers can organize the learning environment and instructional day, teach strategies for managing the learning process, and provide individualized teacher guidance.

For students with impaired executive functions, pull-out, resource-room services in special education may be more confusing than helpful. These children may do better to remain in an organized, coherent learning environment with consistent teacher guidance for the entire school day without disruption. However, they often respond to before-school or after-school tutoring or clubs to supplement the regular instructional program (e.g., Berninger, Abbott, Vermeulen, & Fulton, 2006) and writing (e.g., Berninger, Rutberg, et al., 2006, Study 2).

For many reasons, children with dyslexia, OWL LD, and/or dysgraphia, who tend to have executive function problems, may learn more effectively in the general education classroom than by being pulled out from the regular program. The critical issue for students with impaired executive functions is to have all of the reading or writing instruction provided within the same block of time rather than in separate lessons at different times in the day that are not well integrated. All too often special education pull-out services are not coordinated with the regular program in general education. Children may not transfer skills taught in the resource room to their reading or writing program in the general education classroom unless the special and general education programs are coordinated and explicit instruction is provided. Rather than pulling students out of the general education program, specialized learning environments can be created within the general education classroom that show children how to integrate the various reading and writing skills. Such specialized learning environments are possible if teachers form instructional groupings based on children's reading levels (as described previously in this chapter) or participate in cross-classroom team teaching during common blocks of instructional time (see Chapter 10).

Private schools for students with learning differences tend to create such integrated learning environments that support success in learning, but public schools can too. For examples of teachers in public schools in Seattle, Washington who have done so with excellent student learning outcomes, see Berninger and Richards, Chapters 9 and 12. Often these specialized learning environments were created within a language arts block offered at the same time by all teachers at specific grade levels (e.g., first, second, and third; or fourth, fifth, and sixth). Different teachers assumed responsibility for reading groups at different instructional levels within those grade levels. Children went to the classroom that had the group for their instructional level, which might have been in the classroom taught by their teacher, another classroom taught by a teacher at the same grade level, or a classroom taught by a teacher at another grade level. The instructional groups did not necessarily correspond to the teacher's grade level. Children were under the impression that they "walked about" for reading so that they had an opportunity to interact with other students in the school. The groups were not identified as to the good, average, or poor readers. They all engaged in interesting activities.

See the four sets of lesson plans in *Helping Students with Dyslexia and Dysgraphia Make Connections: Differentiated Instruction Lesson Plans in Reading and Writing* (Berninger & Wolf, 2009) for examples of instructional approaches that create such specialized learning environments. These lessons are not scripts that should be implemented in a rigid, unbending way. Rather, they are highly organized and preplanned in great detail so that the teacher can be continually vigilant and attentive to each student's response to instruction, which is of fundamental importance in teaching students with impaired executive functions. Note that continual opportunities to respond are built into the lessons to maintain attention to and engagement in the task at hand. Attention has three components: 1) focusing on the relevant and ignoring the irrelevant, 2) staying on task, and 3) switching between tasks. Engagement is presence of mind or mindfulness as opposed to detachment from what is happening. Sometimes the response is oral and sometimes it is written. Maintaining attention to and engagement in instruction is often very difficult for students with impaired executive functions. Also note in the lessons how frequently the teacher provides feedback or reinforcement to students for paying attention and staying on task.

Helping Students with Dyslexia and Dysgraphia Make Connections (Berninger & Wolf, 2009) also contains information about instructional strategies for helping students pay attention and stay on task during reading and writing instruction. For example, when a student habituates, which is common in students with impaired executive functions, the student fails to pay attention to or respond to the task at hand after continual exposure to the same stimuli or task. To overcome habituation within a lesson, tasks should be of brief duration and vary frequently; however, within each lesson, the variation should occur in a predictable routine for the order and nature of activities. Collectively, short duration, constant change that introduces novelty, and predictable routine across lessons can help students attend, engage, and self-regulate their learning.

The transition from other (teacher) to self-regulation of learning is fundamentally important for students with impaired executive functions. Also, effective instruction for students with impaired executive functions should be specially designed to overcome the associated impaired timing of component processes in working memory (Berninger, Abbott, Thomson, et al., 2006). The component processes that are taught should be carefully orchestrated in real time to help the learners create functional reading and writing systems in their minds (see Chapter 7).

Not all students in the general education classroom require the same level of teacher guidance and orchestration of instructional components as do children with dyslexia, OWL LD, and/or dysgraphia. As discussed previously, one key to meeting the instructional needs of all students is forming instructional groups for reading based on instructional levels, but then adapting the nature of the instruction and not just the instructional level for the various groups depending on the needs of the students. Some children who have impaired or weak executive functions for their age will require highly explicit and systematic instruction. Other children who have strong executive functions do not need such highly explicit and systematic teacher-directed instruction—they are self-regulated learners who acquire considerable implicit knowledge simply by engaging in reading and writing activities, and they may generate their own strategies for managing the learning process (see Chapter 10). Implementing such flexible plans requires teachers with well-honed executive functions who plan ahead, monitor student response to instruction, and are exceptionally well organized.

Chapter 2 Appendix

INFORMATION FOR OBTAINING
INSTRUCTIONAL PROGRAMS LISTED IN TABLE 2.1

Alphabetic Phonics: ALTA National Office, 14070 Proton Road, Suite 100, LB 9, Dallas, TX 75244; http://www.altaread.org

Association Method: The University of Southern Mississippi Dubard School for Language Disorders, 118 College Drive #10035, Hattiesburg, MS 39406; http://www.usm.edu/dubard

Language!: Sopris West, 4093 Specialty Place, Longmont, CO 80504; http://www.teachlanguage.com

Lindamood-Bell: 416 Higuera Street, San Luis Obispo, CA 93401; http://www.lindamoodbell.com

Orton-Gillingham Approach: Academy of Orton-Gillingham Practitioners and Educators, P.O. Box 234, Amenia, NY 12501; http://www.ortonacademy.org

Project Read: Language Circle Enterprises, P.O. Box 20631, Bloomington, MN 55420; http://www.projectread.com

Slingerland Classroom Approach: Slingerland Institute for Literacy, 12729 Northup Way, Suite 1, Bellevue, WA 98005; http://www.slingerland.org

Sonday System: Winsor Learning, 1620 West Seventh Street, St. Paul, MN 55102; http://www.sondaysystem.com

Spalding Method: Spalding Education International, 23335 North 18th Drive, Suite 102, Phoenix, AZ 85027; http://www.spalding.org

Wilson Reading: Wilson Language Training, 47 Old Webster Road, Oxford, MA 01540; http://www.wilsonlanguage.com

CHAPTER 3

Teaching Oral Language

In this chapter and the ones that follow, references will be cited for publications that are the source of the research-generated findings. However, we also share, without citing other publications, knowledge acquired through experience in teaching students. One purpose of this book is to emphasize that both research-generated and teacher-generated knowledge contribute to effective instruction. As in Chapter 2, in this chapter teacher contributions are presented first followed by researcher contributions.

TEACHER CONTRIBUTIONS

Oral Language Is the Key to Learning at School

Teachers may think of language, reading, and writing as being separate skills and may believe that the purpose of formal education is to teach reading and writing but not oral language. Listening and speaking and reading and writing, however, are all language skills, and success at school requires proficient oral language skills as well as written language skills. Children have to process teachers' instructional talk, which is delivered via oral language, as well as their peer's oral language used in class and on the playground. Slingerland's (1971) classic textbook encouraged teaching children with specific language disabilities rather than only reading disabilities.

Spoken language is a complex process. It begins with a thought in its prelinguistic form, about which researchers know very little. It is assumed the thought is generated in the brain at an unconscious level until it is transformed into language that allows conscious access to thought. To translate thought into oral language, an individual must select the appropriate words, arrange them in the correct syntactic order to convey the desired meaning, recall the phonology (phonetic structure) of words or phrases, and activate the speech mechanism (mouth, tongue, breath) and speak the words that convey the thought. Individuals pass through these processes so quickly and with such seeming ease that we are not aware of the breakdowns that can occur in the thought-to-language translation process. In contrast, as pointed out by Oliphant (1976), when a person is listening to someone else speak, the heard speech must be deciphered before the thought behind the language can be inferred.

Oral language is preparation for written language. Systematically teaching aural (through the ears) and oral (through the mouth) sentence structures enhances children's ability to comprehend and compose written sentences (Haynes & Jennings, 2006). Oral and written language have reciprocal influences on each other. Oral receptive and expressive language aid reading comprehension, and, in turn, reading enhances oral vocabulary growth and syntactic development (Johnson, 1991).

Heard Receptive Oral Language   During informal conversation and instruction at school, children process *receptive language*—that is, the aural language received through the ear. For example, processing requires perceiving sounds in spoken words, understanding vocabulary words, and comprehending the heard message. Children with dyslexia may have impaired ability in phonological processing of heard words and thus difficulty distinguishing close gradations of sound such as /b/ and /p/, /f/ and /v/, or /i/ and /e/; sorting sounds into phonemic categories; or holding a sequence of sounds in working memory. All of these phonological skills are necessary for learning written language. Some students who are distracted or confused by background noises may have difficulty in distinguishing foreground language from nonlanguage auditory stimuli. Some students may have difficulty in processing the morphology (e.g., word endings that mark past tense, number or part of speech) or syntax (e.g., word order) of heard language. Thus, receptive language is complex, and many different aspects of it may break down in a student who has receptive oral language difficulties in addition to reading and spelling problems.

Students with auditory or phonological confusions may be uncertain about what they hear and thus have difficulty in learning to spell words when writing. The first column in Table 3.1 shows the text some eighth-grade students wrote for what they *thought* they heard when common proverbs were dictated. The second column shows what was actually dictated.

Expressive Oral Language   Children with dyslexia may also have difficulty with *expressive language,* which is the organization and expression of their thoughts in oral language. Children with dyslexia may have strengths in thinking even though they cannot express those thoughts easily in oral language. Their speech may be delayed for their age, it may lack organization, and it may be hard to access, or they may have planning or initiating difficulties. However, although expressive language results in oral output, it involves more than speech articulation, and children with dyslexia may have problems with language rather than speech. In fact, whether or not speech is also affected, the fundamental problems in expressive language include delays in vocabulary acquisition, word finding abilities (searching through memory for pronunciations and associated meanings or spellings), syntax abilities (structures for organizing the words in a spoken utterance or sentence unit), or grammar abilities (rules for parts of speech and usage).

Children with expressive oral language problems may use immature or very simple sentence structure. Organization may be affected too. Children who say very little may have difficulty ordering and organizing their language output. Others, who speak a great deal, may express the problem in a different way, which is sometimes masked by their excessive wordiness. For example, they may start at the beginning of a story and try to tell every detail because they do not sort relevant and irrelevant information or arrange ideas hierarchically with a main idea

Table 3.1.   Comparison of heard and actual dictated sentences in students with dyslexia

What students heard and wrote down	What was dictated
Row musnt bill tinted "a."	Rome wasn't built in a day.
Turnip outs fir ply.	Turn about is fair play.
Hum tedium tea set honor wall.	Humpty Dumpty sat on a wall.
Al waits beep a light.	Always be polite.
Diamond died weight for nome ann.	Time and tide wait for no man.

Note: Examples are from B. Wolf's classroom.

and supporting details. Learning written language involves learning to write written symbols that refer to oral language structures in the mind. Thus, oral language that lacks organization and clarity interferes with learning written language.

Some children may perceive and process expressive language well, but the complexity of activating the speech mechanisms—mouth, tongue, teeth, breath—and triggering a response may cause them to lose what they intended to say or deem it not worth the effort. Children who raise their hands, eager to answer a question, only to "lose" their words before they can utter them can become frustrated and embarrassed and are often misunderstood. Soon, the children may become reluctant to volunteer, asking someone else to convey information because the effort is too great to organize their thoughts, retrieve vocabulary, create language in understandable form, and speak. For some children, jotting down notes before raising their hands provides security, however, they may have writing problems as well. While following an oral discussion, some children may lose the words as soon as they try to write. Or, the discussion moves forward and their notes are left behind. One strategy children can use to remember what they want to say is to use a place holder, such as raising an index finger. The place holder signals the child's desire to contribute and sometimes helps the speaker remember what he or she wants to say.

Facilitating oral language development can improve literacy skills because of the close relationship between oral and written language acquisition (Dickinson & McCabe, 1991). As such, all students can benefit from daily oral language lessons as they develop an awareness of the importance of good communication and learn listening and speaking skills. Students who have learned to decode automatically, but who lag in reading comprehension, are most often helped by 1) intensive oral language instruction by well-trained teachers who teach comprehension strategies for oral and written language, and/or 2) oral language therapy by a speech-language pathologist.

Classroom Strategies for Developing Oral Language Skills

Teachers should be prepared to take advantage of any teachable moments during the school day to develop oral vocabulary, listening skills, and language concepts. The following list describes some important strategies for teaching oral language:

1. Encourage conversation. Social interaction provides language practice. Some children may need the teacher to guide them in engaging in conversational language. They will gain experience when the teacher talks to them, asking questions, rephrasing answers, and encouraging oral expression.

2. Expect complete syntactic structure. Although students may not use complete oral syntax in informal speech, doing so in the classroom provides practice in a skill necessary for written language. When students use fragmented syntax, the teacher should model complete syntax.

3. Maintain eye contact with the various members of the class or instructional group. Encouraging students to maintain eye contact helps them gauge the audience's attention and adjust language, volume, or organization to be better understood, communicate more clearly, and receive nonverbal cues about their clarity.

4. Remind students to speak loudly and articulate clearly. Doing so will allow students to feel the muscles used for speech while they are talking. They need to hear their own speech distinctly as they begin to learn written language. It is not easy to sound out a word for reading or spelling when it is not articulated clearly. In the classroom, speakers provide output that becomes aural input for themselves and for their listening classmates. Mumbled or misarticulated speaking will not hold the attention of the group and will not fully benefit the speaker.

5. Explain that tone of voice can change the meaning of what a speaker says. Tone may be related to pitch, volume, speed, and rhythm. Many playground disagreements come about because of misunderstandings when children are using playground voices. It is not the words they use but the volume and pitch that can lead to misunderstanding of motives and attitudes. Conversely, when messages are too soft they can be ignored or hard to understand.

6. Attend to listening skills as well. Teachers need to ensure that students are listening by using consistent cues to get their attention. One school, for example, adopted the phrase, "It's listening time" for all classrooms. Students often are more effectively cued to attention if all school personnel use the same language for reminders. Some students might also benefit from posted written reminders.

    a. Good listeners give feedback to the speaker through eye contact, body language, and nods. They avoid interruption and distraction.

    b. Active listeners need strategies for recall. Direct instruction and practice in using the tools of active listening will help students identify the tools that are most effective for them. These tools may include visualizing, rehearsing, or repeating the items to be remembered; finger counting; using mnemonic clues; or taking notes. The latter is a skill that requires fluent handwriting or keyboarding.

    c. Careful listening prepares students for summarizing or contrasting heard information. Having students verbally summarize or otherwise discuss the information they hear should begin in kindergarten and continue with increasingly difficult questions as children grow older. Teachers should encourage students to ask for clarification when they do not understand something—students can ask the teacher directly or fellow students.

7. Ensure that instructional language is clear. Young children may not understand words or concepts such as *top, center, indent, blanks,* or *missing.* Teachers must be certain that all students understand what is expected of them. For ex-

ample, if a teacher says, "Let's check with Dick" every time a spelling question arises, the teacher should explain to new students that "Dick" is the nickname for the dictionary (rather than a classmate named Dick) and this means they should look for the proper spelling in the dictionary.

8. Make sure students can organize and express thoughts clearly. As students develop reading and writing skills, they are expected to understand the need for capitalizing the beginning of a sentence and placing a period or other punctuation at the end. This expectation assumes that students always recognize sentences, which begins with processing syntax in oral language, even though we do not always speak in complete sentences. By Grade 4, students should reliably write in complete sentences. Being able to organize and express answers clearly first in oral language is a foundation for later writing of organized, clear sentences.

9. Provide help with correct syntax and sentence form by modeling, questioning, and redirecting. Some children have difficulty getting started with the wording of a sentence. Saying the beginning word or phrase for the child can help the child structure his or her response. Give children time for thinking and formulating an oral or written response. Using explicit language with fully developed noun phrases and without ambiguous pronouns can help children's comprehension of reading material.

10. Incorporate a "question of the day" during instruction. Presenting an oral question for students to answer in complete sentences can help students develop clear, well-organized sentences. The question can be a part of each day's opening exercises, for instance before or after taking roll. The students answering the question should speak clearly and loudly enough to be heard, while making eye contact with the audience. The exercise will only take 5 or 10 minutes if just 7–10 students are asked to respond each day. As children practice, this exercise will take less time. Teachers can even write the question on the board so that the students can read it and prepare their answers when they first come into the room. A suggested list of one-part, two-part, three-part, and process questions can be found in Appendix 3A.

   Teachers should encourage students to make use of the language in the question in formulating their answers. If students do not answer in complete sentences the teacher should restructure the answer by modeling and asking the child to repeat the model. In a very short time, students often will become conscious of the *idea* of a sentence and will require little reminding.

   a. Start with one-part questions that require only a simple declarative sentence:

      Teacher: "What is your favorite animal?"

      Child: "My favorite animal is _____."

   b. When children are successful answering one-part questions in complete sentences, move to two-part questions. When they are successful with two-part questions, move to three-part questions. Because two- and three-part questions require more thought and organization on the part of the child, they are usually answered in two sentences:

Teacher: "What is your favorite animal? Why?"

Student: "My favorite animal is _____ because _____."

c.   Process questions are asked to solicit explanations from children:

Teacher: "What is the process for getting on a bus?"

Student: "First you walk up the steps. Then you pay the driver. Then you look for a seat."

d.   Each day, when the selected students have responded to the question, help the listeners summarize what they heard by asking questions such as, "What animal was mentioned most often?" "What reasons did people give for choosing a particular animal?" "What kinds of food did people need for their animals?" Answers should also be in complete sentences.

11.   Ensure students understand the different parts of speech. Parts of speech provide the building blocks for teaching students how to write sentences (Carreker, 2006). The following activity, suggested by Slingerland (1967), builds awareness of prepositions. The whole class can be involved and the teacher can monitor with little difficulty.

a.   Provide each student with three objects, such as a book, a pencil, and a piece of paper. Make sure the objects enable the whole class to be involved and allow the teacher to quickly see whether all students are following directions.

b.   Give a direction and model the appropriate response. For example, "Put the pencil beside the book. Now, where is the pencil? *Beside the book* is a prepositional phrase. It tells where to put the pencil. So, the pencil is beside the book." By using the correct terminology from the beginning, students acquire vocabulary pertaining to parts of speech.

c.   After giving several examples, ask students to respond independently in complete sentences.

Teacher: "Put the paper under the book. Where is the paper?"

Student: "The paper is under the book. *Under the book* is a prepositional phrase; it tells *where*."

Teacher: "Where is the book?"

Student: "The book is on the paper. *On the paper* is a prepositional phrase. It tells *where*.

As students discover prepositions they will place objects *between*, *inside*, and *beside* other objects, and they will excitedly point them out in text and conversations. Students who develop these concepts early have better reading comprehension because they understand phrases and have an awareness of "the words that go together" to tell "where."

12.   Teach students how to build sentences. Sentence building is popular at all grade levels. The following adaptation from Slingerland (1971) allows students to answer editorial questions—who, what, where, when, and why—that lead to better reading comprehension and more effective written language.

a. Choose a subject. The teacher may choose one related to content material or the students may choose a subject. Then ask the students to add more information. For example

Teacher: "What lives on both land and in the water?"

Student: "A frog."

Teacher: "Add two words, adjectives, to describe the frog."

Student: "A big, green frog."

Teacher: "Think of one word—did what?"

Student: "Hopped."

Teacher: "Put it all together to make a sentence."

Student: "A big, green frog hopped."

b. Once an initial sentence is established, ask further questions so that the students can add more information and further build on the sentence. Each added phrase can be completed by a different student—involve as many students as possible. As a phrase is added, the student should repeat the entire sentence with the added phrase. Use as many phrases as the students can handle. For example

Teacher: "Where did the big, green frog hop?"

Student: "Through the grass. A big, green frog hopped through the grass."

Teacher: "How did the big, green frog hop through the grass?"

Student: "Quickly. A big, green frog hopped through the grass quickly."

Teacher: "When did the big, green frog hop through the grass quickly?"

Student: "This morning. A big, green frog hopped through the grass quickly this morning."

Teacher: "Why did the big, green frog hop through the grass quickly this morning?"

Student: "Because he saw a slug. A big, green frog hopped through the grass quickly this morning because he saw a slug.

13. Teach students how to rearrange sentences. Building on the activity described in strategy 12, have participating students stand in a row in the front of the room in the order in which they added their phrases, and ask each one to repeat his or her phrase (e.g., "A big, green frog hopped quickly through the grass this morning because he saw a slug"). Then instruct the students to rearrange themselves and repeat their phrases again. When they do so, new forms of the sentence emerge (e.g., "Because he saw a slug, a big, green frog hopped quickly through the grass this morning," "This morning, a big green, frog hopped quickly through the grass because he saw a slug").

With every new arrangement, the class should determine whether the order makes sense and add suggestions for the order in which the phrases should be arranged. As children are ready, they can make more complex or compound sentences by introducing connecting words such as *and, but, except*, and *then*. Ask students to change the tense to something that is happening now or something that will happen in the future. Introduce a written component: As each phrase is suggested by a child, the teacher can quickly write it on tag board strips. The student can then hold the strips so that the class can see the phrases in the correct order as each sentence is composed and again as phrases are rearranged.

14. Have students build phrases independently. Independent work is a transitional step toward functional use. Students may create their own phrases by combining words from lists provided by the teacher. The words may be from the students' decoding lists or from reading or content texts. The difficulty of the activity may be varied by the words provided. Number words or plural noun markers such as *these, those,* or *some* may be used if the class knows how to form plurals.

   a. Place a list of adjectives, a list of nouns, and a list of noun markers on the board. (See Table 3.2 for an example.) Have students choose one adjective and one noun from each list to create their own lists of noun phrases. The students can also illustrate their noun phrases. Students' lists will vary.

   b. After students are successful with one adjective, have them choose two adjectives for each noun.

   c. Have the students perform the same activity with prepositional phrases. (See Table 3.3 for an example.)

15. Compile a class booklet of students' phrases. Students can create a class booklet by writing a prepositional phrase to complete a sentence (e.g., "When my dog got lost I looked..."). Each student can write and illustrate a phrase to complete the sentence (e.g., *at the grocery store, in the park, under the bed*). When the pages are assembled into a booklet, students can practice reading the very long sentence. They can also write a conclusion to the story.

Abstract and Temporal Oral Language Concepts

Children with language problems often have difficulty with abstract temporal language concepts such as *before, after,* or *following*, and with sequences such as days of the week or months of the year. They also may have difficulty estimating the amount of time needed for an activity or project. Students may have an understanding that seasons—spring, summer, fall (autumn), and winter—are cyclical just as are days of the week and months of the year, but they may have difficulty in recalling them in sequence and associating them with the correct periods of time. For telling time and understanding the calendar, students need to recognize that the cycle of holidays, months of the year, days of the week, time of day, life cycles, and plant growth cycles repeat again and again and that they are related to science, math, and social studies. Regular practice and review will help to make this recall automatic.

Students with language problems may need to see or hear concepts many times and review them frequently in many settings to learn and retain them thor-

Table 3.2.   Building noun phrases

Adjectives	Nouns	Noun markers
far	barn	the
dark	farm	this
sharp	star	a
hard	cart	that
black	jar	
green	chart	
clean	park	
big	yard	
little	scarf	
large	card	

oughly. These skills will be reinforced when the teacher regularly develops, discusses, reviews, and uses activities to strengthen awareness. A formal group language lesson may not be necessary if the teacher regularly and consciously includes these concepts in daily work (e.g., as part of the morning opening exercises, at story time, during "sponge" activities to fill those few minutes in line or before dismissal) and at every natural opportunity.

Regular practice and reinforcement of abstract and temporal oral language concepts is essential throughout the year. The following activities can provide practice for such concepts. However, do not stop practicing them when a child can recite the days of the week or the months of the year. Review these concepts regularly until they are automatic for every child in every kind of oral or written performance. Serial organization or putting items in order is fundamental to learning oral and written language.

Practicing Time of Day   When teaching children to tell time, include practice with an analog clock. The circle of the dial lends emphasis to the cyclical nature of times of day. Include questions about time as questions of the day (e.g., "At what time of the day do you . . . have your favorite meal? wake up? go to bed? feed the dog?").

Table 3.3.   Building prepositional phrases

Prepositions	Nouns	Noun markers
at	barn	the
on	farm	this
under	star	a
near	cart	that
to	jar	
from	chart	
in	park	
	marsh	
	scarf	
	card	

*Practicing **Days of the Week*** Students should be able to name the days of the week in order, starting with any day, and be able to identify what day is before or what day is after any named day. By Grade 3, students should be able to correctly spell the days of the week. As part of the daily calendar work, help students identify various days (e.g., "Today is . . .," "Yesterday was . . .," "Tomorrow will be . . .," "A week ago today was . . .").

*Practicing **Months of the Year*** Use oral activities with all grades and written activities when appropriate.

1. Ask students to name the months in order, starting with any month. Naming in order takes practice, but is an excellent introduction to any new month. "This is April. Let's name all of the months of the year starting with this month."

2. Students can move (e.g., march, tiptoe, hop) in rhythm while reciting the months of the year. When the month in which their birthday occurs is named, they can put their hands above their heads.

3. Ask students to identify which holiday comes in each month and then review holidays for other months in sequence. "Groundhog Day is in February. What holiday is in March? In April?"

4. Ask students to identify the month before or after a given month. "May is before June and after April." "May is between April and June."

5. Have students practice writing the months of the year. If students copy the complete name of the month each time they head their papers, they will have many opportunities to practice the correct spelling. After spelling of months is firmly established, abbreviations may be taught, and students can learn to write the date in various acceptable formats (e.g., February 1, 2008; Feb. 1, 2008; 2/1/2008).

6. Incorporate questions about months in the questions of the day (e.g., "What is the next holiday? When does it occur?" "In what season is [name a month]? What holidays occur in that month?" "What month comes after your birthday?").

*Practicing **Alphabet Order*** A Japanese proverb states that if you wish to know the highest truth, you must begin with the alphabet. Learning the alphabet is a child's first introduction to literacy and to later abstract scientific and logical thinking in Western culture (Logan, 1986). In addition to the alphabet's use in automatic recognition of letters and their names and in communicating language, it is used to classify information through alphabetization, and it relates to functional dictionary use and organizational systems, including understanding telephone books, encyclopedias, and filing systems. Children with dyslexia may have difficulty recalling the alphabet in sequential order. Having the alphabet posted in the front of the classroom or at their desk provides students with a constant point of reference to aid uncertain recall.

1. Start each day by having students recite the alphabet. Have them sing the alphabet song but also recite the alphabet orally. Then put it to use as students put things away by letter or are called to line up or for dismissal in alphabetical order.

Begin with a different letter each time so that students can practice picking up the alphabet from a particular letter rather than always starting with *a.*

2. Ask students to name the letter that comes after or before another letter, or ask them to name the letter that comes between two other letters.

3. Practice alphabetizing. Call three children to the front of the room. They should have clearly printed name tags. Ask class members to arrange the three children in alphabetical order. As the class becomes proficient, increase the numbers of children to be alphabetized. Delay using two or more students whose names begin with the same letter until the performance with *different* letters is automatic. Then bring everyone whose names begin with the same letter to the front. Show how the second letter, or even the third, becomes part of the alphabetizing process.

4. After decoding practice, have the students copy the words in alphabetical order and illustrate each word. Repeat often after decoding and use with science or social studies words.

Play with Language

Language learning occurs as the result of play with language as well as instructional activities. Some students with dyslexia, oral and written language learning disability (OWL LD) and/or dysgraphia benefit from activities that help them gain insight into the use of language for humor. Plays on words and puns require instant recognition of multiple meanings of words and recognition of intonation for understanding exaggeration or to indicate teasing. Donald was such a student in Beverly Wolf's classroom. In fourth grade he was feeling isolated and left out of classroom friendships. The "joke of the day" helped him to understand what made people laugh. Each day, during snack time, the teacher or students read or told a joke. Then they explained why it was funny. Soon the whole class, including Donald, was checking joke books out of the library. Everyone benefited from the analysis and explanations of the nuances of language and the motivation for reading.

Discuss and practice figurative language. Books such as Fred Gwynne's *Chocolate Moose for Dinner* (1976) are good introductions. (See Appendix 3B for further book titles that can help with language learning.) Teachers can read these books to the class and discuss them with students. Teachers can also ask students to illustrate figures of speech, such as "You drive me up the wall!" or "It's raining cats and dogs."

Reading to Children to Stimulate Oral Language Development

Literature provides language stimulation that enriches vocabulary, introduces new language constructions and story grammar, and allows children to discover the joy of language and reading. Reading to children and discussing books with them helps children develop vocabulary and organization of language (Whitehurst, Falco, Lonigan, Fischel, DeBaryshe, et al., 1988). Discussing the text also aids in understanding and prediction (e.g., "What do you think will happen next?" "Why do you think the character did that?"). These open-ended questions promote language and vocabulary growth that is a factor in written language performance. Rhyming stories and poetry develop phonological awareness and can foster a love of the rhythm of language. Reading to children not only opens a world of literature but also improves listening skills—skilled readers listen better and skilled listeners read better.

Literature also provides information to those students who are unable to access it themselves—not just factual information but also information about feelings, points of view, and interpersonal relationships. Literature can give pleasure, provoke thought, teach skills, and provide understanding of other cultures. When introducing literature to children, teachers should begin with illustrated books.

Many picture books, such as Patricia Polacco's *Pink and Say* (1994), are written with concepts most suited for 10- to 12-year-olds. Pictures can aid in clarifying vocabulary, developing comprehension of the text, and illustrating difficult ideas, which is especially important for children with weak auditory skills. Pictures help the audience focus and provide clues to action. Text in picture books comes in shorter chunks than in chapter books, but it expresses ideas with economy and richness of vocabulary. Picture books are tools to help students of all ages to tie words to pictures—to interpret, imagine, visualize, and understand what the author is saying.

A good children's book appeals to adults as well as children. Reading to children helps develop vocabulary, inflection, phrasing, and prosody, all of which may help to develop effective listening. Adults should help children to visualize and be actively involved by asking editorial questions, such as who? what? where? when? why? and how?

Children learn to understand the structure and organization of books by regular informal discussion of such things as author, illustrator, characters, and setting. "How did the characters feel?" "What emotions made them act as they did?" "What words make you think this?" Motivation is the *why* of the story, the source of critical actions. Time and place and mood are all part of setting. Discussing plot leads to clarification of motivation, sequence, action, and resolution. Were issues resolved? Could the same problems occur again? The level of a discussion will vary with the age of the children in the group. Older students should have many opportunities to develop vocabulary and an understanding of the difference between narrative language that tells a story and expository language that may describe, explain, predict, argue, or convey ideas. All of these experiences contribute to competence and confidence in reading.

Summing It Up

Reading, handwriting, spelling, and composing are all language skills. Oral language development is the natural basis for all instruction for all of these skills. If students are allowed to be imprecise or to use oral language incorrectly, they are being denied the tools for learning and for higher level thinking skills. When children do not use oral language correctly, teachers should model correct usage through instructional activities. Appendix 3B contains a list of books for teachers to use in creating that love of language and joy in using it for school learning. Examples are provided for teaching homophones, idioms, play with language, word play, parts of speech, days of the week, and months of the year.

RESEARCHER CONTRIBUTIONS

Researchers in English-speaking countries have conducted large-scale longitudinal studies in which children's oral language is first studied in the preschool years and then reassessed at future stages of language development during formal schooling. For example, preschoolers with problems in oral language were followed through the school years to investigate whether early oral language problems persist and whether these children also develop written language problems in reading and/or writing during the school years. These longitudinal studies (Aram, Ekelman, & Nation, 1984; Bishop & Adams, 1990; Catts, Fey, Zhang, & Tomblin, 1999; Catts, Hogan, & Adloff, 2005) showed that preschoolers with oral language problems may continue to have language learning problems during the school years, may have dyslexia or other reading problems, may have intellectual deficiencies, or may be normal readers. The specific reading problems may be evident in first grade, for example, as children struggle to learn to decode and read words, or the problems may become evident later as curriculum requirements change for reading comprehension.

Other longitudinal studies have focused on development of oral and written language skills in children with diagnosed oral language impairment (Fey, Catts, Proctor-Williams, Tomblin, & Zhang, 2004) or preschoolers at risk for future reading disabilities (Catts, Fey, Zhang, & Tomblin, 2001; Scarborough, 1991). All have documented that oral language skills are essential in learning to read and write and are especially relevant to development of reading comprehension skills—the ultimate goal of reading—and also to writing (Scott & Winsor, 2000; Silliman & Scott, in press). Teaching oral language skills is relevant to developing reading comprehension (Cain & Oakhill, 2007; Carlisle & Rice, 2002) and spelling and written composition (Scott & Winsor, 2000; Silliman & Scott, in press). Schools should not focus only on written language in teaching children to read and write, especially those with learning disabilities involving written language. The instructional program should also include instructional activities to develop oral language skills (e.g., Beck & McKeown, 2001, 2007).

Also, in general education, oral discussion is often used as an evidence-based pedagogical tool for reading, writing, and math instruction (e.g., Nussbaum, 2002; Reznitskaya et al., 2001). Children's relative strengths and weaknesses in listening comprehension and oral expression may influence their ability to participate in such discussions and thus influence their resulting academic achievement. Without a clear understanding of how oral language skills complement written language skills in academic learning, educators may not have the necessary knowledge for optimizing all students' reading and writing.

Thus, the teaching experience and research evidence converge: Oral language is critically important to literacy learning. This chapter has offered many practical suggestions for developing oral language skills of all students, including those with specific learning disabilities in the general education classroom.

Appendix 3A

QUESTIONS OF THE DAY

Sample One-Part Questions

- What school did you attend last year?
- What is your job or responsibility at home?
- What is your favorite food?
- How many children are in your family?
- What pets do you have?
- What would you like to change about yourself?
- What do you do best?
- What do you like best about yourself?
- Where is your favorite place to go?
- What is your favorite after-school activity?
- What is something that bugs you?

Sample Two-Part Questions

- What sport do you play best? Why are you good at it?
- What sport would you like to learn or is hardest for you? Why?
- What school subject is easiest for you? Why do you think it is easy?
- What subject is hardest for you? Why?
- How do you remember a telephone number? What is yours?
- What is one good health habit? Explain.
- What three words describe you best? Why?
- Why do people like you? What do others like best about you?

Sample Three-Part Questions

- If you could buy a gift for someone, who would you buy it for, what would you buy, and why?
- If you could go anywhere, where would you go, why would you go there, and how would you get there?

- If your bicycle has a flat tire, what might you need to fix it, where would you go for help, and who could help you change it?

- What is your favorite sport, how did you learn to play (or when do you watch it), and why do you like it?

- What is your favorite wild animal, where does it live, and what does it do?

Sample Process Questions

A process is the exact order of steps that people or machines follow to get something done. The steps are explained in their exact order. No step is left out. Anyone who follows the same process can do the same thing.

- What is the process for washing your hands?

- What is the process for cleaning up your lunch space?

- What is the process for baking a cake?

- How do you make a peanut butter and jelly sandwich?

- What is the process for tying your shoes?

Appendix 3B

CHILDREN'S BOOKS THAT HELP WITH LANGUAGE LEARNING

Homonyms

Alda, A. (2006). *Did you say pears?* Toronto: Tundra Books.
Barretta, G. (2007). *Dear deer: A book of homophones*. New York: Henry Holt & Company.
Cleary, B. (2005). *How much can a bare bear bear?: What are homonyms and homophones?* Minneapolis, MN: Lerner Publishing Group.
Gwynne, F. (1976). *Chocolate moose for dinner*. New York: Simon & Schuster.
Gwynne, F. (1980). *The king who rained*. New York: Simon & Schuster.
Gwynne, F. (1988). *A little pigeon toad*. New York: Simon & Schuster.
Hambleton, L., & Turhan, S. (2007). *Telling tails: Fun with homonyms*. London: Milet Publishing Ltd.
Terban, M. (1982). *Eight ate: A feast of homonym riddles*. New York: Clarion Books.

Idioms

Arnold, T. (2004). *Even more parts*. New York: Scholastic.
Terban, M. (1983). *In a pickle and other funny idioms*. New York: Houghton Mifflin.
Terban, M. (1987). *Mad as a wet hen! and other funny idioms*. New York: Houghton Mifflin.
Terban, M. (1990). *Punching the clock: Funny action idioms*. New York: Houghton Mifflin.

Play with Language

Scieszca, J. (1991). *Knights of the kitchen table*. New York: Viking.
Terban, M. (1993). *It figures! Fun figures of speech*. New York: Houghton Mifflin.
Also, any titles by Dr. Seuss.

Word Play

Bourke, L. (1991). *Eye spy*. San Francisco: Chronicle Books.
Gwynne, F. (1976). *Chocolate moose for dinner*. New York: Simon & Schuster.
Gwynne, F. (1980). *The king who rained*. New York: Simon & Schuster.
Gwynne, F. (1980). *The sixteen hand horse*. New York: Simon & Schuster.
Gwynne, F. (1988). *A little pigeon toad*. New York: Simon & Schuster.
Juster, M. (1961). *The phantom tollbooth*. New York: Random House.
Terban, M. (1988). *The dove dove*. New York: Clarion Books.

Parts of Speech

Adverbs

Cleary, B. (2003). *Dearly, nearly, insincerely: What is an adverb?* Minneapolis, MN: Lerner Publishing Group.
Heller, R. (1998). *Up, up and away: A book about adverbs*. New York: Penguin Young Readers Group.

Adjectives

Brown, M. (1949). *The important book.* New York: Harper & Row. (Good for generating language for an independent writing activity.)

Cleary, B. (2001). *Hairy, scary, ordinary: What is an adjective?* Minneapolis, MN: Lerner Publishing Group.

Cleary, B. (2007). *Quirky, jerky, extra-perky: More about adjectives.* Minneapolis, MN: Lerner Publishing Group.

Heller, R. (1989). *Many luscious lollipops.* New York: Grosset & Dunlap.

Hubbard, W. (2003). *C is for curious.* New York: Scholastic.

Viorst, J. (1971). *Tenth good thing about Barney.* NY: Simon & Schuster Children's Publishing.

Viorst, J. (1987). *Alexander and the terrible, horrible, rotten, no good, very bad day.* New York: Simon & Schuster.

Yagoda, B. (2007). *When you catch an adjective, kill it: The parts of speech, for better and/or worse.* New York: Broadway Books.

Nouns

Heller, R. (1998). *Merry-go-round: A book about nouns.* New York: Penguin Young Readers Group.

Terban, M. (1986). *Your foot's on my feet and other tricky nouns.* Minneapolis, MN: Lerner Publishing Group.

Pronouns

Cleary, B. (2004). *I and you and don't forget who: What is a pronoun?* Minneapolis, MN: Lerner Publishing Group.

Heller, R. (1999). *Mine, all mine: A book about pronouns.* New York: Penguin Young Readers Group.

Prepositions

Cleary, B. (2002). *Under, over, by the clover: What is a preposition?* Minneapolis, MN: Carolrhoda Books.

Heller, R. (1998). *Behind the mask: A book about prepositions.* New York: Penguin Young Readers Group.

Days of the Week

Carle, E. (1981). *The very hungry caterpillar.* New York: Philomel.

Months of the Year

Sendak, M. (1976). *Chicken soup with rice.* New York: Harper Collins.

CHAPTER 4

Teaching Reading

As in Chapter 3, we begin with teacher contributions and share examples from Beverly Wolf's teaching experience, as classroom teacher or principal, to illustrate some of the knowledge gained from teaching reading to children with dyslexia and/or oral and written language learning disability (OWL LD). We then consider the knowledge generated by research on effective reading instruction for these children.

TEACHER CONTRIBUTIONS

To children, reading is magic. It is a means of delivering the thoughts and language of one person into the language and mind of another. Those children who are resistant or appear to be unmotivated to read typically have been defeated in their efforts by daily failure in their attempts to learn the magic of reading. These children, however, usually long desperately to achieve the ability to read. In Beverly Wolf's classroom, 7-year-old Travis said, "The Christmas presents don't matter. I just need to know how to read." Third grader Raizel said, "My dream is to be a reader."

According to Masland (1979), the magic of reading stems from the complexity of processes that must be mastered so that reading proceeds without effort. These processes include 1) applying the alphabetic principle for grapheme–phoneme correspondences to decoding words that are completely or partially decodable; 2) relating spelling, sound, and meaning in recognizing, pronouncing, and understanding words; and 3) using the structures of oral and written language to comprehend text. Teaching these processes draws on multiple units or levels of language:

1. Phonology: speech sounds (phonemes)

2. Syntax: phrase and sentence structure

3. Semantics: phrase and sentence meaning

4. Discourse structure: organization of connected sentences

5. Pragmatics: use of language for communication acts

Until children are reading without effort, each reading lesson should consist of teacher-directed, explicit, systematic instruction in 1) phonological awareness; 2) applying phonics (alphabetic principle) and morphology to decoding; 3) applying background knowledge already learned to unfamiliar words or concepts in material to be read (activating prior knowledge); 4) both oral reading and silent reading, with appropriate instructional materials; 5) activities to develop oral reading fluency; and 6) reading comprehension. The goal of this instruction is also to develop independent readers who can apply what they learn to reading on their own.

A Brief Review: Organizational Principles and Instructional Materials

To assist teachers in implementing specialized instruction for students with dyslexia or OWL LD in the general education classroom, the following sections review the organizational principles introduced in Chapter 2 and provide an overview of supplementary instructional materials.

Grouping for Differentiated Instruction   Informal reading inventories are administered to determine instructional levels for word reading on a list without context clues and for word reading in the context of a passage. For example, the Qualitative Reading Inventory–4, 4th Edition (QRI-4; Leslie & Caldwell, 2005) is often used for this purpose. Teachers should also consider reading test scores that may be available and students' response to daily reading instruction in forming instructional groups to teach at each student's instructional level.

As one student the authors worked with said, "It's just plain stupid to try to teach a kid to read in a book that's too hard." Sigmund Freud said it in a different way: "Understanding becomes impossible once reading becomes difficult" (Henry, 1999, p. 17). If students cannot recognize at least 90% of the words, they are unlikely to understand what they read (Juel, 1994) or make progress (Honig, 1996). Without challenge, students are also unlikely to grow in reading. If a book is too easy, students are likely not to make progress. A perceptive teacher provides balance between ease and challenge. The key to effective reading instruction is to match the level of instruction to a student's reading level with the right book at a level that challenges the student but is accessible. When students are grouped by instructional level for daily reading instruction, teachers are able to work with text materials as close to each child's reading level as possible and still provide instruction most suited to that group's needs. Small-group instruction will also allow each child more opportunities to respond when the teacher provides feedback. It will also provide the teacher with opportunities for informal daily evaluation of response to instruction that leads to more refined instruction.

By forming three or four instructional groups, the teacher can provide differentiated instruction based on both instructional levels and the nature of instruction needed. For example, one group could be devoted to students with dyslexia or OWL LD, who will require more explicit, systematic, and sustained instruction in various reading skills than classmates in other groups. In forming instructional groups, the teacher needs to take into account whether students' problems are mainly in decoding unknown words, automatic word reading, and/or in reading comprehension and whether students will need extra instruction and practice in one or more of these skills. The teacher also needs to consider whether students' problems are mainly in oral reading fluency, silent reading fluency, or both. Some children need to read out loud and hear what they are reading in order to comprehend, whereas others comprehend better if they can read silently. Another factor to consider is whether children in early grades are masking problems in reading comprehension by drawing on background knowledge to answer comprehension questions rather than drawing on the text as written. Their reading comprehension problems are likely to increase as they encounter more embedded phrases and clauses and technical vocabulary in later grades.

Reading Materials for Balanced Instruction Phonics readers provide decodable leveled materials that are accessible to students and offer many opportunities to practice decoding skills in the context of connected text. (See Chapter 2 for inexpensive or free sources of decoding materials that can be downloaded from the internet.) However, purely decodable materials may not provide enough experience with partially decodable words or rich vocabulary words that are common in spoken language. Older students struggling at low levels will quickly become bored with sentences such as, "The cat sat on the mat." Basal or literature readers provide more variety in linking oral and written language structures in a way that reflects use of language in real-world contexts; however, the word decoding requirements for such texts may be more complex. The ideal is a combination of the two kinds of text. For example, some classrooms spend some time decoding each day and then read from conventional texts. Others alternate between phonics and literature-based readers on different days, providing opportunities for development of both types of skills.

Teaching Phonological and Orthographic Awareness

"Phonological awareness is the ability to notice, think about, or manipulate the individual sounds of words (Torgesen, 1996). Adams (1990) explained that phonological awareness is neither the ability to hear the difference between two sounds nor the ability to pronounce individual sounds. Rather, a beginning reader must first understand that speech can be segmented or broken into small sounds and then learn to relate this awareness of sounds to the awareness of how they are represented in single letters or letter groups in written words (orthographic awareness). That is, readers need to translate printed symbols in written words into corresponding speech sounds, which is the alphabetic principle, and then synthesize the sounds to pronounce whole words. Research shows that phonological awareness enables decoding and decoding enables phonological awareness (reciprocal relationships).

Phonological awareness can be taught, and such teaching makes a difference in beginning reading and spelling achievement. Simply teaching phonics may not be sufficient. The most impressive gains in reading achievement occur when children receive phoneme awareness training along with instruction in the relationships between letters and sounds. The beginning levels of phoneme awareness do not involve written letters or words and, therefore, are not phonics. Later in reading development, phonics—the relationships between letters and sounds—is taught and practiced; in the process, growing orthographic awareness of letter units in written words can lead to growth in phonological awareness of phonemes in spoken words, and vice versa. By convention, sounds are denoted by slashes (e.g., /k/), but letters are denoted by italics (e.g., *c*).

Sixth-grade students who were not making adequate progress in decoding received additional intervention in phonological awareness training following the sequence listed next, proposed by Kaufman (1995).

1. *Rhyming tasks.* Children must learn to attend to the sounds of the words, not the meaning. Teachers should begin by explaining what a rhyme is and providing examples—many children think that words rhyme if they begin with the same sounds, so the teacher should make it clear that only words that share ending sounds rhyme. As children develop proficiency, the teacher can use the cloze procedure in which the students supply the rhyming word (e.g., "Little Jack Horner sat in the _____.").

2. *Categorization tasks.* To promote further development of phonological awareness, the teacher can introduce activities in which children categorize spoken words on the basis of shared sound units. For example, they might indicate the one that does not go with the others on the basis of rhyme endings (e.g., *book, look, like, took*) or beginning phonemes (e.g., *boy, toy, bat, buy*).

3. *Syllable identification tasks.* These tasks (Brady, Fowler, Stone, & Winebury, 1994) are the next developmentally appropriate phonological task. In these tasks, children are asked to find word parts in various positions throughout the word. For example, the teacher can identify a word part (e.g., /all/), and the children must tell whether that syllable appears in the words the teacher names (e.g., *fall, tall, ran, land, always, recall, baker, farmer*).

4. *Word segmentation tasks.* These tasks (Brady et al., 1994) require the insight that words can be isolated throughout a spoken sentence. Teachers may also request that children say a part of the phrase and decide what to omit. Appropriately leveled readers or storybooks can supply sentences, or teachers can make up their own.

5. *Segmenting and blending tasks.* Blending is introduced once the child can segment by words. Next, students are asked to segment spoken words by first breaking off the first phoneme and then subsequent phonemes of a word or syllable. This analytical activity requires insight that sounds can be isolated. Next, they are asked to synthesize; that is, blend. If necessary, the child might repeat /c/ /a/ /t/, then blend *cat*. This synthesizing activity is generally thought to be easier than analytic tasks that break whole words apart. However, it has a memory component that requires children to recall sounds in sequence while resynthesizing before repeating the word.

6. *Phoneme manipulation tasks.* In these tasks, students are asked to manipulate the phonemes in a word and then a nonword (Liberman, Shankweiler, Fischer, & Carter, 1974). The initial or ending consonants may be changed or the vowel may be changed or may be reordered in a word (e.g., *split, spilt*). Or, the child may be asked to add or delete phonemes (e.g., *cap, casp, clasp*). Kaufman (1995) recommended using words that are only partially decodable with older students so that their memory of the spelling of the words does not interfere with the phoneme analysis task.

The sixth-grade students receiving this instruction had a great deal more difficulty in identifying rhyming words than did younger children in other groups. When they were finally able to identify rhyming words in poems, both in and out of context, they were able to zoom ahead through the other activities that followed and their decoding skills improved.

Teaching Decoding by Applying the Alphabetic Principle, Syllables, and Morphology

In addition to phonological awareness, phonics is necessary. Phonics is the system in which symbols (one or two letters) represent sounds (phonemes). The alphabetic principle refers to the correspondence between these graphemes and phonemes. Explicit phonics refers to an organized program in which these correspondences are taught systematically. However, phonics alone is not enough. Students also need to learn to recognize syllable patterns, spelling patterns larger than the letters or letter groups that correspond to phonemes in the alphabetic principle, and the affixes (prefixes at beginning of words and suffixes at the end of words) in written words accurately and quickly. Students also need to understand the morphology of language—how its roots, prefixes, and suffixes can be used to decode and spell longer complex words that they will encounter more often in reading material in Grades 4 and above (Henry, 2003). Affixes give shades of meaning to root words, which are called *base words* if they already have had a suffix affixed to it, for example, *nation* (root word), *national* (base word), and *nationality* (affixed base word). Slingerland and Murray's (2008) *Teacher's Word List* can be used as a source of words in teaching the many strategies of decoding, including, but not restricted to, phonics.

Students benefit from learning the six types of syllables (Moats, 2000):

1. *Closed syllables* have one vowel, which has a short sound, and end with a consonant (e.g., *flip, cast, drop, tub, them*).

2. *Open syllables* end in a vowel, and the vowel is long (e.g., *go, me*). Two-syllable words such as *secret* contain both open (initial long vowel) and closed (final short vowel) syllables.

3. *Vowel–consonant–e syllables* have a vowel followed by a consonant and a silent *e*, which indicates that the vowel before it is long (e.g., *safe, bike, hope, these*).

4. *Vowel team syllables* have two letters together that stand for one phoneme. In vowel digraphs the phoneme is one of the possible options for a letter in the pair (e.g., *m-ai-n*), but in a vowel diphthong the letter-pair stands for a new sound that does not correspond to either single letter (e.g., *j-oi-n*). Point out to children that *w* and *y* are usually consonants but may be vowels in these vowel teams (e.g., *t-ow-n* or *b-oy*).

5. *R-controlled syllables* are letter pairs containing a vowel followed by *r* together which represent a new vowel sound not corresponding to either the vowel letter or *r* alone (e.g., *arm, term, bird, for, hurt*).

6. *Consonant–le syllables* are spelling units in which the sounds are pronounced in a different sequence (/schwa/ → /l/) than they are spelled (*le*). Syllable boundaries between this syllable and the preceding syllable depend on speed of pronouncing the word (e.g., *puddle, giggle*), which might be segmented so that the consonant preceding the *le* syllable is heard at the end of the preceding syllable or beginning of the *le* syllable.

Syllables may also be described by patterns of consonants (C), vowels (V), and consonant blends (two or three letters that are pronounced in sequence very fast to avoid a vowel intrusion as in /b/-/short u or schwa/-/l/ for /bl/). The following sequence, organized by level of difficulty, is often used in teaching decoding:

CVC	hat
CVCC	hand
CCVC	clap
CCVCC	craft
CCCVC	splat

Most approaches to decoding encourage the reader to produce each sound as attentional focus moves across the spelling units in the word from left to right. As a result, reading may have an uneven jerky quality for children with dyslexia who have difficulty directing their attention to sequential spelling units (one- and two-letter units that correspond to phonemes) embedded in written words (see Chapter 7). Others have dysfluent reading because of difficulty in remembering the sounds that go with spelling units—they may forget the beginning sounds in the words and need to start over. Yet others can produce the correct sounds in order but cannot synthesize them to construct a whole spoken word. Vowels often pose the biggest challenge in the decoding process because their position in the word (whether the neighboring letters are another vowel, *r, l,* or a final *e*) determines the sound the spelling unit will make and the number of syllables. Struggling readers may have problems decoding for many different reasons, and the reason often provides the important instructional cue for helping them to decode more successfully.

Prefixes, which give shades of meanings to base words (e.g., *preview*); inflectional suffixes, which change the tense or number without changing the word's part of speech (e.g., *smiled*); and derivational suffixes, which mark part of speech (e.g., *builder*), should be taught. Begin to teach inflectional suffixes in second grade, prefixes in third grade, and derivational suffixes in fourth grade; however, it will probably take a number of years until the affix system is fully mastered (see Nagy, Osborn, Winsor, & O'Flahavan, 1994). For example, *lock* is what we do, *locking* is what we are doing, *locked* is what we did, *locks* means we have more than one lock or tells what someone does, and *locker* means something that locks. Prefixes change the meaning of a base word. *Unlock,* for example, is the opposite of *lock.* Some approaches to decoding recommend students identify the affixes first and then decode the base word and synthesize it with the affixes. Other approaches encourage students to look for known parts of a word to find meaning, and then deal with affixes. In a word such as *reconstruction,* for example, students would look for a word part that they recognize, such as *construct,* and then identify the prefix *re–* and the suffix *–ion.* In either approach, students need not decode each affix. Nunes and Bryant (2006) showed that pronunciation is typically predictably constant across suffix spellings even when alphabetic principle cannot be applied to spell all of the suffix. By identifying affixes first, the student is breaking the word into smaller, recognizable, and manageable pieces and is more able to recognize each unit.

Teachers need to avoid overloading students by asking them to decode words that are too difficult too soon. The goal is to provide practice in the *process* of decoding. Teachers can individualize instruction by offering more difficult words (CVCC or CCVC) to those children who are ready for them. Table 4.1 shows a chart

Table 4.1. A typical decoding list for a daily lesson on the vowel *u*

cvc	cvcc	ccvc	ccvcc
mum	must	slush	stump
sun	lump	stub	trust
sup	jump	grub	slump
sum	hunt	slum	grunt
rug	tuft	stuff	crust
cub	gust	drum	crutch
yum	dump	cluck	plump

Note: c refers to phoneme and not grapheme; *cc* refers to two phonemes.

of words for an introductory decoding lesson using short vowels arranged by levels of difficulty. Table 4.2 shows a list for introducing two-syllable words. Teachers can keep a daily word list on a chart or on the board, which should be visible to all, to provide students with practice in decoding. Individual students can note the affixes, if they have learned them; identify the spelling units in the base word and make their sounds; give its sound; divide the word into syllables if necessary; and then read the word, synthesizing all the sounds that can be decoded. The teacher should begin by calling on a few able children to serve as models for those who are less confident. The goal is to practice a consistent procedure that helps students internalize the steps needed for decoding. Then they can rely on this procedure and develop independence in reading when a teacher is not available to assist. The class stays involved by repeating the word after it is decoded, providing reinforcement. Every child in a class should have an opportunity to decode a word while others watch and repeat. If the teacher must intervene to assist too many children, the list is too hard. Reteaching and returning to a less difficult list is needed. Other children may provide input and reinforcement while one child is practicing the decoding process. This prosocial, cooperative learning approach teaches important social skills along with reading.

Students develop independence by applying decoding skills in many situations, moving from words in isolation to words in text—from guidance to independence. When the teacher is certain that students have mastered the decoding process, decoding practice may be provided in many ways:

1. Decoding from the chart or board, as noted previously.

2. Decoding from a computer generated or photocopied list of words.

3. Decoding from the text before the daily reading lesson begins.

Many students learn to decode words in isolation but do not automatically apply their skills when reading. Practicing decoding within a text helps students transfer their decoding skills to situations with more words in connected text and more opportunities for confusion among words on the same line or for difficulty in maintaining attention to the appropriate line.

Decoding instruction should move from simple unambiguous words with short vowels to phonograms, diphthongs (two vowel letters, one new sound; e.g., *oi*), and vowel digraphs (two vowel letters, sound corresponds to one vowel in

Table 4.2. A typical decoding list for a daily
lesson on two-syllable words

rabbit	signal	optic	imprint
muffin	cactus	index	quintet
bodkin	cutlet	confess	plastic
candid	goblin	suspend	splendid
catnip	wombat	himself	distaff
	rumpus		centric

letter combination [e.g., *ay*]; or two consonant letters, sound corresponds to one sound [e.g., *ch*]), to two-syllable words with two consonants in the medial position (initial closed syllable), and then to one consonant in the medial position (initial open syllable). When teaching words with only one consonant in the medial position, the teacher should begin with open syllable words divided before the single consonant (e.g., *lotus, table, bugle*). When students are confident with this division, the teacher can show what happens when the word is divided after the medial consonant. When words such as *cabin* are divided after the consonant (e.g., *cab´ in*), the consonant at the end of the first syllable makes the vowel short and the second vowel a schwa. Gradually with instruction and practice, children improve their decoding of multisyllable words, use multiple prefixes and suffixes appropriately, and learn the effect of accents on syllables in words. When reading materials require it, children also need specific structured teaching of contractions and possessives. For example, children can be asked to convert two words (e.g., *can, not*) into a contraction (e.g., *can't*) and dissect a contraction (e.g., *don't*) into its word parts (e.g., *do, not*). They can also be asked to use words that are pronounced the same but spelled differently depending on whether the word does signal possession (e.g., *The boys' toys were lost*) or the word does not signal possession (e.g., *The boys lost their toys*).

When each decoding concept is mastered, teachers can play games such as Tic-Tac-Toe with the whole class (see Figure 4.1). However, teachers should use only concepts with which the students are confident. To begin the game, the teacher can divide the class into teams, but only the teacher should know who is on which team (the teacher can keep a list of each team). The teacher chooses the first child. If the child follows the decoding process correctly, he or she may place an X or an O in the box. The next child—either chosen by the teacher or the previous student—is automatically on the opposite team. Because the students do not know which team they are on, every student cheers for everyone. The goal of the game is not only to read the word correctly but also to practice the process correctly.

Preparation for Reading

Johnson and Hook (1978) found that readers with dyslexia had less metalinguistic awareness and were less able to apply strategies using phonological and grammatical features in their reading. Students with dyslexia require more prereading preparation with vocabulary meaning and oral reading of words or phrases that build conscious awareness of language structures than do classmates. Preparatory instruction also activates background knowledge prior to reading a text that will

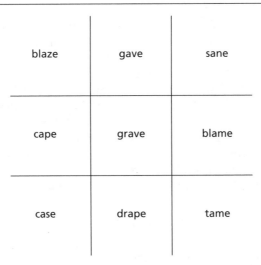

| blaze | gave | sane |
| case | drape | tame |

blaze	gave	sane
cape	grave	blame
case	drape	tame

Figure 4.1. V-C-E Tic-Tac-Toe.

contribute to understanding the text once read, builds confidence in succeeding on language tasks, and stimulates curiosity. Preparation activities such as the following provide awareness of the language of the text and have beneficial effects on reading comprehension when children do read written text.

1. *Eye span.* New information may be processed more accurately and efficiently during the fixations (pauses) between the saccades (forward and backward eye movements) while reading written text (Rayner, 1984) if children are optimally engaged because of the preparation activities.

2. *Phrase awareness.* Beginning readers focus on single words. With preparatory activities and reading experience, they become aware of the structures linking multiple words, such as phrases beginning with prepositions; then phrases with noun markers; and then subject, action, and descriptive phrases. Eventually they become aware of syntax structures underlying sentence organization.

3. *Awareness of inflectional endings in written words.* With preparatory activities, children learn that endings of written words may mark number (singular or plural, as in *cow* or *cows*) or tense (present or past, as in *walk* or *walked*). They also learn how pronouns signal gender (e.g., *him* and *her*) and person (1st, 2nd, 3rd, as in *I, you,* and *they*).

4. *Awareness of links between oral and written language.* With preparatory activities, children learn how capital letters mark the beginning of a new sentence; how punctuation ends a sentence; and how the whole sentence unit is linked to the intonation (musical melody of spoken language) and systematically varies for statements, questions, and commands.

When the preparation steps (Slingerland, 1976) discussed next are used, both word recognition and comprehension are improved. Decoding is applied, vocabulary meaning is developed and clarified, and understanding and recall of text content are strengthened. Low-achieving readers, particularly beginning readers who have not yet mastered decoding skills, need much prereading instruction and practice with both decoding *and* vocabulary at the word level. However, they also need prereading instruction and practice with skills involving units larger than the single word that influence comprehension of text when it is read.

The following *preparation steps* from Slingerland (1976) help develop rhythm for the musical melody of intonation, eye span, and use of the phrase concept to identify new words using context clues. The teacher can select a list of 8–10 words or 6–8 phrases to be read from the material and print the list in clear manuscript on the board or a chart. A pointer can be used to underline each word or phrase as it is read. The reading group or class repeats each phrase as it is read correctly by the teacher or another student. These same steps, followed with words and/or phrases, should also be used at the beginning of each reading lesson before students open their books.

1. The teacher reads each word or phrase from the list and offers clarification as needed. This is a teaching time for noun markers and prepositions, which give clues to meaning. This step provides practice with building awareness of unfamiliar words, punctuation, and linguistic cues. The class repeats the word or phrase.

2. The teacher says a word or phrase from the list and asks a student to point to the correct word or phrase from the list and read it. If the child is correct, the entire class repeats the word or phrase. Several children should have an opportunity to perform until all are confident with the vocabulary and are reading the phrases fluently. This step for guided practice builds security for when students are reading in a book, and it should not be skipped.

3. The teacher provides a concept clue such as, "Find a phrase that tells 'where' the story takes place" (e.g., "in the garden") or "Find a phrase that describes the building in the story" ("the little white house"). Note that both phrases are about places, but only "in the garden" begins with a preposition and tells "where." The child then finds a word or phrase that answers the question. Again, the class repeats if the answer is right. The teacher allows as many children to perform as possible.

4. Finally, the teacher asks various children to read all of the words or phrases. If they have difficulty, the teacher will need to return to steps 1 or 2. Tables 4.3 (for a text for beginning readers) and 4.4 (for a content area text for older readers) show examples of words or phrases to use in this activity.

Table 4.3. Words from a beginning reader

Words written on chart	Clues given orally
New	"Not old"
Out	"A preposition that tells where, opposite of *in*"
Now	"Immediately, not later"
Hello	"A greeting, what we say when we meet someone"
Put	"When you place something, opposite of take"
Bird	"Something with feathers"
Horse	"An animal we ride"
Said	"The word that tells us someone spoke"

Table 4.4. Phrases from a fourth-grade social studies text

Phrases written on chart	Clues given orally
In the Rocky Mountain subregion	"A phrase that tells where, a geographical area"
Gold, zinc, lead, and uranium	"Four minerals, words in a series"
Reminders of the Rocky Mountain gold rush	"What was left after the miners were gone?"
More than a hundred years ago	"When?"
Down a rushing river	"Where?"
A town that once was busy	"A phrase that tells what, a noun phrase, not a ghost town"

Teaching parts of speech builds vocabulary and makes what is often taught as a separate subject a meaningful part of reading and writing. Some concept words to reinforce comprehension can be found in Appendix 4A. Teaching parts of speech introduces students to concepts such as the following that will allow the class to understand and answer the comprehension questions they encounter as they read text:

1. *Noun markers* (determiners) are articles and sometimes number words. They are markers for noun phrases. When students encounter a determiner such as *the,* their eyes should move along the page until they find a noun or naming word. The determiner along with the noun or naming word creates a noun phrase, telling "who" or "what."

2. *Nouns* mark the end of a phrase started by a determiner.

3. *Prepositions* mark phrases that usually tell "where" or "when." As with determiners, the eyes should pause when they see a preposition, then move to the noun. Prepositions and nouns together create prepositional phrases.

4. *Adverbs* tell "how," "when," or "where." Alert students to the importance of the suffix *–ly* that tells "how."

5. *Conjunctions* join words, phrase, and sentences. Appendix 4B lists small words that may require special instruction.

6. *Verbs* are action words. They tell what we do, will do, are doing, or did.

7. *Adjectives* describe size, shape, kind, and how many.

8. *Pronouns* take the place of a noun for subject, object, or possessive cases. Pronouns often cause problems for children with imprecise language. They need practice in determining the referents when pronouns are used. "Who is 'he'?" or "What is 'it'?"

9. *Punctuation* signals the rising intonation associated with questions or the falling intonation associated with statements or commands.

10. *Words can function both as nouns and verbs.* Some words function as more than one part of speech (e.g., *circle, train, coach*).

11. *Accent* affects some words. As accent changes, words may change from nouns to verbs (e.g., *re cord´* versus *rec´ ord*).

Guided Oral and Silent Reading

Teachers should listen to each student read aloud each day in order to check decoding and comprehension skills (Johnson, 2006). During silent reading, students put words together in phrases and sentences to convey thoughts. *Word callers,* who pronounce the words but do not put them together, miss eye span, rhythm, and meaning for text cues. Students with OWL LD must be taught to perceive and integrate phrases so that they understand the writer's meaning. A part of each day's lesson should be devoted to teacher-guided reading to help students develop chunking skills and understanding of the word units that convey meaning. The teacher should begin by structuring the number of words that go together, forming a phrase (Slingerland, 1976). The teacher can help students break the sentences in the text into phrases (e.g., "The first three words tell 'who'"), continuing the phrase work begun during preparation and explicitly teaching the words that go together. Children should not start reading a phrase until they know all of the words in the phrase. The teacher continues to guide reading, helping children to project thought and anticipate the next phrases.

When students have read and studied the sentence, rereading it aloud gives students the opportunity for successful performance and to develop fluency. This strategy moves from small-phrase units to longer sentence units. In the course of time, less structuring is required, but it should not be dropped; only the amount should be modified. If a sentence is not rhythmically phrased, the rhythm should be tapped on the wall, table, or child's shoulder to help her or him feel the cadence of the language. Sweeping the arm from left to right is also a reinforcement of the feeling of the rhythm. Students should reread the whole sentence after they have phrased it to build comprehension of the way the chunks build a cohesive sentence.

Each day, after students have some review and practice with seeing and reading phrases, they should move on to reading without teacher guidance. Children must be taught not to skip words or guess their identity from context. The interpretation of text depends on context but word recognition should not. However, it is not enough for students to correctly call the words. Students must read the sentence with good phrasing with attention to punctuation and prosody if they are to develop fluency and good comprehension skills. The teacher should intervene and restructure or model if a student has difficulty, asking the student to read *the one phrase* that needs improvement. The teacher should remind students of the articles and prepositions in a sentence before which the eyes should pause. Do students know all of the words in the phrase or sentence before they start to read? Do they keep all the describing words together until these words lead to the named word? Teachers should remind children to reread a phrase or sentence when the meaning is unclear. By rereading after studying aloud, children have the opportunity for successful performance. Teachers point out the relationships between the language students read and the language students speak. It is often helpful to remind students to reread as if they are talking.

Bonnie Meyer, a colleague and leader in the Puget Sound Branch of the International Dyslexia Association, has suggested an interesting activity to practice phrase recognition and prepare students for independent report writing: Use consumable text such as a book from Reading A–Z (http://www.readinga-z.com). With teacher guidance (e.g., "Highlight the phrases that name a bird"), students highlight the phrases that provide the answers to comprehension questions. This strategy reinforces the concept that the phrase may be more than just the name of the bird and can include a noun marker as well. "Use a green marker to underline phrases describing what each bird eats." "Use a blue marker to underline the phrases that tell 'where' the bird eats." Even young children who have had the instruction with prepositions discussed previously will have success and visual reinforcement of the phrase concept in written text.

Fluency

Fluency is how rapidly, smoothly, effortlessly, and automatically connected text is read. When children are fluent readers, they read with little conscious attention to the mechanics of reading, such as decoding (Meyer & Felton, 1999). There is a direct relationship between fluency and comprehension because fluent readers attend to the meaning of the text rather than the mechanics of decoding (Adams, 1990). Fluency, however, does not mean speed reading. It means reading with ease, at a decent rate, and with good comprehension (Hall & Moats, 2001). Two skills are especially important for reading fluency (Wood, Flowers, & Grigorenko, 2001): 1) anticipatory processing of stimuli to be read—letters, written words, and written phrases; and 2) automatic, fast recognition time for processing the letters, words, or phrases. Thus, whereas phonological awareness affects the oral reading of words, orthographic awareness of letters in written words may affect reading fluency (Bowers & Wolf, 1993).

Fluent readers decode and read words with little conscious analysis. Their phrasing and intonation mirror their oral speech. They activate their vocabulary and use their prior knowledge of the structure of sentences to project thought for successful performance. Nonfluent readers decode slowly and haltingly. Their speed is inconsistent, with poor phrasing and poor recognition of prosodic features of the melody of spoken language. They may have inadequate sight word recognition and poor recognition of morpheme patterns. They may omit and substitute letters and/or words and ignore punctuation.

The most commonly used method to increase reading fluency is the repeated reading technique (Meyer & Felton, 1999). Beginning readers should practice naming letters, letter groups, and words on lists. It is helpful for them to reread the lists of decoding words used earlier in the lesson. Emerging readers should practice decodable and partially decodable words on lists and have opportunities for repeated reading in class with teacher guidance. The goal is accurate and fluid reading with adequate speed, appropriate phrasing, and correct intonation. Other activities that aid prosody and fluency include the following:

1. *Sentence completion.* The teacher reads a phrase or phrases. When signaled, a child completes the sentence. Then the teacher reads again and signals another child to complete the sentence. This activity provides good modeling of rhythm and inflection by the teacher. This activity also builds reading group skills, as the students must pay attention and follow along in the text while listening to other readers and also anticipate their oral turns.

2. *Round robin repeated reading.* Each child reads a sentence, paragraph, or page, and then the next child gets a turn. The teacher should expect each child to read with rhythm and fluency.

3. *Readers theater.* Fiction lends itself to role playing, in which someone is designated narrator and others read the parts of different characters. Nonfiction can
   be used as students assume the roles of narrators or reporters. This activity
   may be a group rereading for fun or for a performance for an audience.

4. *Choral reading.* The teacher and the class all read a sentence, paragraph, or page
   aloud. Some teachers use this activity when introducing books to beginning
   readers, but this activity can also be used to promote oral reading fluency
   when all students in the group are confident with the material. If any one student is not confident, he or she may get lost in the reading, and the teacher may
   miss insecurities or errors.

5. *Partner reading.* Paired readers choose a quiet, cozy spot to practice reading to
   one another. This activity provides additional practice in reading to a classmate after reading in small groups.

6. *Monitored reading.* The teacher can ask an aide or parent volunteer to listen to a
   student's oral reading. This activity requires that the teacher build the listening skills of the monitor. It may be necessary for the teacher to help the monitor understand that fluent reading does not necessarily mean fast reading. It
   means reading with good phrasing, rhythm, and without hesitation.

7. *Repeated reading.* Parents may assist with repeated reading at home by asking
   children to read orally the same 150- to 200-word passage repeatedly over several days. Children do not have to spend more than 10 minutes rereading each
   night.

Reading Comprehension

Questioning for comprehension helps students think about what they are reading
and focus on what they are to learn from a given passage. Teachers should encourage students to find the specific words that provide the answer when answering
questions about the text. The terminology used will vary according to student age
or experience, but questioning strategies should include the following:

1. Asking students "who?" or "what?" Nouns or noun phrases marked by articles or determiners identify the individual. Noun phrases that include adjectives such as *the little brown dog* describe. Noun phrases may also give details
   about number of something (e.g., *The seven towering hills*).

2. Asking students "where?" or "when?" Students' eyes should pause when they
   see a preposition and then move to the noun. A prepositional phrase gives information, such as where something is located (e.g., *under the umbrella*) or when
   something occurs (e.g., *after lunch*).

3. Asking students to find adjectives and adjective phrases that describe (e.g.,
   smooth and slippery).

4. Asking students to identify verb or action phrases (e.g., *was sliding, had eaten*).

5. Asking students to find what did happen or what will happen to aid understanding of how suffixes and inflectional endings change or shade meanings
   by past, present, future time, possessive, number, gender, and so forth. The suf-

fix –*ly* tells "how," the suffix –*ing* tells what someone or something is doing, and the suffix –*ed* tells what has happened.

6. Asking students to clarify use and meaning of pronouns (e.g., "To whom does *it* refer?" "Who is *she?*").

7. Asking students to demonstrate their understanding of punctuation and the ways it gives meaning in a sentence—including dashes, the many uses of commas, quotations, and others (e.g., "Why does this sentence end with an exclamation mark?" "What mark shows that this is additional information?").

8. Asking students to locate precise vocabulary that gives inferential information (e.g., "What word in the sentence tells how the character feels?").

9. Asking students to predict outcomes (e.g., "What will happen? How do you know?").

10. Asking students to summarize (e.g., "What is the character's daily routine?").

11. Asking students to read the introduction when rereading (e.g., "Where does the story really begin? How do you know?" "Where does the ending or conclusion begin?" "What key words should we look for?" "What kind of story or article is this? Why?").

Comprehension is dependent on a child's own understanding of the structure of language. For example, a second-grade girl in Beverly Wolf's school was reading a book and came across the following sentence: "How quiet it was." A simple sentence, but the girl could not read it. Each time she tried she would say, "How is," and then stop. Then the teacher said, "It's not a question." The child immediately read the sentence correctly. Her anticipation of what would follow the word *How* had made her say *is*. She *expected* a question and tried to make the sentence fit her expectation.

Repetition and review in functional reading situations gradually brings about independence. After guidance through the first two or three paragraphs or pages, children may be able to study the final page or two by themselves. Before asking students to read independently, teachers should provide structure for successful independent reading by reminding them to decode when possible, to use good phrasing or chunking, and to reread to be sure they understand each sentence. When students have studied and completed the whole paragraph or story, they should reread the whole story orally. Group rereading of the story should be for pleasure and fluency alone.

Independent Reading Activities

The following general principles should be kept in mind in designing meaningful independent activities:

1. Activities may be related to any skills previously taught. In general, worksheets can provide additional practice and/or enrichment (extension or stretching) of those skills.

2. Activities should be meaningful, and worksheets that ask students to fill in the blanks should be avoided because they do not encourage children to apply

new learning to constructing meaning or text. Asking students to reread pre-viously read text or to choose a book of interest at the student's independent reading level is likely to do more to reinforce taught reading skills. Asking stu-dents to write their own sentences or text about what they have read is more likely to foster development of their writing skills and integration of writing and reading skills to communicate ideas.

3.   Tasks with functional utility are desirable. For example, children might alpha-betize words on the decoding list for the day, copy them into a personal dic-tionary, and illustrate them. Phrases might also be copied and illustrated and used in booklets children write and use for further reading practice. See Sanderson (1988, 1989) for examples of this kind of independent activity with instructional materials that can be duplicated.

4.   Activities that encourage children to develop metalinguistic awareness of their own learning are helpful. Teachers can give children newspapers and maga-zines and ask them to circle the words they can decode with a green marker and the words they cannot decode with a red marker. Then, the teacher can use those words for further teacher-guided instruction. The sports pages or the front page often have the easiest vocabulary words for students. This activity helps students build awareness of their own abilities to attack unfamiliar words.

5.   Activities that encourage children to apply new learning to a variety of real world applications are helpful. Alternatively, the teacher can ask children to search newspapers or magazines for phrases with particular words, such as nouns, verbs, or prepositional phrases. Using real-world reading material may stimulate their interest in reading on their own and not just when they have to read in class.

6.   See Chapter 2 for additional suggestions.

RESEARCHER CONTRIBUTIONS

We now examine research-generated knowledge that is relevant to teaching reading.

Multimodal, Leveled Language Instruction for Children with Dyslexia and OWL LD

Despite the widespread myth that oral language is auditory and reading is visual, research has shown that reading involves creating maps between written words, based on visual inputs, and spoken words, based on auditory inputs. The early pi-oneers in teaching children with dyslexia knew intuitively that both auditory and visual processes were involved, also in addition to kinesthetic (touch) sensation from writing words, and hence emphasized the multisensory aspects—auditory, visual, and kinesthetic—of teaching reading to students with dyslexia. However, years later, it became clear that more than the primary sensory brain regions for au-ditory input and visual output are involved in reading. Rather, it was determined that 1) association areas in the brain transform sensory auditory input into higher-level phonological representations and transform sensory visual input into higher-level orthographic representations and integrate the phonological and ortho-graphic representations, and 2) motor regions are involved in producing written language. Thus, multimodal sensorimotor instructional approaches are needed for students with dyslexia or OWL LD. In addition, the instructional approaches should be aimed at multiple levels of language, as illustrated in the Teacher Contributions sections in Chapters 3, 4, and 6. (For a review of research leading to these conclusions, see Berninger & Richards, 2002.)

Linguistic Awareness and Working Memory

Mattingly's (1972) insight that linguistic awareness is related to reading acquisition revolutionized how reading and reading disability are conceptualized. Linguistic awareness is conscious reflection about any aspect of language, which can be analyzed at many different levels:

1. Sounds in spoken words (phonological awareness)

2. Letters in written words (orthographic awareness)

3. Morphemes or word parts that convey meaning and may mark parts of speech or other syntactic information (morphological awareness)

4. Syntactic structures in spoken utterances or in written sentences (syntactic awareness)

5. Discourse schema or higher order organization of oral stories or written texts (discourse awareness)

Many functions of the human mind occur outside conscious awareness in what psychologists call *implicit memory*. Conscious awareness of thinking requires explicit memory and working memory (Baddeley & Hitch, 1974), which supports goal-related tasks such as reading. Working memory has limited resources to support storage and processing of information; thus, working memory can make available to consciousness only a fraction of one's mental processes at a particular moment in time.

Researchers also found that learning to read requires linguistic awareness, and children with reading disability have impaired linguistic awareness (e.g., Mattingly, 1972). Linguistic awareness includes the ability to hold words in mind and reflect on their parts. As such, linguistic awareness helps children learn to store and process words in conscious working memory for specific reading goals. For example, phonological awareness of the small sound units called phonemes helps children associate them with graphemes (one- and two-letter spelling units) in learning to decode words. Orthographic awareness of graphemes in written words also contributes to learning to apply grapheme–phoneme correspondences in decoding. Morphological awareness of word parts that signal meaning and grammar also contributes to conscious awareness of written and spoken words in learning to decode written words (Nagy, Berninger, Abbott, Vaughan, & Vermeulen, 2003). The various instructional activities described in the Teacher Contributions section in this chapter develop these kinds of linguistic awareness.

Research has also shown that working memory supports learning to read, and children with reading disability have impaired working memory (e.g., Siegel, 1994; Swanson, 1999a, 2006; Swanson & Ashbaker, 2000). The greater one's conscious linguistic awareness of the task-relevant levels (units) of language, the fewer working memory resources are needed to complete a reading task in explicit memory. Likewise, if some parts of the reading task can be completed automatically in implicit memory outside of conscious awareness, then fewer of the limited working memory resources will be needed to complete the task in explicit memory.

Explicit instruction is designed to 1) bring relevant levels of language to conscious awareness by first reflecting on them in explicit working memory and then 2) develop automatic decoding and word identification in implicit working memory to free up limited cognitive resources in working memory. Such instruction might be referred to as explicit because the teacher-guided dialogue serves to make children aware of different aspects of oral and written language in conscious working memory. It is not direct instruction as implemented with fixed teacher scripts, although lesson plans for teacher-guided instructional activities are used. As illustrated earlier in the chapter, the teacher guides by questioning and gives children ample opportunities to construct responses and practice skills. Many of the illustrated examples of teacher-guided prompts for processing at different levels of language show that teachers are expected to respond flexibly to student response to instruction and adapt instruction as necessary for individuals. Also, in the recommended approach, the teacher is well prepared ahead of time so that he or she can respond flexibly and responsively to the students' instructional needs, as observed in the unfolding teaching–learning interaction cycles.

Students will vary in the degree of explicit instruction they require. Those with dyslexia impairing their word decoding and those with OWL LD impairing their reading comprehension as well as word reading will require the highest levels of explicit teaching, modeling, and teacher-guided student-response construction. Other students in other instructional groups may require moderate to minimal degrees of explicit instruction and may even benefit from student-generated and self-guided learning (for evidence, see Connor, Morrison, & Katch, 2004). Differentiated instruction that meets the instructional needs of ALL students in the classroom provides the appropriate mix of teacher-directed instruction and student-generated learning for each student. Such a mix can be accomplished, but it requires flexible cognitive and language processes of not only the student (see Deák, 2001) but also the teacher (see Chapter 10).

Importance of Three Kinds of Linguistic Awareness

For historical reasons, phonological awareness received more attention than orthographic and morphological awareness at the end of the 20th and beginning of the 21st century. At the time Mattingly (1972) wrote his influential chapter, the prevailing view was that dyslexia was a visual perceptual disorder. Shortly thereafter, Vellutino (1979) presented compelling data to debunk that view, and made a compelling case for the alternative view that dyslexia is a language-based disorder. The notion that reading draws on language processes, which is now the prevailing view, has subsequently received research support from around the world. Just because the eye and visual regions of the brain play a role in the initial processing of written words, it does not follow that dyslexia is a visual perceptual disorder and requires visual perceptual training. Rather, individuals with dyslexia need specialized language instruction. Individuals with and without dyslexia differ in the brain regions that integrate letters with sounds in speech to create orthographic representations of written words (e.g., fusiform gyrus); thus, reading written words involves visible language, but not primarily nonlinguistic visual processes (Berninger & Richards, 2002, Chapter 5).

Many groundbreaking studies pinpointed the role of phonological awareness in learning to read (e.g., Bradley & Bryant, 1983; Bruce, 1964; Liberman et al., 1974; Rosner, 1974). Numerous studies followed (for review of early studies, see Wagner & Torgesen, 1987). The National Reading Panel (National Institute of Child Health and Human Development, 2000) reviewed subsequent studies and concurred that phonological awareness is an essential component of reading instruction (Ehri, Nunes, Stahl, & Willows, 2001; Rayner, Foorman, Perfetti, Pesetsky, & Seidenberg, 2001). As illustrated in the Teacher Contributions section in this chapter, phonological awareness involves a number of units ranging from rhymes to syllables to phonemes. In addition, it involves onset-rimes, the parts of the syllable remaining after the onset (Treiman, 1985). Teachers sometimes refer to the rime parts of a syllable as phonograms (e.g., *and* as in *hand, end* as in *bend, ich* as in *rich, ong* as in *long, ump* as in *bump*) or word families. Children are taught word families for correspondences between multiletter units and speech units that are more predictable in word family units than are single letters or letter groups that correspond to phonemes (e.g., *ight* in *right; ough* in *rough, through,* and *thought*). Berninger (1998b) identified 23 high-utility word families that are more predictable than their internal grapheme–phoneme correspondences.

Research also shows that two other types of linguistic awareness are relevant to learning to read: *orthographic awareness* (Apel, Oster, & Masterson, 2006; Badian, 1998; Berninger, Yates, & Lester, 1991; Bowers & Wolf, 1993; Olson, Forsberg, & Wise, 1994; Olson, Forsberg, Wise, & Rack, 1994; Pacton, Perruchet, Fayol, & Cleeremans, 2001; Templeton & Bear, 1992; Venezky, 1970, 1999) and *morphological awareness* (Bryant, Nunes, & Bindman, 1977; Carlisle, 1995, 2000, 2004; Carlisle & Fleming, 2003; Carlisle & Nomanbhoy, 1993; Carlisle, Stone, & Katz, 2001; Derwing, 1976; Mahony, Singson, & Mann, 2000; Nagy, 2007; Nagy & Anderson, 1999; Nagy, Anderson, Schommer, Scott, & Stallman, 1989; Nagy, Berninger, & Abbott, 2006; Nagy et al., 2003; Pacton, Fayol, & Perruchet, 2005; Pacton et al., 2001; Singson, Mahony, & Mann, 2000; Tyler & Nagy, 1989, 1990; White, Power, & White, 1989). Why, however, has this much evidence been ignored by the experts? The National Reading Panel did not comprehensively review the research on orthographic and morphological awareness and thus all important aspects of linguistic awareness. Yes, phonological awareness is necessary. No, it is not sufficient alone for either beginning or skilled reading. Orthographic and morphological awareness are also needed—both for children with and without dyslexia (Berninger, Raskind, Richards, Abbott, & Stock, 2008).

Venezky (1970, 1999) showed that *English is a morphophonemic orthography that represents speech in a predictable way.* Written English codes a word's sounds, spellings, and morphemes. Thus, three kinds of linguistic awareness for words should be included in the instructional program for reading: phonological, orthographic, and morphological. In Chapters 7, 8, and 9 more research evidence relevant to the importance of teaching children awareness of phonological, orthographic, and morphological word forms and their parts is discussed.

The research evidence clearly supports teaching phonics, especially through third grade, that draws on phonological and orthographic awareness (see Ehri et al., 2001; Foorman, Francis, Fletcher, Schatschneider, & Mehta, 1998; Slavin, Madden, Dolan, & Wasik, 1996; Snowling, 1980). As shown in Table 2.1, more than one effective way for teaching phonics has been developed by teachers for students with dyslexia.

Both students with and without dyslexia also need to develop morphological awareness (e.g., Berninger et al., 2008; Nunes & Bryant, 2006). Typically developing students in the classroom also benefit from morphological awareness instruction, which contributes to word reading, vocabulary, and reading comprehension (e.g., Carlisle & Rice, 2002; Nagy et al., 2006; Stahl & Nagy, 2005). In groundbreaking controlled studies, Henry (e.g., 1988, 1989) showed an advantage for teaching morphological strategies in addition to phonics. Morphology should not be equated with semantics. Morphology refers to word formation structure—root or base words plus prefixes and/or suffixes. As such, morphology is a language concept. Semantics refers to the cognitive representations underlying vocabulary meaning (see Stahl & Nagy, 2005). For example, morphological awareness may be assessed by asking students to decide if two words are related in meaning (e.g., *builder* and *build, corner* and *corn*) or which suffixed word (e.g., *builds, building, builder,* or *built*) fits a sentence context (e.g., "The _____ is making a corner"). Semantics may involve deciding if two words are synonyms (e.g., *baby* and *infant, son* and *father*).

Cross-Word Form Mapping

Children also benefit from instruction in how to coordinate units of phonological, orthographic, and morphological information in pronouncing written words and thinking about their vocabulary meaning. The Teacher Contributions section earlier in this chapter, offered practical suggestions for this instructional goal. Word sorts are another effective way to accomplish this goal (see Chapter 9 and Unit I, Word Detectives, in accompanying workbook, *Helping Students with Dyslexia and Dysgraphia Make Connections* (Berninger & Wolf, 2009). For other valuable instructional guidelines, see Nagy, Osborn, Winsor, and O'Flahavan (1994) and Nunes and Bryant (2006).

Two kinds of mapping across written words and spoken words may be involved in learning to read: *fast mapping,* based on one or two exposures (e.g., naming visual objects and acquiring semantic concepts in acquiring oral vocabulary [McGregor, 2004], and beginning reading and spelling [Apel et al., 2006]) and *slow, effortful mapping,* which requires many more exposures, more practice, and explicit instruction. Fast mapping may explain how children acquire automatic sight word vocabulary. In contrast, slow mapping is based in large part on the alphabetic principle and its transfer to phonological decoding. Both fast and slow mapping may contribute to the creation of an autonomous orthographic lexicon (mental dictionary for written spellings), which has links to pronunciations and word meanings. Early intervention with at-risk first-grade readers showed that a whole-word strategy, in which every letter was named and the whole word was pronounced (fast mapping), and the alphabetic principle (slow mapping) were both effective; no relative advantage for onset-rime strategies was observed for at-risk readers at this stage of reading development (Berninger, Abbott, et al., 2000).

In many readers, the fast mapping orthographic representations are refined by slower mapping during self-teaching, which is decoding words while reading (Share, 2008), or by teacher-guided, explicit instruction during reading lessons (see the Teacher Contributions section in this chapter). Children with dyslexia or OWL LD may have problems in fast mapping so that they have to rely greatly on slow mapping to create the maps for translating written words into spoken words. In Chapter 7, we discuss possible reasons for this impaired fast mapping.

Importance of Word Origin

Henry (1993) showed the importance of teaching Latin and Greek phonemes and morphemes as a word decoding strategy for developing readers beyond the initial stage of word decoding. Explicit reading instruction, however, should not end after the third grade. In fourth grade and above, instruction should focus on mapping strategies related to morphology as well as orthography and phonology and to reading specific words that are likely to be of lower frequency, longer, and more complex than words encountered in previous grades.

Balmuth (1992) and Henry (2003) discussed the historical context and instructional relevance for word origin in teaching reading. The most frequent words in oral language are Anglo-Saxon, a version of English based on old German and English. Compared with the total number of English words, these high-frequency words total only about 1,000 words, and many of them are function words. These function words include conjunctions, prepositions, pronouns, articles, and helping verbs (e.g., *is*), which have no meaning of their own apart from the sentence context in which they occur, but glue the content words (e.g., nouns, verbs, adjectives, adverbs) of the sentence together. Most of the written words in textbooks used in Grades 1, 2, and 3 contain Anglo-Saxon words, which tend to be of one or two syllables; the first syllable is typically accented.

In contrast, the content area subject textbooks in Grades 4 and above have an increasing numbers of words of Latin or French (romance languages) and Greek origin. Individual words of Latin, French, or Greek origin are lower in frequency than words of Anglo-Saxon origin and tend to have three to five syllables; tend not to accent the first syllable, contain schwas (reduced vowels) whose spelling has to be memorized for specific word contexts, and are generally longer and more complex than words of Anglo-Saxon origin. For example, multiple suffixes can be added to a word, as in transforming *inform* (a verb) to *information* (a noun) to *informational* (an adjective). Latin and Greek words are used in the written language of formal schooling, and individuals who have more schooling have more opportunities to learn them (Beeler, 1988). Thus, as Beeler pointed out, children whose parents have more formal schooling are more likely to hear those words spoken in the home than children whose parents have had less schooling. That is why children of less-educated parents are likely to be at an academic disadvantage at fourth grade and above. They have less oral exposure to the kind of words that increasingly appear in written texts in the upper grades. However, the contribution of morphology to word formation in longer, more complex words can be taught at school even if children do not hear those kinds of words at home.

Henry (1990) summarized the important differences in the phonology, orthography, and morphology of words of different word origin. For example, whereas the letters *ch* may stand for the /ch/ phoneme at the beginning of *children* or *chalk* in Anglo-Saxon words, in Greek words it stands for the /k/ phoneme as in *chorus* or *psychology*. Although *sh* is the only spelling for the /sh/ phoneme at the beginning of *should* or *shall* in Anglo-Saxon words, in words of Latin or French origin the

/sh/ phoneme can be spelled with *ti* as in *nation, ci* as in *ancient,* or *si* as in *mission.* The morphology is also different across word origin. Many of the suffixes in Anglo-Saxon code inflection (past tense, plural, comparison of two or more than two), contractions involving function words, or ownership (possessive). Many of the suffixes in Latin or French words code derivation that marks parts of speech and therefore syntactic clues for using a word in sentence context. Greek morphemes, on the other hand, contribute jointly rather than modifying bases, for example, *automobile* (a self-driven motion machine).

See Berninger and Richards (2002) and Chapter 7 for pseudowords from Anglo-Saxon and Latin word origins to use in professional development workshops to expand teachers' linguistic awareness related to word origin and how this knowledge and knowledge of the three kinds of word-level linguistic awareness might be applied to instruction. See the accompanying book of lesson plans (Berninger & Wolf, 2009) for the POM POM Certificate to award to teachers who then grasp the importance of phonological, orthographic, and morphological (POM) awareness in teaching reading and how these may be unique for words of different origin.

The instructional significance of morphology extends beyond its benefits for students with dyslexia or OWL LD. As Nagy (2007) proposed (see Chapter 7), teaching morphological awareness and decoding in school may be the way to narrow the achievement gap between children whose families differ in education and income levels and ethnic or racial backgrounds.

Strategic, Automatic, and Fluent Reading

When a skill can be performed only with application of explicit, controlled strategies (Schneider & Chein, 2003; Schneider & Shiffrin, 1977; Shiffrin & Schneider, 1977), it is said to be strategic. Examples of skills that require strategic processing include decoding unknown words, which may be words never encountered before or words that were encountered but are not remembered, and reading comprehension.

When a reading skill becomes automatic (Samuels, 1985), it executes outside conscious awareness in implicit memory. An example of a reading skill that might become automatic is recognition of a previously encountered word without the reader consciously devoting strategies to decode it. Learning new skills typically requires strategies. Once the skill is practiced and mastered, it may become automatic (direct access without conscious awareness) or fluent (executed quickly and in a coordinated, efficient manner). However, reading comprehension typically requires strategies and cannot be performed completely automatically outside of conscious awareness.

Ehri (1992) provided a conceptual framework for how phonics is coordinated with word-level processes in developing automatic recognition of words. Although automatic recognition of written words is often referred to as a *sight vocabulary,* the use of the word *sight* is somewhat misleading because the visual code is not the only code involved—at least two different codes—phonological and orthographic—are involved.

Automatic word recognition also draws on word-specific representations of written words in long-term memory. These orthographic representations have links to other language (phonological and morphological word forms and their parts) and cognitive (semantic associations and concepts) representations in long-term memory.

When children can recognize single words automatically and use sentence syntax to combine words in meaning units and comprehend the text they are reading orally or silently, their reading is likely to be fluent—smooth, coordinated, effortless reading at the appropriate rate for the task at hand. *Fluency is not just fast reading.* The appropriate speed depends on the task at hand, for example, skimming for information, initial reading before receiving explicit comprehension instruction, subsequent reading and reflective discussion, preparing a written summary with main ideas and supporting details, taking notes for preparing a written report, or studying for a test.

Biemiller (1977–1978) provided the first evidence that reading rate across multiple levels of language, ranging from letters to words to text, contributed to reading fluency. Dowhower (1987) showed that in reciprocal fashion reading comprehension contributed to fluency. Biemiller and Siegel (1997) demonstrated that vocabulary instruction contributed to accurate and fluent reading in children at risk for reading for environmental reasons. Breznitz (1997) reported evidence that computerized accelerated reading programs tailored to individuals' reading rate improved the reading fluency of children with dyslexia. Breznitz (2006); Stahl and Heubach (2005); Stahl, Heubach, and Crammond (1997); and Wolf (2001) reviewed the abundant evidence for the importance of reading fluency.

Research supports a number of teaching approaches for developing reading fluency. Repeatedly reading the same text improved the reading fluency of at-risk second-grade readers (Dowhower, 1987). Prior word-level training for single words that would appear in the text also improved some aspects of reading fluency (Levy, Abello, & Lysynchuk, 1997). For children with dyslexia who had not yet developed adequate knowledge of the alphabetic principle and decoding, combining instruction directed to automatic alphabetic principle as well as repeated readings was more effective than repeated readings alone (Berninger, Abbott, Abbott, Graham, & Richards, 2002).

Vocabulary and Reading Comprehension

The National Reading Panel (NICHD, 2000) also concluded that both vocabulary and reading comprehension should be taught. See Stahl and Nagy (2005) and Carlisle and Rice (2002) for reviews of the research evidence for effective ways of teaching vocabulary and reading comprehension.

Even though dyslexia is a disorder in word decoding, word reading, and spelling, students with dyslexia need more than phonics instruction. They also need to receive instruction in transfer of that phonics to the actual decoding process and repeated practice in applying decoding until word recognition becomes automatic. Students with dyslexia or OWL LD also benefit from systematic instruction in developing vocabulary meaning and reading comprehension. To comprehend a variety of texts, these students need instruction and practice in coordinating the multiple modes of input, output, and their integration and the multiple codes within levels of language in working memory so that they work in concert.

Cognitive Representations and Learning Mechanisms

Reading is a tool for deriving stated meaning from text and constructing meaning that can be inferred from text based on background knowledge of the world and language. The nature of the cognitive representations that are activated or accessed via the written words and text schema is also relevant to teaching reading. On the one hand, some of this knowledge is represented in associational networks (Anderson & Bower, 1973). When a word points to a concept or idea in the network, other concepts are immediately activated to varying degrees along the distributed network. Free association (saying everything that comes to mind when one thinks of one idea) is a window to this kind of cognitive representation in the mind. On the other hand, some of this knowledge is represented in hierarchically arranged categories in which similar information is clustered together because it shares some common features; however, some exemplars of the category may be more representative of the category than other exemplars (e.g., Rosch, 1978; Rosch & Mervis, 1975). Moreover, the same concept can be categorized differently depending on the situation. For example, a pet cat belongs to the category *living things* in the context of life forms and nonlife forms, to the category *animals* in the context of animals versus plants, and to the category *pet* in the context of domesticated animals versus wild animals. *Human cognition is both situated in specific and flexible contexts, depending on the task and context at hand.*

In addition, experiences are coded in episodic memory (Tulving, 2002). These episodic events, which are coded in temporal sequence, are a very different kind of cognitive representation than either associations or categories. None are language representations per se, but via the association regions of the brain, they may be translated into various levels of language. Episodic events track word frequency that affects word recognition, patterns of ordering types of words that affect syntax learning, and sequence of events in stories that affect learning narrative genre. Collectively all contribute to reading comprehension.

Some cognitive representations are declarative and some are procedural (Anderson, 1993). *Declarative knowledge* is factual and conceptual and may draw on the associational network, hierarchical categorical representations, or episodic representations. In contrast, *procedural knowledge* specifies how to do something. Although the goal of reading is to derive and construct meaning from text, the goal of reading instruction, especially during the elementary school years, is to teach procedural knowledge for executing the process of reading—translating written words into both language representations (e.g., spoken words, syntax) and cognitive representations (word meaning and text understanding).

A controversial, unresolved issue in reading is whether learning to read is rule governed and simply requires application of rules or whether it involves computation of connections or associations rather than rule application. Although cognitive scientists continue to disagree vehemently about this issue, teachers may consider the possibility that students may benefit from both approaches: 1) the rules may provide metacognitive guidance to use in self-regulated, independent reading, as long as the students do not interpret the exceptions to the rules as evidence that English is hopelessly irregular; and 2) the associations or connections close in time may improve automaticity and fluency and thus efficiency of working memory supporting the reading process.

Effective teaching methods for reading will draw on a variety of cognitive representations and learning mechanisms. Teaching procedural knowledge may be more related to learning decoding and word reading, whereas teaching declarative knowledge may be more related to learning vocabulary meaning and reading comprehension strategies. Precision teaching methods that create automatic connections close in time may facilitate learning of procedural knowledge for coding written and spoken words and their parts in working memory and translating one code into another (e.g., written words into spoken words in oral reading or written words into morphological word forms in silent or oral reading). Teacher modeling of the decoding process, with students imitating, may help transfer procedural knowledge to the students' own decoding during independent reading. See Chapter 9 for how these learning mechanisms were applied to specialized instruction for students with dyslexia. Instructional approaches that encourage children to access declarative background knowledge during reflective discussions before and after children read a text may also, however, facilitate reading comprehension. Such approaches may also facilitate construction of new declarative knowledge.

Two controversies persist related to teaching students at risk for reading failure. One controversy has to do with the role of the teacher in directing instruction. Some teacher educators firmly believe that children should construct their own knowledge and that teacher-led dissemination of knowledge should be avoided at all costs. For a thoughtful discussion on the potential problems with this approach when taken to an extreme, see Mayer (2004). Many who advocate for the constructivist view of child-directed learning may have in mind a different population of students than those who advocate for the teacher-directed instruction view. The former may be more relevant to students who come from high-literacy homes and enter schools well prepared for literacy learning that emphasizes student construction of knowledge. The latter may be more relevant to students who come from low-literacy, low-income homes or come with biological risk for dyslexia or OWL LD and do not enter schools with all the skills needed for literacy learning. That teacher-directed instruction need not be rote drill and skill, but it needs to be explicit and raise levels of consciousness about levels of language. The evidence from Connor and her colleagues' (2004) research, which won the best research of the year award from the International Reading Association in 2005, showed that both groups exist and benefit from different instructional approaches in beginning reading. Chapter 10 discusses practical suggestions for meeting the needs of both groups in the general education program.

The other cognitive issue that remains controversial has to do with what is meant by *intensive instruction* (see Torgesen et al., 2001). Do students with dyslexia or OWL LD benefit from receiving the same kind of instruction as their classmates over and over for a longer period of time, or do students with dyslexia or OWL LD need a different kind of instruction when they do not respond to the kind of instruction that works for their classmates? Should students who come from families with multigenerational histories of oral language, reading, and writing problems be given only the Tier 1 core curriculum adopted by the school system and monitored for whether they fail to respond? Or, should their weaknesses in language and related processes be identified in kindergarten and first grade so that they can receive specialized instruction from the beginning to increase the probability that they will respond to instruction and continue to do so? These issues will be considered further in Chapter 8.

CONCLUSIONS

In sum, the instructional activities described in the Teacher Contributions section in this chapter converge with growing evidence showing that all students benefit from instructional approaches for reading that teach phonological, orthographic, and morphological awareness and their interrelationships to word decoding and word reading (Sawyer, 2006). In addition, the teacher and researcher contributions converge on the importance of teaching automatic word recognition, fluent oral and silent reading, and strategies for reading comprehension. Both teacher-generated knowledge and research-generated knowledge lead to the conclusion that students with dyslexia and/or OWL LD benefit from a variety of instructional approaches that stimulate different kinds of learning mechanisms and create different kinds of cognitive representations in the minds of readers.

Appendix 4A

CONCEPT WORDS THAT REINFORCE COMPREHENSION

top
through
next to
away from
inside
some, not many
middle
few
farthest
around
over
widest
most
between
whole
nearest
second

corner
several
behind
in a row
different
after
almost
half
center
as many
beginning
side
other
alike
not first, or last
never
below

matches
always
medium sized
right
forward
zero
above
every
separated
left
pair
skip
equal
in order
third
least

Appendix 4B

SMALL, IMPORTANT WORDS
THAT MAY REQUIRE SPECIAL INSTRUCTION

Word	Various meanings/usages
And	Connects words or phrases
	More of the same
	Lists words and phrases in a series
	Also, too, in addition
As	In the same way
	At the same time, while, during
	Because
	Just as or same as
	Like
	While
But	An exception, something different
	Connects two contrasting ideas
	Only
If	Condition
	Reason
Only	Singly—only in its class
	Simply
	Merely
Or	This or that
	Instead of
	Different
	Opposite
Since	Because
	From a certain time until now
So	As a result of
	This came about
Sometimes	Not always, periodically
	Now and then
	Once
	Past, erstwhile
Than	Comparing/inequality
	More than
Then	When
	After that
	At that time
	Following next

Word	Various meanings/usages
To	Tells where
	Attachment
	A direction
	Opposite ends
What	Shows stress
	Asks a question
When	At a certain time
While	Although
	During that time
	As
Yet	A time word meaning *up to now*
	Even so
	However
	Excepting
	Nevertheless
	Still
	At the same time
	It is also the case

CHAPTER 5

Teaching Writing

As in Chapters 2, 3, and 4, we begin with an overview of knowledge generated from teaching writing to students with dyslexia, oral and written language learning disability (OWL LD), and/or dysgraphia. Then we discuss the rapidly expanding body of research knowledge on teaching writing effectively.

TEACHER CONTRIBUTIONS

Students are ready for written expression of ideas when they can write letters and spell words. The composition may be as simple as the completion of a sentence begun by the teacher or as complex as a complete story or written report. Between those two accomplishments come the instruction and guided practice that develop thought patterns and lead to successful independent written language. That guided instruction starts with teaching children to produce automatic and fluent handwriting. Children should be taught to write letters and then the letter or letters that spell the sounds used to spell the words. They will also benefit from activities that help them perceive and discriminate among sounds in spoken words and learn how complex words are formed from adding prefixes and suffixes to base words. Daily guided practice in writing phrases and sentences from dictation is also helpful. Teacher modeling and teacher guidance in constructing well-formed paragraphs are also beneficial. As is the case for reading, well-planned, structured, sequential, and systematic lessons are necessary for developing writing skills.

General Guidelines for Handwriting Instruction

Instruction in beginning handwriting and spelling usually comes before, or concurrently with, instruction in reading, when children are taught letter names and their sounds. Children need direct, explicit teaching of letter formation and much guided practice to develop automatic handwriting and meet the demands of written expressive language. Multisensory associations among visual letters, auditory sounds or names of letters, and kinesthetic touch from using a writing tool help strengthen recall for both reading and writing (Cox, 1992; Slingerland, 1971). The addition of this multisensory component is especially necessary for children who confuse commonly reversed letters such as *b, d, g, p, q,* and *s.* Students with weaknesses in one modality area can use their strengths in other modalities to develop handwriting skill. The strong channel reinforces the weak channel as students write or trace letters while naming them with the goal of providing a legible, automatic means of written expression.

Handwriting Style   When to teach manuscript versus cursive writing depends on the age of the group being taught and school policy. Most public school districts use manuscript print form when introducing handwriting to young children. Many consider it easier than the connected letter forms or cursive writing. Manuscript print writing introduces children to the letter forms they will need to recognize as they begin to learn to read. The use of manuscript print reduces confusion, allowing primary-grade children to see the same symbol forms used for reading, writing, and spelling. However, the way children are taught to write an *a* and a *g* in manuscript does not conform to the letter form on the keyboard for these letters or the written texts they read. Teachers should be sure to point out this difference to children.

Different styles of printing letters are taught, such as ball and stick and slanted D'Nealian letters. The one most often recommended for students with dyslexia is one that uses a continuous stroke, which may facilitate letter writing fluency (Beery, 1982; Slingerland, 1971). This form necessitates that the child lift the pencil fewer times, reducing the opportunity for confusions or reversals. A continuous stroke letter is similar to cursive writing in that lines are retraced whenever possible and the pencil is lifted only when necessary, for example, to cross a *t* or to dot an *i*. Continuous strokes also help prepare the child for a natural transition to cursive writing.

When children are first introduced to manuscript letters, they may need as many as 2 weeks to learn and practice the first few letters, but they often soon move more rapidly to adding a letter or more a week. Likewise, teachers typically introduce a new letter each day for beginning cursive writers. For both manuscript and cursive letters, with connecting strokes, letters with common strokes typically are grouped together for initial instruction.

Cox (1992) and Phelps and Stempel (1987) cited a number of advantages of cursive handwriting, especially for students with dyslexia. To begin with, it provides the student with consistency of knowing that all cursive letter shapes begin on the baseline. Also, it may reduce reversals by eliminating the need to raise the pencil during the process of writing a single letter or series of letters in a word. However, the transition from print to cursive may be problematic for students with dysgraphia (with or without dyslexia) because it requires the child to superimpose a new handwriting form on the one first learned. If students do not have sufficient instruction and practice to become automatic with producing cursive letter forms, they often will revert to manuscript or will mix the two forms.

Handwriting Preference and Pencil Grip   Before handwriting instruction begins, teachers should determine each child's hand preference. For most children, dominance is established by kindergarten age, but a few may be insecure in knowing which hand to use for writing as late as 8 or 9 years. The patterning for instruction and practice of handwriting requires consistent development of *muscle memory* of the form of each letter; that is, the connection between the peripheral and central nervous systems underlying the formation of each letter. Children who switch hands do not establish that memory of letter formation and may start the letter in the wrong place and move in the wrong direction to complete it, resulting in reversals and further confusion. Or, they will recognize the reversal and write over it or waste time attempting to erase the incorrect letter. In most cases, the teachers can determine a student's hand preference with a few simple activities, such as the following:

1. While facing the child, the teacher offers a pencil, piece of chalk, marker, or other writing implement, depending on the writing surface being used. The teacher holds the object toward the child's chest and notes the hand with which the child takes the writing implement.

2. The teacher asks the student to write his or her name with the hand he or she used to accept the pencil. The teacher should note whether the child switches the implement to the other hand, the way the child holds the writing implement, the facility with which it is used, and the consistency of script. The teacher should then ask that the child to write his or her name again with the opposite hand.

3. The teacher repeats the activity by requesting that the student draw a house, first with one hand, then with the other. Again, the teacher should note rate, organization, and quality of the finished product. If the names and houses are completed side by side, it is easy to compare results. Some children know immediately which hand they preferred, and say so. Most can tell which hand is easier for them to use.

4. If a student's hand preference is still not clear, a timed pegboard activity based on the Jansky Kindergarten Index (Jansky & de Hirsch, 1966, p. 14) can be helpful. The teacher places a pegboard and pegs in front of the child and asks the child to place the pegs in the board using only one hand. The teacher allows 30 seconds and should note the number of pegs, their arrangement—in rows or haphazard—and the dexterity with which the child places the pegs in the pegboard. The child then repeats the task with the opposite hand. It is seldom necessary to proceed beyond this activity. If there is still uncertainty about which is the stronger hand, the child can be referred for neuropsychological assessment, or neurological assessment, which typically includes a hand preference test.

When a child's preferred hand is identified, discuss ways that he or she can be helped to remember which hand to use. Some parents provide a watch or bracelet to wear on the writing hand, or teachers can mark the correct hand with a sticker or a marker. It helps students to associate hand preference with the classroom environment. Teachers can mark the correct side of the desk or remind children that when facing the front of the room their writing hand is toward the windows or other classroom landmarks, for example.

Proper Pencil Grip   Check students' pencil grip as they prepare to write. They should use a tripod grip in which the pencil rests on the first joint of the middle finger with the thumb and index fingers holding the pencil in place and the pencil held at a 45-degree angle to the page. Students should hold the pencil firmly with a relaxed arm and hand. The pencil should point toward the shoulder of the writing arm for both left- and right-handed students. An awkward pencil grip is more tiring and may affect letter formation and slant.

> As the demand for writing increases through elementary school, maladroit pencil grip can become an increased liability. Affected children may experience writer's cramp; they may not be able to keep up with the rate requirements for fluent writ-

ing . . . [they] commonly become great misers of writing, producing a significantly diminished quantity of writing. (Levine, 1987, p. 228)

An attentive teacher with consistency and patience can help a student change pencil grip. At any time that incorrect grip is observed, the teacher can redirect the class with the following prompts:

1. "Stop, place your pencils on the desk with the point toward you."

2. "Pinch your pencil." With the index finger and thumb in a pinch position, teachers should ensure that students lightly grasp their pencils approximately 1 inch from the point or where the point begins.

3. "Lift your pencil." As the children lift their pencils, it will fall back into correct writing position and rest on the first joint of the middle finger.

After a few practice sessions, students will only need to hear, "Stop, pinch, lift," to adjust their pencil grip. Teacher perseverance will help students become accustomed to the feel of the new position and use it consistently. After a time, only those children who have continued difficulty will need reminders. The older the child, the more difficulty he or she will have with changing the pencil grip and the greater the need for teacher intervention.

The use of a plastic pencil grip or a metal writing frame can aid students in changing a fatiguing grip to a typical, less tiring one (Phelps & Stempel, 1987; Texas Scottish Rite Hospital for Children [TSRHC], 1990, 1996). Grips come in a variety of forms from plastic triangles and shaped grips to wire frames. Frames have the advantage of eliminating tension when learning to write because the hand simply rests on the frame without gripping the pencil. Children may need to experiment with a variety of pencil grips or frames to determine which one works best for them. Teachers should be aware, however that many children who use grips and frames often become frustrated with them once the novelty has worn off.

Writing Implement   "The complex motor action of writing is overwhelmingly dependent upon accurate, ongoing kinesthetic [reafferent] feedback" (Levine, 1987, p. 226). While children write, they receive feedback in the form of pressure and the pull of the pencil against the paper. Pencils with soft lead require less pressure from the child, thus reducing fatigue. Children with impaired kinesthetic feedback will benefit from using softer leads that will not break as they press firmly in an attempt to receive that feedback when writing (Levine, 1987). A number 2 or softer pencil with no eraser is recommended so that students can trace letters with the unsharpened end without marking the paper. The absence of an eraser eliminates the temptation to spend time erasing, and allows teachers to see the errors children have made so that they know what to incorporate in reteaching in future lesson planning. To encourage self-monitoring and revising (high-level executive functions), teachers can encourage children to put brackets around or draw a single line through mistakes and rewrite the word correctly.

Paper and Instructional Strategies for Beginning Writers   Beginning handwriting instruction starts with activities that involve gross motor movement, which allows the writer to feel in the shoulder and arm the movement necessary to produce the letter and thus improve kinesthetic memory for motor movements. Initial instruction can begin at the chalkboard or dry erase board,

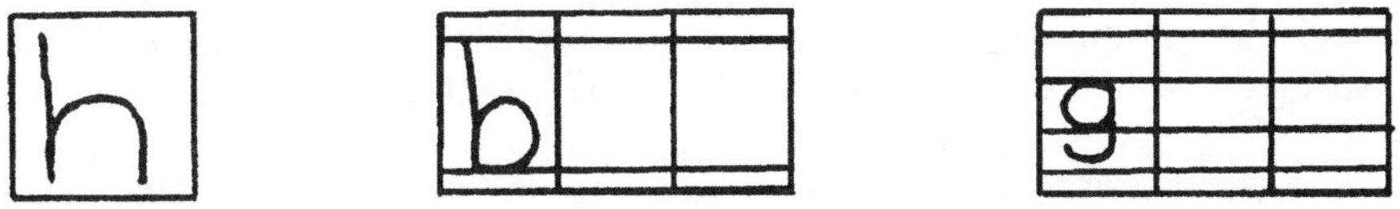

Permanent pattern
9 × 12

Expendable pattern and review
12 × 18

Expendable pattern Reduced
sized folds
12 × 18

Commercial paper sizes: 1-inch spaces, ¾-inch spaces, ½-inch spaces, ⅜-inch spaces

Figure 5.1.   Suggested paper sizes for handwriting. (Duplicating masters are also available from the Slingerland Institute for Literacy, http://www.slingerland.org/)

where the teacher can make large patterns for the students to trace using full arm movements. Instruction can then move to smaller and smaller tracing areas—to folded unlined paper with large spaces 6–8 inches high, then to narrower 3- to 4-inch spaces, then to wide-lined (1 inch) paper, then to primary-grade lined paper, and finally to regular lined notebook paper. The size of the spaces between lines is adjusted downward as the child masters the letter forms. As students write and practice, the teacher should circulate around the room, watching carefully to see that students maintain correct posture, full arm movement, and correct form. If a student's writing deteriorates, he or she may not be ready for reduced-sized paper. Remind students that large (gross) muscle movement helps establish stronger memory of the feel of the letter for writing.

Being able to reduce the size of lines as children's formation of letters becomes automatic will happen much more quickly with older students than with younger ones. Remind students that if they continue to use good form while using a full arm movement, they may continue on narrower lined paper. See Figure 5.1 for suggested paper sizes for handwriting.

Paper Position   Many handwriting programs recommend that, when using manuscript writing, right-handed students keep their papers parallel to the bottom of the desk to help them keep their manuscript letters straight but that left-handed writers keep the edge of the paper parallel to the writing arm, which should be at about a 45-degree angle to the edge of the desk. When using cursive writing, right-handed students should keep the right corner higher than the left, whereas left-handed students slant in the opposite direction, with the left corner higher than the right. This approach allows students to see what they are writing and avoids smudging as their arms move across the page. It also prevents "hooking," or a curled wrist, that is common among left-handed writers. Some teachers draw a line or place tape on students' desks at about a 45-degree angle to serve as a guide for paper alignment until students are able to keep the slant for themselves. In all cases, students should anchor their papers at the top with their non-writing hands.

Developmental Sequence   Manuscript writing is taught throughout the year, typically beginning in kindergarten or first grade. A shorter period of instruction or review at the beginning of second grade followed by daily practice will prepare students for functional writing. Cursive writing is usually taught within the first 4 or 5 weeks of the school year, typically in third grade. Letter forms should be taught before they are practiced in a word, phrase, or sentence so that, when needed, letters can be formed automatically without conscious effort.

The Daily Lesson   Attention to detail before instruction begins and while students participate in the lesson will build standards for successful, automatic performance. Before each lesson, the teacher should check students' posture, paper position, and pencil grip. If necessary, the teacher should stop the lesson periodically to remind students of posture and grip and emphasize the importance of naming the letters before writing them. Having students name the letter just as their arms start to move strengthens the automatic intersensory association of the letter name and its formation. This daily attention to handwriting helps students learn the letter forms; increases their automatic writing; and facilitates the connections between the letters and corresponding sounds, which facilitates word reading and spelling. Students should be instructed to write, then lightly trace over each letter, rather than writing the same letter over and over again because the quality of the repeatedly written letter often deteriorates as students write it again and again.

Teaching New Letters   Handwriting generally is not taught in alphabetical order. It is more effective to introduce the letters grouped by formation strokes. This approach allows students to master one type of movement before focusing on another. Figures 5.2 and 5.3 show examples of both manuscript and cursive letters grouped by strokes. Lowercase letters should be taught first in both manuscript and cursive handwriting. Handwriting programs vary as to whether they begin with capital or lowercase letters, but because lowercase letters are used more frequently in writing and appear more often in written text, teaching them first may have an advantage.

Teachers provide the guidance for establishing or changing writing habits. Students will tire less easily and feel more confident as they see and feel the success of their efforts. Students with dysgraphia, many of whom also have dyslexia, need direct, explicit instruction in letter formation and much guided practice to achieve automatic handwriting performance before the letters are used to write a word, phrase, or sentence.

Each lesson should provide time for teaching new letters until all upper- and lowercase letters are introduced and then periodically reviewed until firmly established. If teaching cursive writing, letter connections are also practiced until firmly established. At the beginning, while students are still learning new letters, the writing lesson may be as long as 30 minutes. As letters are learned, the time spent on review is no more than 10 minutes. The same lesson sequence and time allotments apply to both manuscript and cursive writing. Teachers should teach, practice, and review so that students can recall each letter automatically as a single unit. As noted previously, cursive writing should be taught within the first 4 or 5 weeks of the school year so that it becomes a useful tool for producing written language during the rest of the school year and so that students have time to build consistent automatic performance. It is confusing for students who are learning a new writing style to switch between manuscript and cursive during this period.

Uppercase letters are used in only about 2% of writing and are introduced initially only as needed for student names or sentence beginnings. After students can write all lowercase letters legibly and automatically, teachers can then place greater

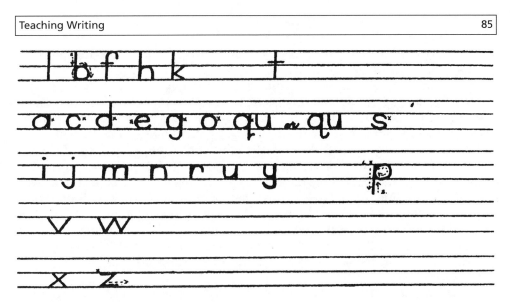

Figure 5.2.   Manuscript letters grouped by strokes.

emphasis on teaching uppercase letters and writing them automatically. Teachers should keep written work to a minimum until lowercase writing is functional.

When teaching specific letters or letter connections, the teacher should integrate them into all succeeding parts of the daily written lesson so that there is consistent practice and reinforcement in using them in phrases, sentences, compositions, and other written work. Before letter writing is automatic, teachers should encourage students to name the letters they will write as they start to move their arms to write. This strategy helps strengthen the memory for letter name and letter formation. Necessary descriptive phrases should be repeated each time the let-

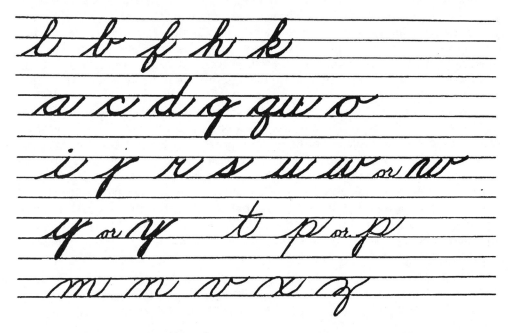

Figure 5.3.   Cursive letters grouped by strokes.

ter is traced or written to reinforce motor memory until the letter production is automatic (TSRHC, 1996; Slingerland, 1971).

Students recall the sequence of movements for a given letter better if the instructor teaches verbalization of consistent, precise directions for each letter. These descriptions often accompany teacher manuals for writing programs. For example, when writing the letter *d*, students might say, "Around like an *a* and tall stem up and down to the writing line." When writing the letter *b*, they might say, "Tall stem down and away from my body" (if right handed) or "Tall stem down and across my body" (if left handed; Slingerland 1971, p. 62). The same verbalization is true for both manuscript and cursive writing. Verbal input for writing will provide a consistent tool for children, who are uncertain when encountering the letters *b* or *d* in reading. If there has been enough verbal input, a child can recognize the letter while blindfolded at the board when the teacher guides the hand. He or she will discover that muscle memory helped with recall of the letter form.

Reviewing Letters   When all letter forms have been taught, a 5–10 minute daily review of those needed in the daily lesson, difficult letter forms, or easily confused letter forms will help students maintain standards and automatic performance. Berninger (1998b) recommended a daily 5-minute warm-up before written composition in which children practice each letter once or write letters that come before or after other letters in the alphabet.

In the Alphabetic Phonics Approach (see Chapter 2, Table 2.1), students can practice during the handwriting part of the daily lesson, focusing on their individual levels and goals. All students should strive for rhythmic movement from one letter to another as the teacher names them. The teacher should establish a focus or goal for each practice and review session. The focus or goal may be using correct posture or pencil position; naming the letter when writing; modifying letter proportion, especially of tall letters; or repeating individual strokes, such as "pull down straight" strokes, circles, release strokes, and lower loops.

In Orton-Gillingham based approaches (see Chapter 2), handwriting practice and review are integrated into the written language lesson to provide success with spelling and written language tasks. For example, if students will be expected to write the word *work*, they will practice the letter forms and connections necessary to successfully write the word (e.g., *wo, or, wor, rk*).

In the Slingerland approach, each day starts with a writing lesson when students are at their most rested and freshest to prepare them for the daily written work of the day. Examples of skills in daily practice include 1) moving from one letter to the next smoothly to develop a rhythmic tempo and 2) forming one dictated letter, then tracing, and then writing and tracing the next one as it is named. If the students are unable to write a letter satisfactorily, the teacher returns to the tracing step at the board or on large paper patterns or to forming letters with large muscle groups in the air. Students should also practice rhythm, fluency, and the spacing between letters. Guidelines for selecting letters for review should meet the following requirements:

1. Review those letters needed for successful written performance in the daily spelling and written composition lesson. These may include letters with which students have had difficulty or those with difficult connections between letters.

2. Review groups of letters that share common formation components. In manuscript it may be those beginning with a down stroke (e.g., *l, h, b, m, n, r, p, k*) or

those that begin with the formation of *a* starting at the "2-o'clock" position (e.g., *c, d, g, qu, s*). In cursive, letters would also be grouped by similar strokes. See Figures 5.2 and 5.3.

3. Teach alphabet order as preparation for dictionary skills.

4. Practice a series of letters that spell short words (e.g., *are, was, for*).

5. Students who have learned both manuscript and cursive should practice copying from the board or a chart, manuscript to manuscript, cursive to cursive, and manuscript to cursive or cursive to manuscript. They should begin with single letters, then groups of two or three letters, and finally short words.

Teacher judgment will determine the amount of structure required during review. Children should move from forming the letter in the air before writing to a more automatic step to develop rhythm and fluency. The class writes, names, and traces about three times, until the next letter is given. Each time the children write the letter, they should name it and, if necessary, remind themselves verbally of the correct formation. The teacher corrects very little.

Letter Connections in Cursive   Teachers should teach and practice cursive connections with special attention to the difficult ones. All but four cursive letters end with a connecting stroke near the writing line. The exceptions are those that connect at the midline—*b, o, v,* and *w*. The connections to these letters require specific instruction and consistent review. When teaching difficult connections, the teacher should provide the class with prepared patterns to be traced, copied, and written from memory. Extra practice should be provided for frequent combinations such as *br, oa, vi,* and *wh* (see Figure 5.4 for the example of *or*). Henry (2003) pointed out that third graders often need practice in these linkages when they are using cursive writing for spelling more complex words.

General Guidelines for Spelling Instruction

Handwriting—that is, letter production—supports written word production—that is, word spellings—which are the building blocks for generating written text that expresses ideas.

Language Processes Contributing to Spelling   Spelling is a complex process. It is not rote memorization that relies totally on visual recall. Spelling written words is related to sound sequences, letter patterns, and morphemes (base words and affixes). The sound sequences, letter patterns, and morphemes depend to a large extent on word origin—whether a word is of Anglo-Saxon, Latinate, French, or Greek origin (Henry, 2003; also see Chapter 4). Words connected by meaning are also connected by spelling. The silent *b* in the word *bomb* is articulated in the words *bombard* and *bombardment.* Morphology often preserves the spelling of the meaningful parts of words, though pronunciation may vary, as in *define* and *definition* or *doubt* and *dubious.*

Multisensory Approach to Spelling Instruction   The various multisensory teaching methods use slightly different approaches to spelling instruction, although they each follow sequential steps that lead to successful performance. Whatever the method of instruction, students should be taught to repeat the

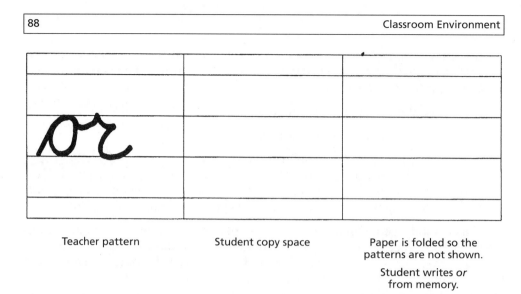

Teacher pattern   Student copy space   Paper is folded so the
                                                 patterns are not shown.

                                                 Student writes *or*
                                                 from memory.

Figure 5.4. Practicing letter connections in cursive writing with letter connections for the word *or.*

word, listen to the sounds in sequence, think of each vowel sound in the word, associate it with the letter or letters that spell the vowel sound, repeat the word, recall the sounds of words in sequence, and spell the whole word. Repeating the word helps students hear sounds in sequence and feel the speech production in sequence. Listening for the vowel sounds allows students to address difficult and ambiguous parts of the word first. Repeating the word again allows students to once more hear and feel the sounds in sequence and associate them with their letter counterparts, necessary for spelling the word in writing.

Sequence for Phonics Instruction in Spelling   Teachers should consider the order in which phonics elements are introduced for spelling in writing dictated spoken words. After teachers introduce student to five or six consonants, they can then introduce the letter *a* that stands for the short vowel sound /short a/. Without introducing more vowels, the teacher works with the students to develop the procedure for spelling words with /a/. Presenting too many phonic elements at once can overload students and does not allow sufficient practice to build for functional use of spelling.

Instruction should begin with words that are regular for reading and spelling, following unambiguous sound–symbol relationships. These are usually short vowel words. Continue to words that are not ambiguous for reading, but are ambiguous for spelling (i.e., alternate spellings for the sounds are plausible), such as *pale* and *pail*. To spell these words, the speller must know the various options available for spelling, and recall the correct option for a particular word with a specific meaning. Focus on encoding a particular spelling unit (e.g., *ee*) until students are able to confidently spell *ee* words, such as *feet, seed, meet, beef,* and *sheep.* Then the teacher can introduce another vowel unit, such as *oa;* however, enough time for guided practice in perception of the sounds is necessary before providing opportunities for discrimination between *ee* and *oa.* At another time, the teacher can introduce a third unit that stands for /long e/, such as *ea.* Students are introduced to the concept of determining which spelling of /long e/ is to be used for specific dictated words with specific meanings by listening for the / long e/ sound, considering its placement in the word and word origin, and selecting one or another based on experience with decoding or spelling the specific word. The teacher serves as a dictionary, answering student questions about which alternative to use. When the correct choice is made, the child spells the word. First- and second-grade students may not go beyond this step.

Use of Dictionaries in Spelling

Use of Dictionaries in Spelling   Teachers can help older students check the dictionary for correct spellings while the class observes. Depending on the age and reading ability of the students, the teacher or a student may read the definition. If the word does not appear in the dictionary, try an alternative spelling. Eventually students may check the dictionary independently.

As students progress, they learn the generalizations that help them make more accurate spelling decisions. Students learn words that sound the same, are spelled differently, and have different meanings. Beginning dictionary use should occur when students know the spelling alternatives open to them and are able to use the dictionary to locate them. Teach students to use the most common alternatives first. They should learn that when they hear /long a/ at the end of a word they will have several choices of spelling, but that some (e.g., *ai, a-e, ei*) will not occur at the end of the word. Thus, position of a sound or letter in a word is also informative in addition to spelling–phoneme correspondences and syllables.

Influence on Spelling Beyond Phonics   Students need to understand the factors that govern spelling word origin, syllabication, and generalizations. Many words in reading texts and children's written productions in the first three grades are one- or two-syllable high-frequency words of Anglo-Saxon origin. Many of the words in textbooks and children's written production in the upper grades, however, are of Latinate origin and tend to have three to five syllables and unaccented schwas or are of Greek origin with some different spelling–sound correspondences and morpheme patterns than words of Anglo-Saxon origin (Balmuth, 1992; Henry, 2003; see Chapter 4). The alphabetic principle and the six syllable types (Moats, 2000) for Anglo-Saxon words discussed in Chapter 4 are also relevant to spelling. In addition, vowel sounds and spellings are often governed by their placement in the word. Here are a few examples:

1.   If the syllable is closed (consonant–vowel–consonant), the vowel sound will be short.

2.   Vowels at the end of accented syllables are usually long, as in *baby, secret, tiger, pony,* and *music.*

3.   The vowel at the end of an unaccented syllable may have a schwa (reduced vowel sound) as in *away* or *afraid.*

4.   These multiletter consonant groups—*ck, dge, tch*—occur immediately after a short vowel.

5.   The letters *f, l, s,* and *z* are doubled at the end of a one-syllable short-vowel word.

Morphological Contributions to Spelling   Morphology is also relevant to spelling. Words that share the same root may have similar spellings (e.g., *sign, signal*). After learning how to spell base words, students should practice adding prefixes and suffixes. Prefixes give shades of meaning to words and suffixes indicate tense, number (singular or plural), or part of speech. Understanding the past tense suffix *–ed* is important in beginning spelling. It may be pronounced /d/, /t/, or /ed/, but spelling errors are less likely to occur if students understand that the past tense suffix is spelled *ed* for all three sounds (except for a few exceptions that remain from Old Anglo-Saxon English, such as *knelt, slept,* and *crept*). Students unlock the power of language when they understand the ways in which morphology contributes to their understanding of the meanings of words. On both oral and written language tasks, good language learners have been shown to be more sensitive to derivational relationships and to use this knowledge more productively than have poor language learners (Rubin, 1988; Stolz & Feldman, 1995). For example, a graduate student with a history of learning disabilities explained to B. Wolf her superior performance on the Miller Analogies Test by her ability to identify base words and their affixes and then attach the word to analogous meanings. This understanding builds vocabulary, improves reading skills, and allows students to express themselves with greater precision and facility in writing.

Spelling Rules   There are three consistent spelling rules for adding suffixes to one-syllable words:

1. *The doubling* or *1-1-1 rule* refers to words of one syllable ending in one consonant after one vowel. The final consonant is doubled IF the suffix being added begins with a vowel (e.g., *running*).

2. *The silent e rule* refers to the silent *e* being dropped if the suffix being added begins with a vowel (e.g., *hiked*). If it does not begin with a vowel, simply add the suffix (e.g., *wisely*).

3. *The y rule* refers to changing the *y* to an *i* if the suffix being added begins with a vowel (e.g., *candied*) except when the suffix begins with an *i* (e.g., carrying).

Written Expression

Both handwriting and spelling contribute to text generation. Children with dyslexia, OWL LD, and/or dysgraphia require explicit instruction in composition. Simply engaging in the writing process is not sufficient for them.

Phrases   Written expression begins when words are combined to convey meaning. In daily spelling lessons, children should be given practice in spelling not only single words but also phrases. For examples of independent activities with phrases, see Chapter 4.

Sentences   Sentence building is an integral part of the daily writing and spelling lesson. The phrases created as part of the daily lesson can be combined to form sentences. Students love to anticipate what the sentence will be and add multiple phrases or rearrange them in novel ways. In planning, the teacher creates the sentence first, using words from the spelling lesson, and then identifies phrases to be written before assembling them into a sentence in a text. Begin by combining spelling words, partially decodable words, and familiar words into phrases (e.g., *when spring comes, in the sun, some children*). Then combine phrases into sentences (e.g., Some children have fun in the sun when spring comes). Discuss ways to add details to sentences by answering more of the editorial questions (Who? What? Where? When? Why? How?). Children can also spell their own sentences.

Paragraphs   After students begin to understand how to organize and compose sentences to express an idea, they are ready to write paragraphs. Paragraph writing requires integration of several tasks that lead toward eventual independent written work. The student must not only organize his or her thoughts and retrieve the language for each sentence to produce a cohesive sequence of ideas that express the thoughts but also spell conventionally and use capitalization and punctuation appropriately. A good paragraph should have a clear topic sentence that tells the reader what the paragraph will be about. The body of the paragraph gives specific details that support and strengthen the topic sentence. The concluding sentence provides closure or leads the reader to the next paragraph. The goal is to develop proper paragraph writing with organization of thought and functional use of spelling, punctuation, and correct placement on paper. This approach allows students to integrate cognitive and language processes in writing. Guidelines for teaching written expression include the following:

1. Point out to the students during the Question of the Day (Chapter 3) that their answers to a three-stage question can be the basis for a paragraph.

2. Ask them to brainstorm ideas on specific topics (e.g., what they do on a rainy day). Create a topic sentence to use in step 3.

3. As part of the Question of the Day, provide a topic sentence and ask students to create two or more sentences for the body of the paragraph and a concluding sentence.

4. Students may add to a teacher-generated topic sentence to create their own paragraphs. Class discussion of individual paragraphs can help students develop understanding of cohesion in written language.

5. Continue these oral activities until all students are secure with the concept of topic sentences. Daily practice with writing sentences leads to weekly practice in constructing clear, well-organized paragraphs independently. Writing multiparagraph papers provides a structure for notetaking and multipage reports.

Independent Writing Activities   Meaningful independent writing activities for instructional groups can be done in groups or individually. For example, students can

1. Brainstorm lists of words and create class charts or lists students can keep in their notebooks for use during independent writing lessons. This activity will help add variety to writing and eliminate the worry of incorrect spelling.

2. Compile a list of synonyms for the words *speak* or *said.*

3. Compile a list of synonyms for the word *movement.*

4. Compile a list of synonyms for the word *hungry.*

5. Add suffixes or prefixes to base words (see Table 5.1) or start with the whole word and identify root, prefix, and suffixes (see Table 5.2; the teacher provides lists of base words, prefixes, suffixes, and whole words).

6. Practice with parts of speech is a practical application of written language skills. Even beginning writers can sort nouns, verbs, and adjectives if they understand that nouns are naming words and verbs are action words. Begin by providing lists as shown in Chapter 4. Then have students write their own sentences.

7. Expand on activities suggested in Chapter 4 by constructing sentences that include the following parts of speech: noun markers, adjectives, and nouns; prepositions, adjectives, nouns; articles and nouns; articles, adjectives, and nouns; prepositional phrases; spatial (where) phrases; and temporal (when) phrases.

8. Provide a matched list of homonyms. Children copy the paired words on folded, half-ruled paper and then illustrate both spellings (e.g., *sale, sail; pane, pain; plane, plain; pale, pail; pare, pair, pear; cell, sell*).

9. The teacher provides a list of base words and points out the list of known prefixes and suffixes that are posted in the room. Students copy the base word, the prefix, and the suffix they are using in the appropriate columns. The whole word is written in the last column.

Story starters allow students to apply their writing skills. They may be more effective for some students with OWL LD if they are allowed to verbalize their ideas before writing.

Computer Use

The computer is an invaluable tool for writing activities—it can help a student eliminate frustration with handwriting and correcting spelling errors, and it aids in producing a clear and readable product. A computer also permits more flexibility in correcting, editing, and reorganizing text, which may promote new cognitive styles. When keyboarding is automatic, it saves the student time, and the ease of production can produce a positive attitude toward learning. More than two decades ago, Logan (1986) predicted that computer technology would enhance literacy. Indeed, computers may help those students with handwriting, spelling, and expressive writing difficulties to develop more flexibility in generating and processing written language.

However, they still require explicit writing instruction. Whether students with dysgraphia with or without dyslexia benefit from use of computers in written expression may depend on whether they receive explicit, systematic instruction in keyboarding, spelling with the computer, and composing with the computer. The same processing skills that interfere with their learning to write with a pencil or pen could interfere with their learning to use the computer to write. Teaching keyboarding skills requires the same explicit systematic instruction as does teaching handwriting skills. King (2005) theorized that some students with dyslexia have difficulty learning the keyboard because they are attempting to superimpose a new alphabet order (asdf) on the original learning (abcd). She suggested that students be taught the conventional keyboard in alphabetical order using a multisensory approach. The authors know of no controlled research showing that students with dyslexia benefit from a nonstandard keyboard.

RESEARCHER CONTRIBUTIONS

Defining Writing

The word *writing* is used to refer to many aspects of the complex writing process. Writing may refer to the act of producing written letters (handwriting) or words (spelling) or the complex cognitive processes of generating ideas, planning what to write and how to write it, translating the ideas and plans into written text, and reviewing and revising the text to make it better. The planning, translating, and reviewing/revising cognitive processes in the Hayes and Flowers (1980) model of writing benefit from explicit instruction (for review, see Wong & Berninger, 2004). Research shows that handwriting, spelling, and composition are separable processes, but when all of these component processes are adequately developed, they work in concert in the functional writing system (see Berninger & Richards, 2002, Chapter 9). Thus, the instructional program should devote time to teaching each of these separately and to integrating them.

Although many teachers, drawing on whole-language or constructivist philosophy, no longer use systematic handwriting and spelling programs to teach these transcription skills and believe that engaging students in authentic composing activities is sufficient (see Graham & Harris, 1994), research evidence supports explicit teaching of handwriting, spelling, and composing (Graham & Perrin, 2007a, 2007b). Explicit instruction brings the transcription and composition skills into conscious awareness, which supports application of strategies to writing (see Chapter 4 for explicit reading instruction to bring reading into conscious awareness). Before reviewing evidence-based instructional approaches to teaching writing skills explicitly, further clarification of what dysgraphia is and how it is related to dyslexia is provided (also see Introduction and Chapter 8).

Dysgraphia

Dysgraphia is unusual difficulty with handwriting and/or spelling that may occur alone or with dyslexia (impaired word decoding, word reading, and spelling) or OWL LD (impaired morphological and syntactic awareness and comprehension). Children with dysgraphia who have difficulty with handwriting may have illegible letter formation and/or excessively slow, nonautomatic letter writing. The handwriting problems may also interfere with their spelling and written composition (Berninger & Amtmann, 2003). Children with dysgraphia who have difficulty spelling experience difficulty in translating all their ideas into written language. Not only children with dysgraphia but also children with dyslexia and OWL LD have writing problems. *Dyslexia is not just a reading disorder—it is also a writing disorder because of the spelling problems that interfere with development of written composition* (Berninger, Nielsen, Abbott, Wijsman, & Raskind, 2008b). Spelling problems may be more difficult to remediate than the reading problems in dyslexia (Lefly & Pennington, 1991), especially if not treated early and throughout the school years.

In order to group students for instructional purposes and plan sufficient explicit instruction for them in specific areas of written language, it is important to know whether individual students have difficulties in handwriting only; spelling only; word reading and spelling only, whether writing problems are related to dyslexia, OWL LD, and/or dysgraphia; or handwriting, word reading, and spelling. Gender differences occur in writing rather than reading (Berninger, Nielsen, Abbott, Wijsman, & Raskind, 2008a): Boys tend to have more difficulties than girls in handwriting, spelling, and executive functions for self-regulation of composing, and girls are more likely than boys to compensate for both reading and writing problems in their adult years (Berninger et al., 2008a).

Handwriting

Although handwriting is considered a low-level mechanical skill in the writing process, both legible letter writing and automatic letter writing contribute uniquely to amount and quality of written composition in Grades 1–6 (Graham, Berninger, Abbott, Abbott, & Whitaker, 1997). Explicit instruction in handwriting in the first two grades may prevent more significant written composition problems in the later grades for all students. Zaner-Bloser (Columbus, OH; www.zaner-bloser.com/fresh/handwriting-overview.html) publishes handwriting programs that can be implemented in the general education program for all students. Effective handwriting instruction need not involve a large part of the instructional day or mindless copying of the same letters over and over. In fact the brain may habituate, that is fail to attend to and benefit from repeated writing of the same letter(s) over and over without some novelty in the instructional activity (Berninger & Richards, 2002). For the most comprehensive review of the motor processes that are involved in handwriting, which is a very complex skill, see Graham and Weintraub (1996).

Manuscript Writing Rutberg studied children who already showed unusual difficulty in letter writing at the beginning of first grade. She compared the instructional approaches used by occupational or physical therapists with those used by educators (first study in Berninger, Rutberg, et al., 2006). The results showed that the treatment that worked on muscle strength and fine motor control prior to teaching letter formation resulted in more accurate letter formation. The treatment that only taught and practiced letter writing resulted in more automatic letter writing. However, only the first treatment resulted in improvement on a verbal mediation task. Verbal mediation (self-talk to guide the letter formation process) may be an appropriate part of initial instruction in letter formation but not of subsequent instruction aimed at learning automatic letter writing.

The most effective instruction, compared with control and alternative treatments, for improving automatic manuscript letter writing that transferred to amount composed within time limits (compositional fluency) included the following instructional components for each of the 26 letters (Berninger, 1998a; Berninger et al., 1997):

- Children study the numbered arrow cues in a model letter

- Children cover the letter and hold it in the mind's eye for a few seconds

- Children use numbered arrow cues in the model letter as a strategy to write the letter from memory and compare the letter they wrote with the model letter

At each step of the strategy, the teacher should name the letter because letter names serve as letter form retrieval cues (Berninger et al., 1997). Brooks showed that this treatment also reduced reversals in letter writing compared with a control treatment (see Berninger, Rutberg, et al., 2006). Graham, Harris, and Fink (2000) also showed that explicit handwriting strategies benefited beginning writers with handwriting problems and transferred to improved written composition

Children must learn not only how to produce letters automatically but also how to retrieve letter forms automatically from long-term memory as they prepare them for production. This automatic retrieval depends on searching and accessing a specific letter form among the 26 letters stored in long-term memory. Storing them in alphabetical order has an advantage for automatic letter form retrieval. The before and after alphabet letter game can help students develop automatic letter retrieval. In this game, children are asked to tell or write the letter that comes before or after another letter in alphabetic order. In a writing tutorial, the children who played these before and after games wrote longer compositions than those who did not play the games, suggesting some transfer to written expression of ideas (Berninger, Abbott, Whitaker, Sylvester, & Nolen, 1995). See Berninger 1998b for lessons with before and after letter-writing activities.

Big Strokes for Little Folks (Rubel, 1995) teaches component strokes in letter formation by groups of letters that share common strokes and includes supplementary activities for developing small motor and muscle skills related to writing. For lessons for combining instructional activities for developing automatic letter retrieval and production with composing on-topic prompts, see Berninger (1998a) and Berninger and Abbott (2003, Lesson Set 3).

Cursive Writing *Loops and Groups: A Kinesthetic Writing System* (Benbow, 1990) is a program for teaching cursive writing that incorporates many of the general principles of handwriting instruction under the Teacher Contributions section in this chapter. Another useful instructional resource is *Handwriting without Tears* (Olsen, 2004).

Relatively less research has been devoted to cursive than manuscript handwriting, but the authors' research has found that children who have not mastered manuscript writing may have extreme difficulty in making the transition to cursive writing instruction, but other children transition easily from manuscript handwriting to cursive writing instruction. Whether a student with dyslexia also has dysgraphia may influence how the student responds to either manuscript or cursive handwriting instruction.

Handwriting Versus Keyboarding For children with severe dysgraphia, a decision has to be made as to whether instruction should focus on just manuscript or perhaps also keyboarding to use in operating a laptop for written assignments. Comprehensive neuropsychological assessment of graphomotor planning and other relevant processes may yield useful information in making this decision (Berninger, 2004b). Even if children with dysgraphia cannot learn to write legible cursive letters, they should be taught to read cursive letters that others use. If a decision is made that a student with dysgraphia should, as an accommodation, be allowed to use a laptop for all written assignments, then explicit instruction in keyboarding should be provided. One instructional resource for providing explicit keyboard instruction is *Computer Keyboarding for Beginners* (Fry, 1993).

In typically developing children, both common and unique neurodevelopmental processes explain manuscript and cursive writing across the elementary school grades (Berninger, Abbott, Augsburger, & Garcia, 2008; Berninger, Richards, et al.,

2007; Hayes & Berninger, in press). Two research findings have been surprising for typically developing students: 1) good writers often use a mix of cursive and manuscript or revert to manuscript (Graham, Berninger, & Weintraub, 1998; Jones, 2004); and 2) typically developing children write more, write faster, write more-complex syntax, and express more ideas when writing by pen than by keyboard (Berninger, Richards, Stock, Trivedi, & Altemeier, 2007; Hayes & Berninger, in press). Thus, the keyboard is not a substitute for handwriting, and quality hand-writing instruction and practice in composing with pencil or pen is important for both writers with and without writing disabilities.

Attention   Teachers should monitor children's attention during writing in-struction and writing activities in the classroom and share with parents. Aspects of attention teachers should observe include 1) focusing on the relevant part of a task and ignoring the irrelevant parts of the task, 2) staying on task, and 3) switching from one task to another or one part of a task to another. Writing in the air in Slingerhand handwriting instruction may engage the frontal attention system via the large motor movements of the arm, which are also regulated by the frontal system.

Some children with dysgraphia also have attention deficit disorder and do not respond to handwriting instruction or produce legible letter writing until they receive medication for their attention deficit disorder. The improvement in hand-writing is often dramatic and rapid once medication is started. Many psychologists have training relevant to diagnosing attention deficit disorder, but in most states, only physicians can prescribe medication for it and need to be involved, along with the parents, in making the decision as to whether medication may be helpful for treating the attention problems. If the decision is to try a trial of medication, teach-ers should continue to monitor attention and handwriting in the classroom and share their observations with the child's parents, physician, and other relevant pro-fessionals. Decisions to use any medication for learning problems should be made cautiously, based on careful diagnosis, and monitored closely. When more than one drug is prescribed for a child, the possibility of adverse drug interactions should be considered. Teachers can help raise appropriate questions for the parents, physicians, and psychologists to consider in prescribing medication for problems at school in learning or producing written language.

Spelling

Research on spelling is rapidly expanding knowledge of the language processes that contribute to this complex writing skill.

Relationship of Word Spelling and Reading   Spelling is related to word reading, but it is not the mirror image of word reading. For example, if one applies the alphabetic principle to spelling words, the number of correspondences be-tween a phoneme and a grapheme (one- or two-letter spelling unit) is greater in the direction of translating spoken words into written words than in the direction of translating written words into a spoken words (Berninger, 1998b). For example, the single letter *a* is typically associated with a /long a/ sound (in an open or silent *e* syllable), a /short a/ sound (in a closed syllable), or a /schwa/ (reduced vowel). However, the /long a/ phoneme could be spelled with the letter *a* in a closed or silent *e* syllable, or the letters *ai* as in *gain; ay* as in *say; ey* as in *they; eigh* as in *weigh;* or *ea* as in *great.* That is, in the sound-to-spelling direction, English has more alternations or options than in the spelling-to-sound direction. These options can be called *substitutes* in teaching students to spell; see Berninger and Abbott (2003; see the Reproducibles section) for charts of substitutes that children can keep at their desk to help them review the options. A good analogy that teachers can tell students is that just like a coach substitutes players so one player does not get too tired, English substitutes different spelling units for the same sound so that no one spelling unit is overworked or gets too tired. English, however, is not hopelessly irregular—it is a predictable system with options that need to be learned for slow mapping that refines the initial fast mapping of spoken and written words (see Chapter 4).

Also, effective instruction may differ for word reading and spelling. The first author and colleagues found that for word reading, the most effective instruction for learning taught and transfer words (same graphemes or phonemes but in different word contexts) was the alphabetic principle or whole-word naming of letters and words (see Chapter 4). For word spelling, combined naming of letters and the whole word *and* training in onset rimes transferred best to taught and transfer word spelling, but the alphabetic principle (in the phoneme-to-grapheme direction) transferred best to spelling during independent composing (Berninger et al., 1998).

Thus, the most effective way to teach word reading and word spelling may not be identical. Also, just because a child is learning to read words it does not follow that the child can spell all those words. Both word reading and word spelling need to be taught and monitored for all students in the general education class to make sure both are developing to grade-appropriate levels (see Chapter 8).

Controlled (Strategic) and Automatic Processing in Spelling   English spelling is *not* a mere mechanical skill as many assume. It is a complex language process (Venezky, 1970, 1999) that draws on multiple components (Berninger & Fayol, 2008), including the following:

- Phonology, orthography, and morphology (Silliman, Bahr, & Peters, 2006)

- Vocabulary (semantics, which is a system for linking words in the language system with concepts in the cognition system, see Stahl & Nagy, 2005; Wilkinson, Bahr, Silliman, & Berninger, 2007)

- Word origin (Balmuth, 1992; Henry, 2003)

- Phonotactics (Treiman, Kessler, Knewasser, Tincoff, & Bowman, 2000) and orthotactics (probable sequences and positions of sounds and letters, respectively; Apel, Oster, & Masterson, 2006; Pacton et al., 2001)

Morphology (Carlisle, 1994, 1996; Derwing, Smith, & Wiebe, 1995; Green et al., 2003) is important for both learning to spell and applying spelling to composing. *SPELL-Links to Reading and Writing: A Word Study Program for K–Adult* (Masterson, Apel, & Wasowicz, 2002) provides individually tailored assessment that can be translated into spelling instruction. Teachers can consult with the school's speech-language pathologist, sometimes called a communication disorders specialist, who may be able and willing to help implement this assessment–intervention program to pinpoint which children may have phonological, orthographic, or morphological problems interfering with their spelling development and to assess the vocabulary development of poor spellers. School psychologists also may have the training and tools to assess these skills. See Gentry (2004) for spelling strategies for use with all general education students, including those with dyslexia and dysgraphia.

Although some evidence points to strategic stages in spelling development from phonological to orthographic to morphological (e.g., Templeton & Bear, 1992), other evidence suggests that all three processes—phonological, orthographic, and morphological—contribute jointly to spelling throughout writing development beginning in the elementary school years (Garcia, 2007); although how the three word forms and their parts are related to each other may change with writing development (e.g., Berninger, Raskind, et al., 2008). For example, when first learning to spell a new word, one may rely on conscious strategies for transforming phonological units into orthographic and morphological units (e.g., Treiman, 1993). Once the word is familiar and practiced until the spelling is recalled automatically (e.g., Steffler, Varnhagen, Friesen, & Trieman, 1998), spelling then relies on accessing or retrieving a word-specific, precise spelling in the autonomous orthographic lexicon. As one learns to spell longer and morphologically more complex words, one relies on morphological spelling rules that specify spelling at the end of a base word and beginning of suffixes that are affixed to the base word (e.g., Dixon & Engelmann, 2001). When all the language processes are working together in concert, the autonomous orthographic lexicon supports automatic direct retrieval of word-specific spellings from implicit memory. Then spelling may appear deceptively on the surface to be a mechanical skill because it does not require conscious attention to integrate it with composing processes in a fluent manner. However, the facts show that *spelling is a complex skill drawing on many language processes acquired over time.*

Language Processes in Skilled Spelling   The spelling bee, once a mainstream instructional activity in the little red school house in rural America, is regaining a surge of popularity. Local, state, regional, and national competitions are being held, and both television and movies are featuring stories about spelling bees. Many spelling bees allow children to ask before spelling a word if they are uncertain about a particular word. The types of questions children ask are revealing about the processes that contribute to word spelling. Some ask for the meaning, a definition. Some ask for the word to be used in a sentence. Some ask for it to be pronounced again. Others ask for word origin. Students who participate in spelling bees typically use meaning cues, the associated sounds, and the sound and morpheme cues specific to word origin to help them remember or construct the most probable word spelling. Spelling is a meaning-driven skill that draws on phonological, orthographic, and morphological aspects of words and is fundamentally important in transcribing thoughts in creating written text.

Contemporary Immigrant Words in the Language   In addition to words of Anglo-Saxon, Latinate and French, and Greek origin discussed in Chapter 4, other words are making their way into American English from computer technology and the large waves of families moving to the United States from all over the world. For example, in the Seattle area, a recent count by one of the large school systems in the region showed that 83 languages were spoken by families of children in the school system. Words are dynamic, flexible linguistic units that are continually being added to the spoken and written language. General education teachers can include some of these words from the languages spoken by children in their classrooms in the spelling program.

Fast and Slow Mapping in Spelling Good spellers may be able to rely on fast mapping (one or a few exposures) to initially learn how to spell words (Apel et al., 2006) as well as how to read them (see Chapter 4). Because good spellers are sensitive to the phonotactic and orthotactic structures (probable sequencing and positioning of sounds within spoken words and letters in written words, respectively) within implicit memory, fast mapping results in accurate spelling, and they may seem like natural spellers. In contrast, children with dyslexia or dysgraphia impairing spelling do not have typical phonotactic and/or orthotactic sensitivity and cannot rely on fast mapping to the same extent as good spellers in learning to spell. Rather, they need to rely on slow mapping (see Chapter 4) in which they apply phonological-orthographic strategies, such as the alphabetic principle (phoneme-to-grapheme direction), onset and rime, lexical naming of spoken words and all the letters in a word, and morphological strategies in conscious working memory to learn to spell words.

General education teachers can accommodate both students who do and do not learn to spell easily through fast mapping because all students benefit from explicit instruction and instructional activities focused on slow mapping of phonological, orthographic, and morphological word forms and their parts. Such explicit instruction does not have to be confined to direct transmission of information. It can also include activities to promote enjoyment of words, including word play for humor, as in riddles and puns; multiple meanings for the same sound patterns, as in homonyms; and word hunts to find words that have certain morphological or other characteristics. (For examples of this kind of instruction, see Chapter 9 and the Mommylongwords contest in Lesson Sets 9 and 10 in Berninger & Abbott, 2003.) One tutor in the after-school clubs designed to help students score better on the state's high-stakes test (Lesson Set 10) shared her surprise when play with words was combined with direct instruction strategies. Four reluctant fourth-grade writers started consulting *spontaneously* with a dictionary and were engaged in a meaningful discussion about word spelling and word meaning related to an independent writing assignment.

Relationship of Spelling to Written Composition Spelling influences the written composition of children and adults with dyslexia (Berninger, Nielsen, et al., 2008b; Connelly, Campbell, MacLean, & Barnes, 2006) and of typically developing writers (Abbott, Berninger, & Fayol, 2008; Graham et al., 1997). One father of a child with dyslexia reported that he wished he could have gone through college writing what he knew on essays instead of worrying about words he thought he could spell correctly; he envied students who could just write their ideas without worrying about spelling. The transfer of spelling to written composition is most likely if spelling lessons are followed immediately by composition activities in which children write freely on grade-appropriate topics (Berninger et al., 1998) or are asked to use grade-appropriate, high-frequency spelling words in their compositions (Berninger, Vaughan, et al., 2000).

Evidence-Based General Principles for Spelling Instruction   Research supports the following guidelines for teaching spelling to students with spelling problems due to dyslexia or dysgraphia:

1. *Less is more.* In what might be the first scientific research on instructional practices, Rice (1897, 1913) studied spelling instruction in classrooms throughout the country. The results showed that children who received just 15 minutes of daily spelling instruction achieved higher spelling scores than those who received 1 hour a day of spelling instruction. What may matter more than absolute amount of time spent on spelling is the nature of the spelling instruction received. More time should be spent teaching spelling strategies and less time relying solely on assessing spelling once a week on dictation tests.

2. *Beginning spelling (Grades 1–3) is affected by word frequency in the language, and so is developing spelling in the upper grades, but learning word formation strategies for low-frequency, morphologically complex words also becomes important in the upper grades.* Fry (1996) incorporated the 1,000 most-frequent words in the language into his spelling lessons for Grades 1–6; these were developed and validated over the years for children who received services in his Rutgers University clinic for learning problems. Each spelling lesson begins with teaching and practicing explicit strategies for learning to spell single high-frequency words, which are called Instant Words. This strategy instruction and practice is followed by sentence dictation activities in which children practice spelling the same words in sentence context, which clarifies the meaning of each word. Sentence dictation requires that children hold multiple words in sentence syntax in conscious working memory as they spell, much as they must do when composing.

    Graham, Harris, and Loynachan (1994) created another list of grade-appropriate, high-frequency words to use in spelling instruction at different instructional levels. This list is based on the high-frequency words children use in their own compositions at various grade levels. See Lesson Set 5 in Berninger and Abbott (2003) for examples of how these high-frequency words for writing can be used in written composition activities to encourage children to learn to spell them correctly in their own writing and not just on a dictated spelling test.

3. *Use effective strategies.* Effective strategies for teaching beginning spelling using high-frequency words include selective reminding; combining the alphabetic principle, onset rimes, and whole-word naming; developing syllable awareness for the six syllable types in English and the phonemes in the syllables; spelling the same words repeatedly in different sentence contexts from dictation; sorting function and content words by phoneme–grapheme correspondences; and word play.

    a. For selective reminding, based on Hart, Berninger, and Abbott (1997), children practice spelling a small set of high-frequency words in each lesson, but on subsequent trials only practice those missed in the prior trials (see Berninger, 1998b).

    b. To ensure that children transfer spelling knowledge beyond the taught one-syllable words to other one-syllable words and to their own composing, they need to learn multiple spelling strategies for phoneme-to-grapheme correspondence, onset rimes, and whole words (naming all the letters and the whole word; Berninger et al., 1998;Berninger & Abbott, 2003, Lesson Set 4). Fry (1996) also includes activities for applying the alphabetic principle to spelling.

c. Games for developing syllable awareness and phoneme awareness within syllables that improved spelling of two-syllable words are included in Lesson Set 5 (Berninger & Abbott, 2003), which is based on a study by Berninger, Vaughan, et al. (2000). In that study, a minimum of 24 repeated practices in spelling a word as part of sentence dictation was required for at-risk second-grade spellers to reach mastery for spelling second-grade, high-frequency words. The programmatic spelling research of Dreyer, Luke, and Melican (1995) showed that what differentiated good and poor spellers was memory for word spelling in the long run not the short run. Thus, instructional programs for spelling should consider distributing repetitions of spelling practice for particular words across time intervals that span several months and not just sequential days within the school week.

d. All or most of the phonemes in content words (nouns, verbs, adjectives, and adverbs) tend to correspond predictably to graphemes; but function words (conjunctions, prepositions, pronouns, helping verbs, articles) tend to be only partially decodable compared with content words (i.e., have fewer phonemes that correspond to conventional graphemes). However, training automatic phoneme–grapheme correspondences; sorting phonemes into categories for alternative possible graphemes on a substitution card (e.g., /z/ can be spelled with s or z), and playing spelling bingo for the high-frequency, partially decodable function words improved children's spelling of function as well as content words (Berninger, Vaughan, et al., 2002; also see Lesson Set 7 in Berninger & Abbott, 2003). Also, see Bear, Ivernizzi, Templeton, and Johnston (2000) for sorting activities that facilitate spelling development.

e. Play with language through the humor in riddles, puns, and jokes can also be an effective instructional component for spelling (e.g., Berninger, Abbott, Abbott, Graham, & Richards, 2002). Children at risk for spelling (and reading) problems may develop understanding of how language is used to create humor at a slower rate than typically developing readers and spellers. For example, a sixth grader who had participated in several of the treatment studies finally "got" the jokes and riddles used at the beginning of each session when younger children in that treatment study still struggled with perceiving the humor in the word play. In a before-school club that always began with about 10 minutes of children choosing their favorite riddle, pun, or joke of the day from paperbacks and other collections the researchers provided (Berninger, Rutberg et al., 2006, Study 4), one second grader asked his teacher in all seriousness if jokes always had to be funny. Until children reach a certain level of linguistic awareness, the humor in language may not be readily apparent. Word hunts for words with specific syllable or morpheme patterns were part of the effective writing instruction that improved writing on state high-stakes tests as well as individually administered standardized tests of composition (Berninger, Rutberg et al., 2006, Study 4).

4. *Effective strategies for teaching spelling beyond the beginning stage* include ortho-
    graphic strategies such as Photographic Leprechaun and Proofreader's Trick,
    which are in the Mark Twain spelling lessons (Unit II) in the accompanying
    workbook, *Helping Students with Dyslexia and Dysgraphia Make Connections: Dif-
    ferentiated Instruction Lesson Plans in Reading and Writing* (Berninger & Wolf,
    2009), and visual search (finding correctly spelled words in the horizontal, verti-
    cal, or diagonal rows of otherwise random letters) and anagrams (unscrambling
    letters to find correctly spelled words) in *Spelling Through Morphographs* (Dixon
    & Engelmann, 2001). Examples of effective morphological strategies include
    adding morphological awareness activities from Dixon and Englemann (2001;
    building words from roots and affixes; decomposing words with affixes into
    their roots, prefixes, and suffixes; morphological spelling rules), and Henry
    (1990, 2003) and Henry and Redding (1996; phonological, orthographic, and
    morphological units in words of Anglo-Saxon, Latinate, and Greek origin). Fry
    (1996) also includes morpheme variants that develop morphological awareness
    as applied to spelling.

Composition

To facilitate transfer of transcription skills to composition and to integrate the various writing components in resource-limited working memory, which may have
reduced storage or processing capability in children with dyslexia and/or dysgraphia (see Chapters 4 and 7), transcription and composition instruction should
be taught close in time in the same lesson so that they become functionally integrated (Berninger et al., 1995; Berninger et al., 1997, 1998; Berninger, Rutberg, et al.,
2006; Berninger, Vaughan, et al., 2000, 2002). Explicit strategies should be used for
not only the transcription skills but also high-level cognitive processes of composing (Auman, 2003; Berninger et al., 1995, 2002; Carlisle, 1996; Graham & Harris,
2005; Graham & Perrin, 2007a, 2007b). Examples of explicit composition instruction are teacher modeling of the Plan, Write, Review, Revise (PWRR) strategy
(Hayes & Flowers, 1980; e.g., thinking aloud as the teacher plans, translates, reviews, and revises and models each of these processes for the students) and teacher
guidance in constructing well-formed paragraphs (e.g., asking questions and offering suggestions as children plan, compose, and review and revise). Following
this kind of explicit writing instruction, poor writers at the transition between third
and fourth grade improved in their composing and self-reported less writing
avoidant behaviors when they could write better (Berninger et al., 1995). This transition is critical because the writing requirements of the curriculum increase and
become more complex in fourth grade and above. Children need to be monitored
and given supplementary instruction if needed during this transition.

  Children also benefit from explicit strategy instruction in learning different
writing genres, such as narrative and expository—informational, compare and
contrast, and persuasive (e.g., for review of research, especially the programmatic
research of Wong, on this topic with middle school and high school students, see
Wong & Berninger, 2004). For example, Berninger et al. (2002) showed that third
graders at risk for writing improved in expository writing when they were explicitly taught how to plan, translate, and review and revise this genre (Berninger &
Abbott, 2003, Lesson Set 7).

  For children with dyslexia, OWL LD, and/or dysgraphia, many of whom
have problems in executive functions for self-regulation of the writing process

(Graham, 1997; Hooper, Swartz, Wakely, de Kruif, & Montgomery, 2002; Hooper, Wakely, de Kruif, & Swartz, 2006), and for other students in Grade 4 and above, simply engaging in the authentic communication process is not sufficient (Graham & Perrin, 2007a, 2007b). Students benefit from explicit instruction (raising cognitive awareness of the processes) and strategy instruction (Graham & Harris, 2005) in each of the cognitive processes of writing. They also benefit from explicit instruction in the six traits of writing (Culham, 2003), which some states' high-stakes tests use in evaluating whether students meet state standards in writing. *The Writing Lab Approach to Language Instruction and Intervention* (Nelson, Bahr, & Van Meter, 2004) is a valuable source of writing instruction activities and software to support the composing process for general education teachers because it is based on research that included students with a variety of language problems including OWL LD.

Teaching Writing to English Language Learners

Learning to write (or read) English should not be delayed until oral, conversational English is mastered. In fact, written language can support learning a second language in its oral as well as written format. (See http://techno-ware-esl.com/engdisc.html for resources for teaching writing to English language learners.)

Computers

The need for explicit instruction in spelling continues even in the technological era with spell checks, which flag possible spelling errors that can only be fixed if the computer user knows the correct spelling. Often students with dyslexia, OWL LD, and/or dysgraphia do not. Spell checks do not recognize the spelling errors of many students with dyslexia and/or dysgraphia because their spelling departs so much from conventional spelling. One seventh grade student with dyslexia was ecstatic when the spell check, which probably requires a spelling level of fourth to fifth grade, could finally detect his spelling errors.

Computers might be used in the revising process and to scan grade-appropriate text into computer programs that then read that text back to writers who cannot read the grade-level texts sufficiently well on their own. This computer application gives students with dyslexia, OWL LD, and/or dysgraphia access to grade-appropriate content, despite reading problems, for completing grade-appropriate writing activities. Spelling problems can be addressed during the revision of multiple drafts of compositions.

CONCLUSION

Both the teacher-generated knowledge and research-generated knowledge led to the conclusion that children with writing problems benefit from explicit instruction in handwriting, spelling, and composition, beginning as early as first grade and continuing thereafter. The research showed that it is possible to combine explicit transcription instruction with authentic composing activities to improve student writing outcomes. The research also showed that by directing instruction to all levels of language (see Chapters 3 and 4) close in time helps struggling writers overcome working memory inefficiencies.

CHAPTER 6

Teaching Across the Language Systems with Intellectual Engagement

General education teachers have an important role to play in developing the cognitive and multiple language skills (listening, speaking, reading, and writing) of all students including those with dyslexia, oral and written language learning disability (OWL LD), and/or dysgraphia. In this chapter examples from teaching experience and research studies are provided to illustrate effective ways of accomplishing these instructional goals.

TEACHER CONTRIBUTIONS

The weaknesses of students with dyslexia, OWL LD, and/or dysgraphia in written language frequently deprive them of the very experiences in which they may excel, such as creative and insightful thinking outside the box (Arieti, 1976). Instead, their instructional program may overemphasize drill and practice of the written language skills with which they struggle. As a result, these students may be cheated of opportunities to explore, discover, and create, which are normal avenues toward motivated, self-directed learning and thinking.

An integrated curriculum using material from across content areas may set the stage for intellectual engagement and provide a context within which students with dyslexia, OWL LD, and/or dysgraphia can learn the more difficult written language skills. On the one hand, working with high-interest materials may allow these students to use their intellectual skills to find success apart from written language and then transfer that success to reading, spelling, and composing with satisfaction and confidence. On the other hand, multisensory instruction may enhance attention to instruction and engagement in the learning process.

Students with dyslexia are often described as being "kinesthetic learners" who benefit from hands-on learning activities. Kinesthesis is a sensory input system that registers touch, especially touch associated with sequential motor movements on or of the hands. Multisensory teaching may be necessary to help students with dyslexia integrate information across sensory input modalities and link these modalities with motor output and internal language systems (see Chapters 5 and 7 as well as this chapter for reframing multisensory learning as multimodal sensorimotor learning). According to Birsh (2006), multisensory strategies simultaneously involve visual, auditory, and tactile-kinesthetic sensory systems and can be linked with the articulatory-motor components of speaking, thus serving as a bridge for linking listening, speaking, reading, and writing. Multisensory teaching in which children are engaged in listening, looking, touching, reading, speaking, and writing activities in all lessons may serve to 1) integrate all sensory input modalities and 2) capitalize on those modalities that are strengths, which may help overcome weaknesses in other modalities.

In other words, using both intellectually engaging content material and a multisensory approach may capture and maintain students' attention during instruction. Also, learning activities that involve teacher–student interactions and allow for discovery in learning may increase academic engagement in learning in students with dyslexia, OWL LD, and/or dysgraphia (Torrance, 1963). Immersing a class in new material by involving as many curriculum areas and modalities of input as possible also offers students opportunities to make new and creative cognitive connections.

Teachers have provided multisensory instruction in various ways for students with dyslexia. In one class, for instance, the letter *m* became memorable when beginning readers sang the folk song "Miss Mary Mack" and learned about machines. They created the sounds of machines during music and rhythm, created their own machines during art, and developed oral language skills as they described the purpose and operation of their inventions. This immersion made them acutely aware of the letter *m* while they were moving, creating, and learning about science.

When the letter *a* was introduced, each child received an apple and was instructed to draw pictures of the different things they could do with apples. Then the children took their apples home to use in some way and then bring back to show the class. The following day, they produced turkeys and clowns made of apples and marshmallows. One child recited "Peter, Peter *apple eater*" and showed Peter's house made of an apple. And the food! Johnny Appleseed would have been proud of the apple pies, apple cakes, apple cookies, apple sauce, and apples and dip that the children brought to share. Having so many good things to eat motivated the class to assemble an apple cookbook that included apple pictures and apple poems created from a class-generated vocabulary cache of words to describe apples. They also sang Malvina Reynolds's apple tree song, "If You Love Me" (1974); planted an apple tree at their school; and tasted a variety of apples and graphed their preferences. They found books about apples and watched *The Legend of Johnny Appleseed*. Learning about the letter *a* generated science, nutrition, math, art, music, and oral language activities.

Second-grade students in another class learning that the letter combination *ow* sounds like /ow/, as in *cow* were motivated to practice and remember by learning about clowns. Each student created his or her own clown face on paper, and then parent volunteers painted the student's faces. Some students designed costumes and others planned the funny things that they would do.

Students also practiced creating /ow/ words during independent activities. They added the suffixes *–ing* and *–ed* to /ow/ verbs (e.g., *bowed, frowning, howled, vowed, plowing, crowned*) and used them with /ow/ nouns (e.g., *cow, frown, town, sow, crown*) to build their own sentences, which began, "A clown came to town and . . ." Some clowns fell down or turned upside down, and others put on fancy gowns.

Multimodal Instruction across the Curriculum

Primary grade teachers commonly bring this sense of fun and exploration to the language curriculum. Unfortunately, as children grow older or as they are confronted with weaknesses in written language, these adventures in learning typically are neglected. They need not be, however. For example, one sixth-grade activity in a school for students with dyslexia began with a social studies lesson about food production. The teacher, recognizing that food is a motivator for many children, used chocolate to demonstrate the steps involved in bringing a product from its source to the home.

During a math lesson, she gave each student a Hershey's chocolate bar and used the candy to lead the class through a simple fraction lesson. The bars were easy to break on the dividing lines and easy to manipulate. The teacher also used M&Ms during a graphing activity. After the lesson, while students were eating their chocolate bars fraction by fraction, the teacher led a discussion of the origins of chocolate and students' favorite chocolate foods.

During a reading lesson, students read *All about Chocolate,* an upper elementary/middle school nonfiction booklet from http://www.readinga-z.com. These consumable, high-interest books allow teachers to develop comprehension and note-taking skills in an appropriate book for a child's reading level. The students used many words related to the production of chocolate (see Table 6.1) for decoding practice and a vocabulary discussion, which prepared the students for the text. The words also allowed them to practice the new skills of decoding multisyllable words with both open and closed syllables and those with suffixes, with an emphasis on words that are changed when a suffix beginning with a vowel is added. The students also practiced reading many phrases that appeared in the book (see Table 6.2).

The teacher guided the students through reading the book and helped them to make connections to prior knowledge and relate the information in the text to the information in the timelines, illustrations, and charts in the booklet. The students also used the comprehension extensions suggested by Bonnie Meyer (see Chapter 4) to prepare for note taking and written reports. They then reread the book and, with teacher guidance, selected phrases from the book in which they used to answer comprehension questions. Instead of writing in the book, however, the students used transparent overlays over the text, highlighting certain phrases with different colors and numbering processes. For example, the teacher directed the students to use yellow to highlight phrases describing the beans, use light green to highlight phrases describing the process, and number the order in which the processes took place.

Table 6.1. Words for decoding practice

fermented	consumption	protection	remaining
complicated	plantation	affordable	flavor
process	popularity	making	kilograms

Table 6.2.   Phrases selected for reading preparation

begin to smell like chocolate
any remaining pulp or pieces of the pods
from the fermented dried beans
a very long and complicated process
in order to bring out the chocolate flavor
from around the world
the cleaned and blended beans
in the cacao (kah–kow) pod

On another occasion, with different materials, the students used colored markers to identify noun phrases, descriptive phrases, and prepositional phrases while the teacher led them through the beginning steps of outlining. The week's spelling lesson was also about chocolate. The teacher wrote the following paragraph, which included often troublesome words, on a chart for students to copy:

> People around the world love chocolate. Have you ever wondered where chocolate comes from? Chocolate grows on trees. You can't pick a chunk of chocolate from a tree branch and eat it. Chocolate starts from beans, but getting from beans to chocolate is a very long and complicated process.

Each day's lesson also included practice with phrase and sentence writing using some of the words the students generated for decoding practice. After the students practiced writing independently, they were paired, and, using their highlighted booklets, they wrote a paragraph of a paper about one step in the process of bringing chocolate to market. The paragraph the teacher provided during the spelling lesson became the introductory paragraph of the students' papers, followed by their own paragraph and a concluding paragraph the teacher supplied. After the students gained more experience following this model and writing multiparagraph papers, the teacher planned to have the students follow the same steps generating notes and writing multipage reports.

In addition to writing activities, the students participated in oral language activities, including an oral report on their homework assignment to make something from chocolate. Some students discussed the physical changes as milk, cocoa, and sugar became fudge. One student thought the gases that make a cake rise were most interesting, and he demonstrated cake baking in class. Others wrote poetry or used candy wrappers for a collage.

The week's lesson also provided review and practice with phonic elements such as short vowels; letter combinations; soft *c;* multisyllable words and partially phonetic words such as *come, from,* and *people;* and contractions.

Teachers should always consider their specific goals to be accomplished when planning integrated activities. How will each activity help move the lesson forward? How will it provide success for the range of children in the classroom? What adjustments are necessary to make it do so? Is there enough flexibility for different skill levels? Is it engaging?

Teachers should not expect students with reading problems to acquire all of their information through reading assignments, nor should they expect those with difficulties in written expressive language to submit only written assignments. Subject knowledge can also be acquired through teacher-guided, hands-on activities and oral discussion in which all students participate. Children can also demonstrate what they have learned by audiotaping or dictating their oral productions. Content areas not only contain new vocabulary and concepts to expand knowledge but also introduce students to known vocabulary in new ways (e.g., math vocabulary uses the words *times* and *into* in ways that may confuse students). Student activities, tied to content, are limited only by teacher and student imagination. Students do not need apples or chocolate if they can be drawn into the search for knowledge through imagination alone.

RESEARCHER CONTRIBUTIONS

Because of the commitment of many teachers in the International Dyslexia Association, a nationwide effort has been providing professional development in structured, multimodal language instruction for teachers who work with students with dyslexia, OWL LD, and dysgraphia. During the past four decades, researchers have made important progress in understanding the multidimensional aspects of language, which is a complex ability. In this chapter we bring together methods and insights that have resulted from both kinds of contributions.

No End Organs in Language System

Early in his career, Alvin Liberman (1999) proposed the Motor Theory of Speech Perception, according to which speech is perceived in terms of its motor production, that is, articulation of sounds. Liberman's theory was startling because it suggested that understanding speech depended on more than analyzing the auditory input through the ears. Research over the years supported the motor theory of speech perception, or at least the idea that speech perception is the result of analyzing both auditory features in the incoming speech signal and articulatory gestures in producing speech. Put another way, input and output systems work together during perception and production. Neuroscientists refer to the input and output systems of the brain as the *end organs* because these are the systems that have direct contact with the external environment. Many other brain systems have only indirect contact with the external environment through these end organs. That is why incoming sensory and outgoing motor processes can influence higher order language and cognitive processes.

Multimodal Language Team

Over the course of his career, Liberman (1999) had another groundbreaking insight: Because language has no end organs of its own in the brain, it teams with the sensory input and motor output systems of the brain. In other words, language is an internal code. When language teams with the ears, a functional system for listening develops for receiving information from the environment on the aural channel (ears). When language teams with the mouth, a functional system for speaking develops for acting on the environment via oral-motor movement of mouth in speech that produces oral language productions. When language teams with the eyes, a functional system for reading develops. And, when language teams with the hands, a functional system for writing develops for producing written language via graphomotor movements of the hand. A review of functional brain imaging studies showed that not only common but also unique brain regions activate for listening, speaking, reading, and writing tasks (Berninger & Richards, 2002), so these language systems work together to some extent, but the brain does not have a single, simple language system.

This insight, which is as important as Mattingly's insight about linguistic awareness (see Chapter 4), has an important implication for how reading and writing are taught to all students, not just those with dyslexia, OWL LD, and/or dysgraphia. A multimodal brain system with two sensory input systems (auditory listening and visual reading) and two motor output systems (oral motor productions through the mouth and graphomotor productions through the hand) support literacy learning (also see Chapter 4). Optimal literacy instruction, therefore, draws on all four modalities.

Dynamic and Stable Language Profiles for Listening, Speaking, Reading, and Writing

The insight that language is an internal code is also important because typically developing readers and writers have language profiles that show individual differences within each child as to the level to which listening, speaking, reading, and writing are developed. These individual differences, which can influence how children respond to the same literacy instruction, may change over the course of development, but in some cases, possibly because of genetic influences (see Chapter 7), relative strengths or relative weaknesses in these profiles may remain stable over the course of development (Berninger & Abbott, 2008).

Multimodal Language Instruction

General education has increasingly adopted oral discussion as an effective instructional tool for reading, writing, and math instruction (e.g., Beck & McKeown, 2001, 2007; Nussbaum, 2002; Reznitskaya et al., 2001). However, children with relative weaknesses in listening comprehension and oral expression may need instructional activities to develop these language skills sufficiently to be able to participate in these discussions (see Chapter 3 for suggestions). Also, teaching oral language skills is often relevant to developing reading comprehension (Cain & Oakhill, 2007; Carlisle & Rice, 2002; see also Chapters 3 and 4). Alternatively, some children with dyslexia may have relative strengths in listening and/or oral expression despite their relative weaknesses in reading and writing, and can learn and actually shine in front of classmates in these oral discussions.

In addition, a writing-across-the-curriculum movement has influenced mainstream general education practices since at least the 1980s. Children are expected to write in all content areas, not just in language arts, and many states' high-stakes tests require that students write answers and not just choose multiple-choice answers.

The point is that literacy instruction in schools should not focus only on reading and writing; rather, it should focus more broadly on all of the multiple modes of language—listening, speaking, reading, and writing. Chapter 10 provides suggestions about how general education teachers can capitalize on this multimodal teaching approach for students in general and for students with dyslexia, OWL LD, and/or dysgraphia in particular.

Intellectually Engaging, Hands-On Learning

Language is a system that not only makes contact with the external world through end organs (sensory and motor systems) but also makes contact with the internal mental world of cognition. Some refer to this mental world as *intellect*. Language supports the translation of ideas in this mental world into a code that can be communicated with the outside world by mouth (speaking or oral expression) and/or by hand (writing or written expression). Effective instruction must engage multiple modes of language and intellect. Two instructional strategies for creating and sustaining intellectual engagement, which can be integrated with literacy instruction involving listening, speaking, reading, and writing, are 1) thematic units on developmentally appropriate topics of interest, and 2) embedding hands-on activities in multimodal language instruction. In addition, hope themes can be used to inspire struggling learners that they, like others, can overcome obstacles and succeed.

Role of Intellectually Engaging Themes and Hope Themes in Thematic Instructional Units.
Instructional studies have validated the effectiveness of instructional approaches that integrate explicit instruction with high-interest, intellectually engaging activities and hope themes for struggling students. These were validated on the basis of both behavioral and brain change evidence. An instructional study showed that phonological processing in the brain could normalize in students with dyslexia after they received multimodal, multicode instruction that included science experiments for high intellectual engagement and used Einstein's early struggles in school, which he overcame, as a hope theme (see Chapter 4; Berninger, 2000, Lesson Set 15; Berninger & Abbott, 2003).

In the accompanying workbook, *Helping Students with Dyslexia and Dysgraphia Make Connections: Differentiated Instruction Lesson Plans in Reading and Writing* (Berninger & Wolf, 2009), in the Word Detectives Curriculum (Unit I), two themes are used to intellectually engage students with dyslexia in the curriculum designed to improve their reading (Berninger et al., 2003): Sherlock Holmes solving word mysteries and aliens learning about language on earth. In the Mark Twain Writers Workshop (Berninger, Winn, et al., 2008, Study 1), Unit II in the workbook, the theme of Mark Twain as a writer, public speaker, and humorist is used to spur interest in writing. In addition, Mark Twain's life, which, like Einstein's, did not get off to a successful start but finished well, is used to promote hope. In the John Muir Science Writers Workshop (Berninger, Winn, et al., 2008, Study 2), which is Unit III in the workbook, the theme of John Muir, a scientist and writer who survived an accident and founded the American National Park system and the environmental movement, is used to spur interest in writing about science. In the Sequoyah Writing Readers Workshop (Berninger, Stock, Lee, Abbott, & Breznitz, 2007), Unit IV in the workbook, the theme is Sequoyah, the Cherokee who at age 50 gave his people written language and for whom the giant redwoods in California are named. Sequoyah's life accomplishments, despite his physical disabilities, are used as a hope theme.

Role of Hands-On Activities in Intellectual Engagement
As a reading specialist in the schools, the first author discovered that combining hands-on science experiments with reading instruction was particularly helpful for students with reading disabilities. Collectively, results from various studies discussed next provide clues as to why this is so.

One study demonstrated that children with dyslexia had difficulty with self-regulation of attention and this difficulty had a probable genetic basis (Hsu, Wijsman, Berninger, Thomson, & Raskind, 2002). A subsequent study showed that children with dyslexia had trouble paying attention to written words on orthographic tasks but not to spoken words on phonological tasks (Thomson et al., 2005). Thomson et al. proposed that the visual motion detection region of the brain, which had been shown to differ in individuals with and without dyslexia (Eden et al., 1996), might be disrupted by attentional mechanisms and that, in turn, the visual motion region disrupts nearby regions involved in orthographic processing. Results of Winn et al. (2006) were consistent with this proposal. Winn et al. found that individual differences in the visual motion region of the brain were related to individual differences in rate of performing visual tasks in children with but not without dyslexia. A subsequent instructional study (Chenault, Thomson, Abbott, & Berninger, 2006) showed that attentional training prior to spelling and composition instruction led to greater improvement in writing than did the control treatment, possibly because attention training improved ability to pay attention to written words during instruction.

Winn et al. (2006) also found that the children with and without dyslexia performed comparably in accuracy on visual tasks, but those with dyslexia performed more slowly on visual tasks that were timed. Thus, having dyslexia did not convey a special talent for those individuals in the visual domain but did impair them more in the rate than accuracy of visual processing.

Richards et al. (2007) found that, following the hands-on virtual reality training in navigating the Puget Sound to find Luna, a lost orca whale, the brain normalized in the visual motion region on a task that required children to pronounce written pseudowords. The normalization occurred in a region associated with touch sensation of the hands, which is near a center for phonological processing. Thus, hands-on, intellectually engaging activities may help overcome the visual motion impairment and related impairment in phonological decoding of written pseudowords, which requires initial orthographic processing followed by phonological recoding of graphemes, via the touch sensation (kinesthetic input). This role of kinesthetic input in overcoming dyslexia was proposed by the pioneers in the field of dyslexia (see Chapter 1). The *Helping Students with Dyslexia and Dysgraphia* workbook (Berninger & Wolf, 2009) includes hands-on, intellectually engaging activities along with lesson plans for explicit reading and writing instruction.

CONCLUSION

Both teaching experience and research findings (see the workbook *Helping Students with Dyslexia and Dysgraphia Make Connections* [Berninger & Wolf, 2009] for specific lesson sets) support the conclusion that effective instruction for students with dyslexia, OWL LD, and/or dysgraphia includes instruction to develop oral (listening and speaking) and written (reading and writing) language systems in the mind as well as high-interest, intellectually engaging, hands-on activities. One study even showed that students without these specific learning disabilities benefited from and enjoyed these lessons. The lessons can be implemented in general education classes or special education classes.

Blending Science and Educational Practice

Some people there are who, being grown, forget the horrible task of learning to read. It is perhaps the greatest single effort that the human undertakes, and he must do it as a child . . . [it is] the reduction of experience to a set of symbols. For a thousand thousand years these humans have existed and they have only learned this trick—this magic—in the final ten thousand of the thousand thousand.... I remember that words—written or printed—were devils, and books, because they gave me pain, were my enemies.

The Acts of King Arthur and His Noble Knights
(Steinbeck, 1976, p. xi)

CHAPTER 7

Contributions from Science Disciplines

In contrast to the chapters in the previous section, each chapter in this section begins with researcher contributions from specific biological or behavioral disciplines followed by teacher reflections on these contributions.

From 1995 to 2006, the National Institute of Child Health and Human Development (NICHD) at the National Institutes of Health funded the University of Washington Multidisciplinary Learning Disabilities Center (UW LDC). The first author served as principal investigator of the UW LDC that generated findings relevant to understanding the biological basis of dyslexia, which are shared in this chapter. Following the overview of research findings, the second author discussed how she has implemented evidence-based instructional approaches in her own classroom.

RESEARCHER CONTRIBUTIONS

Research-generated knowledge from human genetics, neuroscience, linguistics, and cognitive science is discussed in this section.

Lessons from Genetics Research

Twin studies (e.g., Kovas, Haworth, Dale, & Plomin, 2007; Olson, Wise, Connors, Rack, & Fulker, 1989; Willcutt, Pennington, & DeFries, 2000) have offered evidence that dyslexia has both genetic and environmental influences. Family aggregation studies directed by Wendy Raskind, M.D., Ph.D., at the UW LDC showed a probable genetic basis for specific phenotypes (measures of the behavioral expression) of dyslexia and related learning disabilities: accuracy and rate of pseudoword reading and real-word reading; spelling; and related phonological, rapid naming, attention, and executive function (e.g., Hsu, Wijsman, Berninger, Thomson, & Raskind, 2002; Raskind, Hsu, Thomson, Berninger, & Wijsman, 2000).

The genetic basis of dyslexia may be heterogeneous, meaning many different chromosomes and gene locations on the chromosomes are involved; specific chromosome linkages are related to the phenotype studied (Brkanac et al., 2007; Cardon et al., 1995; Grigorenko et al., 2001; Smith, Kimberling, Pennington, & Lubs, 1983). For example, different chromosome linkage is reported for real-word and nonword reading (Chapman et al., 2004; Igo et al., 2006) and for accuracy and rate

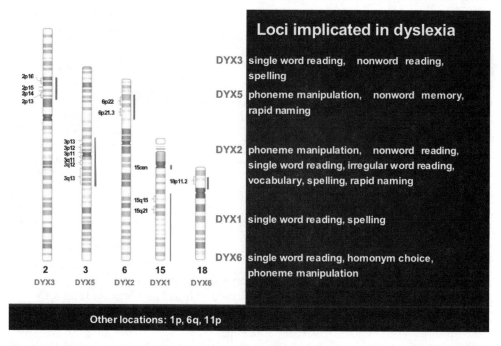

Figure 7.1. Chromosomal loci for which linkage to dyslexia or dyslexia-related phenotypes have been reported. (From Richards, T., Aylward, E., Raskind, W., Abbott, R., Field, K., Parsons, A., et al. [2006]. Converging evidence for triple word form theory in child dyslexics. *Developmental Neuropsychology, 30,* 547–589; www.informa world.com; reprinted by permission of Taylor & Francis.)

of nonword reading (Raskind et al., 2005). Spelling, which many think of as a purely visual or orthographic process, has a genetic pathway from phonology in dyslexia (Wijsman et al., 2000). See Figure 7.1 for the various chromosomes reported to be associated with developmental dyslexia.

The locations of genes on chromosomes have also been studied. Two specific gene locations associated with dyslexia have replicated across research groups—one on chromosome 15 and one on chromosome 6. Based on case control studies involving individuals who had the specific allele (variant gene) on chromosome 15, the UW LDC found that their mean score on a phonological phenotype (nonword repetition) was lower than that of individuals who had the unaffected gene in the same location. Also, individuals with the allele on chromosome 6 scored lower on an executive function phenotype (rapid alternating switching attention) than did individuals whose gene in the same location did not show that variation (Berninger, Raskind, Richards, Abbott, & Stock, 2008).

The acquired dyslexias—in which individuals who can read at some point lose the ability to read or lose specific aspects of reading—are typically due to injury or disease rather than genetic causes.

These genetic findings have educational implications. Genes may contribute to two core types of impairments typically found in children with dyslexia: phonological (Morris et al., 1998; Rack, Snowling, & Olson, 1992; Stanovich & Siegel, 1994) and executive function (Lyon & Krasnegor, 1996; Swanson, 1999b). Genetic variation in processes affecting reading and writing acquisition may make it more difficult but not impossible for affected individuals to learn to read and write if taught in a way they can learn. The approaches to teaching that work for them can be implemented by general education teachers in the regular classroom. Not only genes but also experiences in the instructional and learning environment affect their learning.

Research in human genetics has made major advances, in large part because of the Human Genome Project and other initiatives worldwide. Research on phenotype–genotype associations is rapidly expanding knowledge of the heterogeneous nature of dyslexia. See Raskind (2001) and Thomson and Raskind (2004) for glossaries defining the terminology used by geneticists so that nongeneticists can understand this rapidly expanding body of research. These sources also contain reviews of the research on the genetics of developmental dyslexia.

Genes may influence brain development in at least three ways (see Berninger & Richards, 2002, Chapter 4). First, genes may affect how the brain is wired during early fetal development. Second, genes may affect maturation of the brain after birth by guiding the process of forming sheaths of myelin, a white fatty substance, which forms around axons that transmit electrical signals from one neuron to another neuron and thus connect spatially separated neurons functionally in time. This process called myelination improves the speed and efficiency of neural conduction. One reason some students fail to respond to instruction may be that parts of the brain needed to learn from that instruction, for example frontal regions, which are the last to undergo myelination, have not yet undergone myelination but may in the future. Third, regulatory genes may influence the protein chemistry in the cell bodies of neurons in the brain that regulate their moment-to-moment operating systems, which in turn influence the learning process. Thus, brain variables also contribute to the biological basis of dyslexia, as discussed next.

Lessons from Neuroscience Research

One study found that children with and without dyslexia differed in the size of three structures in their brains—the left and right inferior frontal gyrus and the right cerebellum—all of which were larger in proficient readers than in children with dyslexia (see Figure 7.2; Eckert et al., 2003). Another study found differences between proficient readers and children with dyslexia in word-form areas in the back of the brain (mainly in temporal and parietal regions; Eckert et al., 2005). Other researchers have also reported differences between proficient readers and students with dyslexia in the word-form regions (e.g., Pugh et al., 1996).

Functional magnetic resonance imaging (fMRI) of the brains of children without dyslexia while they performed phonological, orthographic, and morphological tasks showed that these word-form tasks had common and unique neural signatures (Richards, Aylward, Raskind, et al., 2006; see Figure 7.3), that is, significant blood oxygen level dependent (BOLD) activation. Because brain regions at work consume glucose fueled by oxygen, this measure shows where the brain is at work during a particular kind of task. Following instructional treatment (see Chapter 9), frontal brain regions involved in the working memory architecture and executive functions in language or in word-form storage and processing normalized on phonological (Aylward et al., 2003), orthographic (Richards, Aylward, Berninger, et al., 2006), and morphological (Richards et al., 2005) tasks that children performed during the fMRI scanning. All three types of word-form storage and processing are needed for reading and writing outcomes, but what matters the most is learning to coordinate their interrelationships (see Berninger et al., 2008, and Lessons from Linguistics Research section later in the chapter).

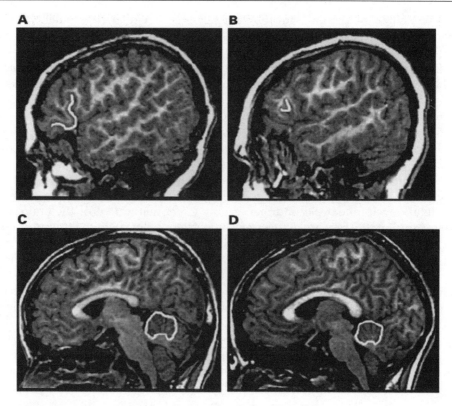

Figure 7.2. Structural magnetic resonance imaging (MRI) differences between children without dyslexia (left column) and children with dyslexia (right column) in inferior frontal gyrus (larger in good readers in A than in readers with dyslexia in B) and right cerebellum (larger in good readers in C than in poor readers in D). (From Eckert, M., Leonard, C., Richards, T., Aylward, E., Thomson, J., & Berninger, V.W. [2003]. Anatomical correlates of dyslexia: Frontal and cerebellar findings. *Brain, 126*[2], 482–494; reprinted by permission.)

fMRI functional connectivity studies with adults have examined which brain regions activated together in time when seed points originated in each of the working memory components identified in the MRI studies comparing children with and without dyslexia. For both adults (Stanberry et al., 2006) and children (Richards & Berninger, 2007), differences in functional connectivity were observed between those with and without dyslexia in this functional architecture. For the children with dyslexia, the connectivity normalized after the instructional treatment in the Mark Twain Writers Workshop (see Chapter 9). Diffusion tensor imaging of structural connectivity among white fiber tracts emanating from the same seed points showed differences between the fathers with and without dyslexia in structural connectivity as well (Richards et al., 2008). The functional and structural connectivity studies were done with fathers because mothers appear more likely to compensate (overcome earlier reading and spelling problems) than fathers (Raskind, 2001).

Taken together, these findings suggested that structural differences in three components of working memory, which support conscious processing of words, might explain why children with dyslexia have more difficulty than children without dyslexia in learning to read and spell (Berninger et al., 2008; Richards, Aylward, Raskind, et al., 2006). The first component in word-form areas stores words in

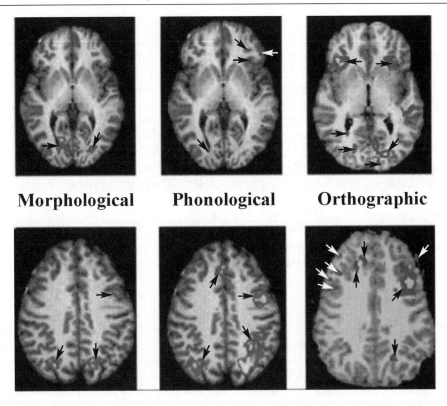

Figure 7.3. Functional MRI (fMRI) of phonological, orthographic, and morphological word forms. Each column contains the fMRI overlay onto structural MRI at the same two anatomical axial sections of the brain. The first column of brain images contains the fMRI during morpheme mapping, which is the contrast between the morphological task (Does the top word come from the bottom word?) and the synonym task (Do both words mean the same?). The second column of brain images contains the fMRI during phoneme mapping, which is the contrast between the phonological task (Can the pink letters in the top word sound the same as the pink letters in the bottom word?) and the letter strings task (Do the top and bottom letters strings match exactly?). The third column of brain images contains the fMRI during orthographic mapping, which is the contrast between the spelling task (Are the top and bottom words both spelled correctly?) and the letter strings task.

The arrows show the areas of brain activation, which for morpheme mapping are in the occipital, parietal, and frontal lobes; for phoneme mapping are in the parietal, frontal, and cingulate areas; and for orthographic mapping are in the occipital, temporal, parietal, and frontal lobes in proficient readers. See http://www.brookespublishing.com/Berninger for a link to images in which activated regions are in color. (From Richards, T., Aylward, E., Raskind, W., Abbott, R., Field, K., Parsons, A., et al. [2006]. Converging evidence for triple word form theory in child dyslexics. *Developmental Neuropsychology, 30,* 547–589; www.informaworld.com; reprinted by permission of Taylor & Francis.)

different formats or codes: phonological (sounds in spoken words), orthographic (letters in written words), and morphological (word parts that affect meaning). The second component is the phonological loop (neural pathways between right cerebellum and left inferior frontal gyrus), which guides the cross–word-form mapping process (e.g., naming written words or spelling spoken words). The third component is executive functions that include supervisory attention. The frontal lobes house many executive functions and the left inferior frontal gyrus is thought to be the highest level of executive function for the language system.

An *n-back test* is an imaging task used to study tracking information in working memory over short time intervals. In an fMRI study, children with and without dyslexia, all of whom had significant spelling problems, differed in fMRI BOLD activation in brain regions associated with working memory when asked to decide if the displayed sea creature was the same as the creature displayed two trials before (Richards et al., 2009).

These brain findings have educational implications. Word-form storage and processing are important for learning to decode (pronounce) and encode (spell) written words *accurately*. The working memory components of a system must work in concert, that is, be orchestrated in time like the musical instruments in an orchestra (see Posner, Petersen, Fox, & Raichle, 1988), for individuals to learn to read and write *fluently* (quickly with smooth coordination). For additional information, readings, and Internet resources on how the brain might inform reading and writing instruction for children with and without dyslexia, oral and written language learning disability (OWL LD), and/or dysgraphia, see Berninger and Richards (2002, 2008b).

Children with dyslexia may compensate, that is, perform like children without dyslexia on behavioral measures of reading or spelling achievement or normalize in specific brain regions, but unless they normalize in functional connectivity, the temporal connections among those regions (Shaywitz et al., 2003), they may not fully overcome their dyslexia. Children with dyslexia may face a lifelong challenge of orchestrating components of their working memory system to support written language processing. This challenge may be invisible to others. Children with dyslexia in the UW LDC studies reported the experience of having to exert considerably more mental effort and time to accomplish the same reading and writing tasks as others do. Their literacy problems typically are not due to a lack of motivation, but they may require extraordinary motivation to persist and succeed in school work. Growth mixture modeling of classes of response across rows on rapid automatic naming captured this invisible difficulty in sustaining over time effortful mental activity involving the coordination of orthographic and phonological codes (Amtmann, Abbott, & Berninger, 2007). Whereas proficient readers often decreased in naming time across rows, children with dyslexia started and stayed slow or started slow and became slower.

Lessons from Linguistics Research

Venezky (1970) showed 1) that speech is represented in English orthography, and 2) how spelling represents speech sounds is predictable to a large extent. Venezky debunked the myth popularized by playwright George Bernard Shaw, who complained perhaps in jest that, based on the different sounds the letters *ough* make in *though, thought, rough,* and *through,* English is a hopelessly irregular language in letter–sound and sound–letter relationships. To grasp the predictable patterns requires two fundamental insights.

First, the *predictability is often not at the single-letter level.* Graphemes are one- and two-letter units that correspond to phonemes. In English, these graphemes often involve two-letter spelling units such as *th* in *thing* or *this, or* as in *fork* or *word,* or *ng* as in *sing* or *ring.* Also, blends such as the *bl* in *blend* are best treated as two-letter spelling units because the corresponding sounds have to be produced faster in time than the single sounds for each of the single letter constituents in order to avoid an unwanted vowel sound intrusion, such as a schwa in between the /b/ and /l/ in /bul-end/ instead of /blend/. Therefore, children should be taught to parse written words into the one- or two-letter units that correspond to a phoneme rather than to try to decode words or spell words one letter at a time in left-to-right order.

Second, the *predictability does not involve one-to-one mapping* of letters onto sound or sound onto letters *but rather alternations, which are permissible options.* Some letters have more than one sound associated with them, such as the letter *c*, which can stand for the /k/ or /s/ sound. Note that the /th/ in *thing* and the /th/ in *this* are alternations (a different phoneme is associated with this common spelling unit). Likewise the /or/ in *fork* and *word* are alternations for the common *or* spelling. The /ng/ in *sing* does not correspond to the single phoneme associated with either the letter *n* as in *not* or the letter *g* as in *go*. Teaching alternations provides an alternative strategy to use when decoding or encoding written words (see Berninger, 1998b).

When these two insights were pointed out to a child in the summer between third and fourth grade, she began to bloom in spelling and told the neighborhood and extended family that she could not believe that her teachers had never told her about these two secrets of English spelling. Many teachers probably do not know about Venezky's insights about spelling because they were not taught them by their own elementary school teachers or professors in preservice teacher education programs. Conventional phonics often does not teach these two fundamental insights either.

Had George Bernard Shaw had a teacher who taught him that some spelling–sound relationships are more predictable at units even larger than the one- or two-letter graphemes in the grapheme–phoneme correspondences of alphabetic principle, he might have better appreciated the predictability of English spelling, which when pronounced sometimes is at the level of word families (see Berninger, 1998b). For example, the alternations for the *ough* word family are /long o/, /aw/, /short u/, or /oo/, respectively, for *though, thought, rough,* and *through.* Those 4-to-1 odds are reasonably predictable considering that no one complains about the many sound–meaning associations English speakers handle all the time with ease in implicit memory. Consider /t/ /oo/, which can mean *also, a quantity more than one but less than three, moving in the direction toward,* and so forth.

Linguists call this ability to map multiple meanings onto the same sound form *polysemy* (Stahl & Nagy, 2005). Presumably, children enter school with varying degrees of insight about these sound–meaning relationships in oral language. Spelling knowledge can in fact remove the ambiguity and identify the correct meaning in words pronounced the same. Little research has been done on polysemy, but reflection about variable meanings for the same spoken word could be an important part of the early literacy program as children add on spelling knowledge to the sound–meaning–spelling relationships. Such knowledge can enhance vocabulary development as well as phonological decoding in reading (pronouncing written words) and phonological encoding in spelling (writing spelling units to stand for sounds in spoken words). Phonological, orthographic, and morphological awareness contribute to decoding and spelling and other reading and writing outcomes (e.g., Nagy, Berninger, & Abbott, 2006; Nagy, Berninger, Abbott, Vaughan, & Vermeulen, 2003). Moreover, it is the ability to interrelate awareness of these three word-forms and their parts that underlies the various reading and writing skills of both students with and without dyslexia (Berninger et al., 2008).

Research has shown that added morphological awareness treatment to phonics practice was more effective than added phonological awareness treatment to phonics practice in normalizing chemical activation in the brain (Richards et al.,

2002) and improving rate of phonological decoding on a behavioral measure in children with dyslexia who had completed fourth, fifth, or sixth grade (Berninger et al., 2003). The instructional activities for developing both morphological and phonological awareness used in this study are in the Word Detectives lesson plans in Unit I in *Helping Students with Dyslexia and Dysgraphia Make Connections: Differentiated Instruction Lesson Plans in Reading and Writing* (Berninger & Wolf, 2009).

Morphological awareness and its relationship to phonology and orthography may be more important (have larger path coefficients for some outcomes) for students with dyslexia than for those without dyslexia; however, for both proficient readers and students with dyslexia, phonological, orthographic, and morphological awareness contributed uniquely via an underlying factor based on their interrelationships to reading and writing outcomes in third and fifth graders (Berninger et al., 2008). Also, discriminant function analyses of children who were consistently poor, average, and good spellers in Grades 1–4 or 3–6 showed that phonological, orthographic, *and* morphological composites contributed to their spelling ability and differentiated among the three spelling ability groups (Garcia, 2007).

Lessons from Cognitive Science

Attention Links to Orthography   Self-regulation of attention may be particularly relevant when orthographic symbols are involved in literacy learning (Thomson et al., 2005). Some individuals with dyslexia appear to have difficulty self-regulating their attention across the letters in left-to-right direction within written words to identify the spelling units that correspond to phonemes (Richards et al., 2007). This impairment can interfere with phonological decoding as much as phonological awareness problems can. Chapter 9 discusses teaching approaches for helping children improve their attentional focus to letters and spelling units within written words during the decoding process. Lessons in the *Helping Students with Dyslexia and Dysgraphia Make Connections,* a workbook of instructional activities that is a companion to this book (Berninger & Wolf, 2009), contain teaching strategies for helping children focus their attention, stay on task, and switch between tasks.

What the National Reading Panel Overlooked   In 2000, the NICHD report on teaching children to read concluded that effective reading instruction consisted of five components: phonological awareness, phonological decoding, reading fluency, vocabulary development, and reading comprehension. All of these components certainly are necessary, but probably not sufficient. Considerable research has shown that orthographic and morphological awareness are also important for both reading and writing outcomes (e.g., Berninger et al., 2008; Berninger & Fayol, 2008; Nagy et al., 2003, 2006; also see Chapter 4).

Likewise, the report did not give sufficient attention to instruction designed to help students with weaknesses in executive functions to become self-regulated readers and writers. The National Reading Panel was geared to the general education program without consideration of the kind of learning differences in beginning literacy identified by Connor, Morrison, and Katch (2004). They showed that beginning readers differ greatly in the literacy knowledge they bring to school and the amount of explicit, teacher-directed instruction they require. Teachers need to differentiate instruction along the dimension of student-required, teacher-guided assistance in self-regulation of learning.

Students who have biologically based attention or executive function impairment require more other-regulation from adults, who provide guidance and serve as their executive functions, to learn self-regulation of language learning. Those who have attention and executive functions for their age fall within the normal range and are better able to engage in child-directed learning (see Connor et al., 2004). Students with dyslexia may require explicit instruction in reading and writing throughout schooling, but not all students in the classroom require the same degree of explicit, teacher-directed instruction. Chapter 10 discusses optional plans for meeting the needs of students with dyslexia who require more explicit, teacher-guided instruction than classmates. Special education is not the only option, although it may be advisable to have a special education individualized education program that documents diagnosis of an educational disabling condition, specifies the nature of explicit instruction in self-regulation strategies needed in the least restrictive environment (general education classroom), and details a progress monitoring plan. Accommodations alone are seldom sufficient for students with significant executive function impairments.

Lessons from Cognitive and Developmental Science

Need for Explicit Writing Instruction Throughout Schooling Research in these disciplines points to the need for early intervention as well as explicit instruction throughout schooling in the cognitive processes of writing. Reading impairments are relatively easy to overcome compared with writing impairments in students with dyslexia (e.g., Berninger, 2006; Berninger, Nielsen, Abbott, Wijsman, & Raskind, 2008b). Early in schooling dyslexia manifests itself as difficulty in naming letters and associating sounds with letters. These difficulties interfere with learning to decode written words. In addition, some children have difficulty writing letters. However, when they are given explicit instruction in phonological and orthographic awareness, naming and writing letters, and decoding written words, most begin to learn to read reasonably well.

The curriculum requirements in school change after the primary grades when the primary literacy tasks are learning to read orally—pronounce written words—recognizing words during silent reading, and associating meaning with pronounced or recognized written words. In later grades, children are expected to complete longer, more complex written assignments, which often require them to write about what they read, that is, integrate reading and writing (Altemeier, Abbott, & Berninger, 2008). Children who had problems in phonological decoding earlier in development may now have trouble with completing written assignments and integrating writing and reading unless given specialized instruction in these skills (see Chapter 9). Although a recent meta-analysis (Graham & Perin, 2007a, 2007b) showed that at fourth grade and above students in general require explicit and strategic writing instruction, many schools do not yet provide such instruction. Hopefully, readers of this book will learn how to do so (see Mark Twain [Unit II], John Muir [Unit III], and Sequoyah [Unit IV] lesson sets in *Helping Students with Dyslexia and Dysgraphia Make Connections* [Berninger & Wolf, 2009]) and share this new knowledge with colleagues.

TEACHER REFLECTIONS ON RESEARCH CONTRIBUTIONS FROM THE SCIENCES

When educators work with students with dyslexia, they may be working with parents who have biologically based dyslexia, OWL LD, and/or dysgraphia as well. Parents' persisting reading and writing problems and possibly oral language problems can complicate communication between the school and the home. Letters, time lines, and comprehension of oral and written communication may be affected. Parents, who are sensitive to their own learning problems may find a diagnosis for their children comforting because they are relieved to have a name, finally, for their own problems. The label also gives them powerful empathy for their children's struggles. It may make them better advocates for their children to obtain accommodations, such as extended time for assignments or tests or special services. The diagnosis may also remind them of the painful experiences they themselves had in school as they struggled with reading and/or writing. Educators should be sensitive to these cross-generational experiences that may influence parents' relationships with their children's schools and teachers.

In Chapters 3, 4, and 5, the second author emphasized the importance of systematic, structured, sequential instruction in oral and written language, which is important in both visual and auditory processing of written language by both eye and ear. If students who have dyslexia do not see words as wholes, they must be taught to process constituent letters in each word from left to right. Many do not fixate on the beginning of the word and may look at any part of it, sometimes randomly. As a result, word recognition is erratic. The teacher must guide them in learning left-to-right progression for decoding single words as well as for reading across the page. These students may have particular difficulty with sight words. They can use some decoding skills to begin access to a word such as *the* in which the *th* corresponds to a phoneme but the *e* corresponds to a schwa or reduced vowel rather than a full phoneme with predictable spelling. Automatic recall requires many, many exposures—sometimes as many as 200—in isolation and in phrases. Fortunately *the* is a very high-frequency word to which students will have many exposures. When students have mastered words in isolation, they need to learn to "chunk" groups of words into meaningful phrases for reading with fluency and comprehension. Some strategies for chunking are offered in Chapter 4.

Similarly, students often respond with enthusiasm when they are shown that what they hear when they say a word influences the spelling of the word. Security with each spelling component gives them power over spelling. However introduction of too many elements in too short a time can result in confusion and frustration. Teachers need to pace the introduction of each new element so that the child can feel success with both single words and sentences.

In providing research-based instruction, the teacher can set the student on the road to success, but the transfer from the acquisition of teacher-supported skills to independent performance requires careful guidance and monitoring. The length and complexity of assignments may be increased as each student performs successfully at his or her own level. This success is especially important, because the student is not always able to judge his or her own progress. Students with dyslexia or related learning disabilities must expend more effort to accomplish what those without dyslexia may do with ease. Therefore, they view themselves as less competent. Teachers can help them to identify their own strengths and talents while helping them to feel pride in their accomplishments. Although they may not produce the same product, these students may have been working harder than anyone else in the class. One high school student told Beverly Wolf, "Having dyslexia is like climbing the mountain on your hands and knees while everyone else rides the chair lift."

CONCLUSION

Research generated by the basic biological and behavioral sciences has led to the conclusion that a teacher who keeps abreast of research developments can apply these insights to classroom practice in literacy instruction for students with dyslexia, OWL LD, and/or dysgraphia. Research has shown that these students are vulnerable in the following areas and thus need very explicit instruction in these skills to overcome the biologically based weaknesses: 1) phonological, orthographic, and morphological storage and processing of word forms and awareness of these and how they can be coordinated to support reading and spelling; 2) mechanisms for integrating the internal representations in the word forms with the end organs; 3) executive functions for self-regulation of internal learning processes; and the 4) time-sensitive working memory architecture within which these processes operate and have to be coordinated in time.

CHAPTER 8

Contributions
from Clinical Disciplines

In most schools, the focus of a multidisciplinary assessment is on determining students' eligibility for special education services rather than diagnosing whether a student has a specific learning disability such as dyslexia, oral and written language learning disability (OWL LD), or dysgraphia. Accurate diagnosis is important because it has implications for which processes may be impaired and can explain a student's struggle in learning to read and/or write. An accurate diagnosis also has implications for treatment planning—how the regular instructional program may need to be modified with specialized instruction in the general or special education classroom.

In research conducted by the University of Washington Multidisciplinary Learning Disabilities Center (UW LDC), parents often expressed more interest in accurate diagnoses and understanding why their children struggled with reading or writing than in their children qualifying for pull-out special education services (i.e., meeting eligibility criteria) (see Berninger, 2008b). They believed that knowing why a student struggles more than classmates would provide instructional clues in the general education classroom.

The family genetics research yielded information about which clinical measures were likely to capture the behavioral expression of the underlying genetic basis of developmental dyslexia and dysgraphia in children and adults. These behavioral markers are referred to as phenotypes. For example, the UW LDC family genetics study validated behavioral markers of developmental dyslexia, OWL LD, and/or dysgraphia in children and adults within a working memory architecture: three kinds of word-form storage and processing (coding and reflective phonological, orthographic, and morphological awareness); phonological and orthographic loops; and executive functions related to inhibition, rapid attention switching, and sustained processing over time (Berninger, Abbott, Thomson, et al., 2006). Problems in orthographic coding, phonological coding, phonological loop, and executive functions were found to be associated with dyslexia (Berninger, 2008a; Berninger, Abbott, Thomson, & Raskind, 2001; Berninger et al., 2001; Berninger, Raskind, Richards, Abbott, & Stock, 2008). Problems in orthographic, phonological, and morphological coding; syntactic awareness; phonological and orthographic loops; and executive functions were found to be associated with OWL LD (Berninger, 2007, 2008b; Berninger, O'Donnell, & Holdnack, 2008; Berninger, Raskind, et al.,

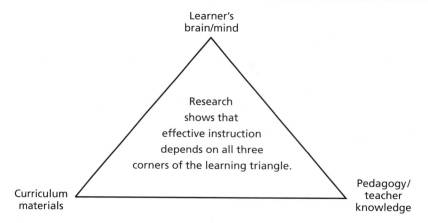

Figure 8.1.   Learning triangle: Interactions among the learning writer; the writing teacher; and the instructional materials, tools, and curriculum for writing. (*Source:* Berninger, Stage, Smith, & Hildebrand, 2001.)

2008). Problems in orthographic coding and orthographic loop and executive functions were found to be associated with dysgraphia (Berninger, 2004, 2008b; Berninger et al., 2008; Berninger, Raskind, et al., 2008). For guidance in clinical diagnosis of dyslexia, OWL LD, and dysgraphia, see Berninger (2007).

The learning triangle in Figure 8.1 provides a context in which to understand the relevance of evidence-based diagnosis. Children's learning is the result of interactions among the three corners of the learning triangle. The foundation of instruction is represented as the base of the triangle, including the teachers' knowledge and pedagogy (teaching methods) in one corner and the curriculum (including instructional materials and tools) in the other corner. The top corner of the triangle represents the processes in the child's brain or mind, which are also important because they influence response to instruction (Berninger & Richards, 2008b). These processes, which are influenced by genes, brain variables (structures, functions, structural connectivity, functional connectivity), and instructional experiences, exhibit individual differences that mediate response to intervention. Learning, therefore, is never the result of just the teacher's instruction or just the student's characteristics—learning is the product of all three corners of the triangle.

However, teachers are seldom given sufficient professional development regarding what the relevant learning processes are, how they can be assessed, and who on the multidisciplinary team of educational professionals might do the assessment and interpret the results. Unlike medical and speech and language professionals who are given training in both diagnosis and treatment, in education teachers are prepared to treat and psychologists are prepared to assess. As a result, teachers must partner with psychologists and speech and language specialists in the school to link assessment and instruction in meaningful ways.

The sections that follow discuss UW LDC's clinically relevant research about the learning processes (phenotype markers) in students with dyslexia, OWL LD, and/or dysgraphia. The goal of this chapter is to educate educators about how this research might inform the top of the learning triangle for teachers who work with students having these specific kinds of learning disabilities. Just because a student has reading problems does not mean that the student has dyslexia.

DEFINING DYSLEXIA

Two studies funded by the National Institutes of Health have shown that an individual's verbal IQ score is a better predictor of reading achievement than nonverbal performance IQ (Greenblatt, Mattis, & Trad, 1990; Vellutino, Scanlon, & Tanzman, 1991). Verbal IQs reflect ability, compared with age peers, to reason with language. Nonverbal IQs reflect ability, compared with age peers, to think in ways that do not necessarily require language. Review of a growing body of research has shown that reading pseudowords—pronounceable words without meaning—and reading real words on a list are better indicators of a reading disability than reading words in passages in which context clues could mask an individual's true word decoding abilities (Stanovich, 1986). Other research has pointed to the importance of reading rate and fluency in identifying subtypes of reading disability (Lovett, 1987). Reading disability also can be associated with persisting spelling impairments (Berninger, Nielsen et al., 2008b; Bruck, 1993; Lefly, & Pennington, 1991). Dyslexia, a word of Greek origin, can also be defined on the basis of morphology (Berninger, 2001; see Introduction). The prefix *dys–* means *impaired,* the base *lexia* refers to the lexicon or mental dictionary for words, and the suffix *–a* has been added and the *con* of *lexicon* dropped to indicate that it is a state of being impaired in words.

Defining something also necessitates defining what it is not. The written language problems of individuals with dyslexia, for instance, cannot be explained on the basis of any other neurogenetic, developmental, or learning disorders. For example, such problems cannot be explained by intellectual disability across the five domains of development (cognitive, oral language, motor, social emotional, attention/executive function), pervasive developmental delay in two or more developmental domains, autism, primary language disorder (developmental aphasia), fragile X syndrome, Down syndrome, Williams syndrome, Turner syndrome, Kleinfelter syndrome, brain injury or disease, psychiatric disorder, emotional trauma, or environmental issues.

The UW LDC (1995 to the present) defines dyslexia as unexpected difficulty in accuracy or fluency of word reading or phonological decoding in isolation or in a passage or in spelling; it is of neurobiological origin and related to impaired phonological processing. This definition is comparable to the definition The International Dyslexia Association (IDA) adopted in 2003 (Lyon, Shaywitz, & Shaywitz, 2003). The only difference is that the UW LDC found that dyslexia is also associated with processing impairments in orthographic and rapid automatic naming (RAN; Berninger et al., 2001). Also, the IDA did not define how to assess unusual difficulty, and the UW LDC did so on the basis of verbal reasoning ability. Likewise, Wadsworth, Olson, Pennington, and DeFries (2000) reported that reading disability had a genetic basis if discrepant from IQ, but not if reading was not discrepant from IQ. However, the UW LDC studies do not show that children with dyslexia have only an IQ–achievement discrepancy (e.g., between verbal IQ and word decoding or spelling) but rather they also have associated impairment in specific phenotypes (behavioral measures)—phonology, orthography, RAN, and RAS (Berninger, Abbott, et al., 2006).

The number of students with dyslexia in the general population is often estimated to range from 15% to 20%, but the exact number is unknown due to differences in samples and how the disorder is defined (see Berninger, Nielsen, Abbott, Wijsman, & Raskind, 2008a).

DEFINING ORAL AND WRITTEN LANGUAGE LEARNING DISABILITY

The UW LDC research team also studied children who did not meet the research inclusion criteria for dyslexia, many of whom did not exhibit IQ–achievement discrepancy, and found that they had significant problems in reading comprehension, oral reading of real words, morphological awareness, syntactic awareness, and word retrieval. That is, they showed the same behavioral markers as selective language impairment and language learning disability. The UW LDC researchers coined the term *oral and written language learning disability* (OWL LD) to emphasize that these children have oral as well as written language problems. In contrast, those with dyslexia often have oral language skills (morphological and syntactic awareness) that are average or better except in phonology (analyzing sounds in spoken words). The problems associated with OWL LD are primarily with accurate and automatic reading of real words for which meaning cues can be used, oral reading accuracy and fluency when reading words in the context of passages, reading comprehension, written spelling, and syntax construction in written composition. That is, children with OWL LD have word-level oral reading and spelling problems *and* text-level reading comprehension and fluency and written expression problems (see Catts, Fey, Zhang, & Tomblin, 1999, 2001; Catts, Hogan, & Adloff, 2005; Fey, Catts, Proctor-Williams, Tomblin, & Zhang, 2004; Scott, 2004; and Scott & Windsor, 2000). Their reading and writing problems are probably related to their oral language problems (phonological, morphological, and syntactic awareness; listening comprehension; and fluency in word retrieval).

DEFINING DYSGRAPHIA

Dysgraphia is a transcription disability (TD) that affects handwriting and/or spelling. For additional information about its definition and diagnosis, see the Introduction, Chapter 5, and Berninger (2004b). Contrary to widespread belief, dysgraphia is not purely a motor problem, but rather also due to underlying problems in orthographic coding, the orthographic loop that coordinates orthographic coding and graphomotor output by the hands and fingers, and the executive functions involved in letter writing (Berninger, 2004b). Incidence of dysgraphia involving impaired letter form writing by hand (Berninger, 2004b) may increase from 4% due to handwriting difficulties in the primary grades to 20% or more in the middle school grades when written composition requirements become more complex (Hooper, Knuth, Yerby, Anderson & Moore, in press). However, the probable number of children in the population who have handwriting only; spelling only; combined handwriting and spelling; and related orthographic, fine motor, orthographic–motor integration, and executive functions related to these transcription problems is unknown.

Many children with dysgraphia cannot complete written assignments that are legible, meet grade-appropriate standards for content and length, or finish assignments within time limits. Because the federal laws over the years for educationally disabling conditions define one of the specific learning disabilities as problems in written expression, the state code for implementing federal law often does not consider a handwriting disability or spelling disability to be a specific learning disability. An analogy from the reading domain would be qualifying students for special education only on the basis of reading comprehension and not word decoding or automatic word recognition problems. States that do not recognize handwriting disability as a specific learning disability may not be aware of a growing body of research literature on the link between handwriting problems and written expression (e.g., Berninger & Amtmann, 2003; Graham, Berninger, Abbott, Abbott, & Whitaker, 1997) and spelling problems and written expression (Berninger, Nielsen et al., 2008b). Many parents and teachers ask why it is not obvious from looking at a student's written work that the student has handwriting and/or spelling disability. Even though a special education category does not exist for transcription disability (TD)—impaired handwriting and/or spelling—TD does exist and is responsible for many (not all) written expression problems.

Many teachers and psychologists have complained that students who do not complete their written assignments are not motivated. However, teaching, clinical, and research experiences suggest otherwise—many of these students are highly motivated to write but emotionally traumatized that others cannot read their writing or they cannot write adequately to succeed in school (Berninger, Abbott, Whitaker, Sylvester, & Nolen, 1995). Many of these children also suffer from emotional problems (e.g., impaired self-esteem, self-efficacy, or heightened anxiety) due to undiagnosed and untreated dysgraphia, rather than emotional or motivational problems causing incomplete work. After continually failing to keep up with the written assignments or written tests at school, some children with dysgraphia will begin to avoid written work and are described as writing avoidant (for further discussion of these issues, see Berninger & Hidi, 2006). The important point is that emotional problems are often the consequence, not the cause, of writing disabilities. Gifted children with intellectual talent often have significant handwriting and/or spelling disabilities that compromise their ability to express their ideas in writing and complete written assignments even though they excel at learning with oral language (Yates, Berninger, & Abbott, 1994).

INSTRUCTIONAL IMPLICATIONS OF DIFFERENTIAL DIAGNOSIS

The distinctions among dyslexia, OWL LD, and dysgraphia (Berninger, 2006, 2008a; Berninger, O'Donnell, et al., 2008) have instructional implications. If a child has dyslexia, the child needs specialized instruction in phonology, oral reading accuracy and fluency for single words and passages, and written spelling. If the child has OWL LD, the same kind of instruction as for dyslexia is necessary but is not sufficient.

If children with OWL LD receive only instruction in phonological awareness and phonological decoding, they are likely to make progress in those areas but not necessarily in real-word reading or spelling skills, which also require morphological awareness treatment (see Chapter 7). Moreover, without morphological and syntactic awareness treatment, they are unlikely to make progress in reading comprehension or in written expression of ideas. Children with OWL LD who are not getting morphology, syntax, and comprehension treatment for both their oral and written language are increasingly being referred to the UW LDC. They tend to respond to phonics instruction and overcome their decoding problems but continue to have persistent problems in real word reading, reading comprehension, and written composition unless they receive instruction tailored to their underlying problems in morphological and syntactic awareness and word retrieval. Many of the students who fail to respond to instruction in general or special education or fail to meet IQ–achievement discrepancy criteria meet diagnostic criteria for OWL LD (Berninger, 2007). Relevant criteria for OWL LD diagnosis are impaired morphological and syntactic awareness and word retrieval in individuals whose intellectual ability, based on nonverbal or verbal IQ, falls at least within the lower limits of the normal range. However, they are often not discrepant from IQ in their reading and writing achievement. An initial case study suggests that reading comprehension can improve if the treatment is expanded beyond phonology to include morphology and syntax in oral and written language as well. If a child has dysgraphia, the child needs specialized instruction in handwriting and/or spelling.

Figure 8.2 summarizes which kind of word-form storage and processing impairments are associated with a specific diagnosis—dyslexia, OWL LD, or dysgraphia.

Dyslexia, OWL LD, and dysgraphia can be differentiated on the basis of orthographic, phonological, and morphological/syntactic measures (Berninger, Raskind, et al., 2008). Students impaired only in orthographic awareness may benefit from orthographic awareness instructional activities. Those who are impaired in orthographic and/or phonological awareness will need phonological awareness instruction as well. Those who also have impaired morphological or syntactic awareness will also need instructional activities to develop these kinds of linguistic awareness.

Teaching Students with Dyslexia

A second wave of phenotyping studies conducted by UW LDC found that dyslexia is both a reading and writing disorder. The children and adults with dyslexia in the study also had spelling problems, and those spelling problems were directly related to their written composition problems in expressing ideas in writing (Berninger, Nielsen, et al., 2008b). Males with dyslexia tended to be more impaired in writing than did females with dyslexia (Berninger, Nielsen et al., 2008a). Teaching students to overcome their oral reading and spelling problems requires explicit instruction in orthographic and phonological awareness of written and spoken words and their parts and mapping procedures for orthographic–phonological correspondences that may be complex (not one-to-one but rather involving options; see Chapters 4, 5, and 7). They also benefit from specialized orthographic strategies and strategies that render reading and spelling automatic (Berninger, 1998b; Berninger, Nielsen, et al., 2008b; see Chapter 9, and Units I–IV in the companion workbook, *Helping Students with Dyslexia and Dysgraphia Make Connections: Differentiated Instruction Lesson Plans in Reading and Writing* [Berninger & Wolf, 2009]).

Teaching Students with OWL LD

Federal special education policy under the Individuals with Disabilities Education Improvement Act (IDEA) of 2004 (PL 108-446) specifies that students with learning disabilities in listening comprehension and oral expression are to be identified and given appropriate education in addition to those with learning disabilities in reading comprehension and written expression. However, those with oral language learning disabilities may be underidentified and underserved in an era with national focus on literacy defined on the basis of written language achievement. Improving written language may require teaching oral language skills to those with oral language impairment (Scott & Windsor, 2000). The authors suspect that

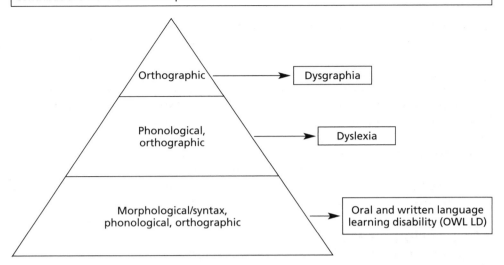

Figure 8.2. Relationship between word-form deficit and diagnosis. (From Berninger, V.W. [2007]. *Process Assessment of the Learner, second edition [PAL-II] user guide.* San Antonio, TX: Pearson Assessment; reprinted by permission.)

more children may have OWL LD than dyslexia, but until schools identify both groups, these statistics are not available. Chapter 3 offered many practical suggestions for classroom teachers to provide the kind of modeling and explicit instruction that students with OWL LD require in oral and written language and their integration. The list of books at the end of the end of Chapter 3 is a valuable instructional resource for developing many aspects of oral language.

Teaching Students with Dysgraphia

Transcription (handwriting and/or spelling) is but one of the cognitive processes in written expression, yet one of the most important for written school work (Berninger & Amtmann, 2003). Problems in handwriting and spelling can negatively affect a student's ability to translate ideas into written language and even revise writing to improve its quality. Although computer keyboards may make it easier to produce letters, evidence shows that children write longer compositions and write them faster by pen than by keyboard (Berninger, Abbott, et al., 2008; Berninger, Richards, Stock, Trivedi, & Altemeier, 2007; Connelly et al., in press; Hayes & Berninger, in press). Thus, not only in the early grades but also throughout schooling, students with handwriting and spelling problems benefit from explicit instruction in transcription (handwriting, keyboarding, spelling by pen and keyboard, and composing) (see Chapters 5 and 9) and not just accommodations that allow them to use computers and have more time on task. The authors are not suggesting that the accommodations be eliminated but that they are used in conjunction with explicit instruction in handwriting or spelling, as needed, until writing by pen is legible and automatic, and composition.

The key to effective handwriting and spelling instruction is to draw students' attention to the orthographic word form in written words and the constituent letters. Chapter 5 provides an overview of some of the evidence-based approaches for teaching orthographic awareness of letter forms during handwriting instruction. Chenault, Thomson, Abbott, and Berninger's instructional study (2006) for students with persisting writing problems in the upper elementary grades showed that pretreatment in attention training (Kerns, Eso, & Thomson, 1999) was more effective than pretreatment in reading fluency on students' response to the written composition instruction that followed. Based on the research reported in Chapter 7 that showed a direct pathway from self-regulation of attention to the orthographic word form, this finding makes sense. This finding also suggests that teachers should incorporate explicit strategies for teaching students to pay attention to word spellings as part of spelling and composition instruction. Another study found that rapid automatic naming predicted transfer of taught spelling to one's own compositions (Amtmann, Abbott, & Berninger, 2008). This finding highlights the importance of teaching the alphabetic principle in phoneme-to-grapheme direction until it is automatic and teaching specific, grade-appropriate spelling words through repeated, daily sentence dictation until spelling is automatic.

ARE DYSLEXIA, OWL LD, AND DYSGRAPHIA JUST LANGUAGE DISORDERS?

The impaired word-level reading and spelling skills in dyslexia are associated with impaired processing in working memory components (Swanson, 1999b, 2006), all of which have a phonological core deficit (Berninger, Abbott, Thomson, et al., 2006; Morris et al., 1998; Stanovich & Siegel, 1994). The phonological core deficit interferes with accuracy of oral reading and decoding, but the working memory deficit interferes with fluency (temporal coordination; see Chapters 7 and 9). Executive functions are also critical for integrating reading and writing (Altemeier, Abbott, & Berninger, 2008; Altemeier, Jones, Abbott, & Berninger, 2006). That is, dyslexia is both a language disorder and working memory disorder (Berninger, Abbott, Thomson, et al., 2006; Swanson, 2006).

This working memory architecture is relevant to all three specific learning disabilities affecting written language acquisition. Within the working memory architecture, students with dyslexia may be impaired in any of the components in Figure 8.3, particularly in orthographic and phonological word-form storage and processing and in the phonological loop. Students with OWL LD may be impaired in any of the components in Figure 8.3, particularly in the orthographic, phonological, and morphological word-form storage and processing, in the syntax storage for processing accumulating word forms, and in the phonological and orthographic loops. Students with dysgraphia may be impaired in any of the components in Figure 8.3, particularly in the orthographic word-form storage and processing and in the orthographic loop. Executive function impairment is common across all three specific learning disabilities interfering with written language acquisition.

Oral-motor function, which is related to the oral reading, and graphomotor function, which is related to the written expression of students with dyslexia (Berninger, Nielsen, et al., 2008a, 2008b), are also included in Figure 8.3 because they are part of the phonological and orthographic loops, respectively. UW LDC genotyping case control studies to date point to gene variants in the phenotypes associated with phonological storage and processing and executive functions for regulating switching attention. (See Berninger, Raskind, et al., 2008, and Chapter 7 for further discussion of these findings.) Children may overcome the phonological, orthographic, and/or morphological word storage and processing problems but continue to have executive function weaknesses throughout schooling, which is why they continue to need teacher-guided, explicit instruction in written language.

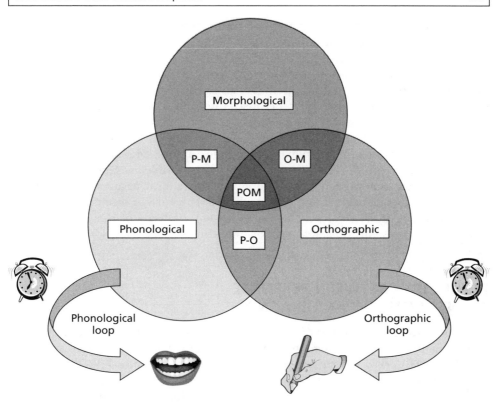

Figure 8.3. Executive functions: Inhibition, set switching, task maintenance, and retrieval fluency. (From Berninger, V.W. [2007]. *Process Assessment of the Learner, second edition [PAL-II] user guide.* San Antonio, TX: Pearson Assessment; reprinted by permission.)

DO SOME CHILDREN HAVE COMBINATIONS OF DYSLEXIA, OWL LD, AND DYSGRAPHIA?

Although many students appear to have just dyslexia, just OWL LD, or just dysgraphia, others show signs of having more than one disability (Berninger, et al., in press). Some students with dyslexia also have dysgraphia—handwriting subtype—but others do not. Some students with higher IQ scores show signs of both dyslexia and OWL LD (morphological and syntactic awareness problems despite strong oral vocabularies) and even have higher verbal than nonverbal performance IQ scores. Children with multiple disabilities need an instructional program to include treatment components, as the diagnosis indicates, for handwriting, spelling, composition, and oral language morphology and syntax.

ASSESSMENT MODELS

Some reasons for referral require comprehensive assessment using many different approaches to describe a student's profile. These profiles are unique for each individual. Nevertheless, researchers have identified patterns (configurations of phenotypes) in the writing, reading, and oral language profiles of school-age children that have diagnostic and treatment implications. The diagnoses of dyslexia, OWL LD, and dysgraphia are evidence based.

Regrettably, the federal legislation guaranteeing students a free, appropriate education does not guarantee them free evidence-based diagnosis and evidence-based instruction linked to those diagnoses. Thus, the special education categories used for children with disabilities are simply labels for qualifying students for services. Some students have a profile that enables them to receive pull-out or other kinds of special education services. Because education is under local control, which students have such a profile depends on state and often the local school system where students live. *Free and appropriate* is not the same as *evidence based.*

If the reader finds this perplexing, so do the authors, who believe the solution is for educational professionals to provide the best possible evidence-based assessment and instruction proactively. Nothing in state, federal, case, or legislative law prohibits that. See Berninger and Holdnack (2008) for further discussion of the differences among individual profiles (snowflakes), patterns of diagnostic phenotypes (constellations), and categories for providing services (labels) in assessment of learning disabilities.

DISTINCTION BETWEEN RESPONSE TO INTERVENTION AND DIAGNOSIS

All good instruction includes an assessment component (progress monitoring) to determine if a student is learning what the teacher is teaching or to set an educational goal. However, progress monitoring should not be confused with a diagnosis. The 2004 IDEA reauthorization (PL 108-446) stipulates that response to instruction may be a part of comprehensive assessment; it does not indicate that response to instruction alone can replace comprehensive assessment. Moreover, qualifying students for special education services is not the same as evidence-based diagnosis grounded in science and best practices in relevant disciplines, such as psychology, speech and language, physical and occupational therapy, and specializations in medicine (see Berninger, 1998b; Berninger & Holdnack, 2008). Progress monitoring requires analysis by the teacher of the particular instructional needs of the student, not merely assessment of growth or lack of it.

Next we raise issues for practitioners to think about as they carefully plan to incorporate in their teaching insights from clinically relevant research. First, we raise the issue and then we propose what we think a reasonable answer is.

Why is it important to base instruction on careful diagnosis of whether a student may have oral language weaknesses beyond phonological processing that also need to be taken into account in planning and delivering written language instruction? If the other oral language problems are not diagnosed, they will not be treated, and the reading and written language problems may persist even if the student improves in phonics and phonological decoding.

Why is it important to understand that some children have only decoding problems, some have both decoding and reading comprehension problems, and some have only comprehension problems? Because these individual differences exist, students differ in the intensity and nature of instruction they require in their general education reading and writing programs in these skills.

Why is it important to understand that some children have a problem in decoding words despite good vocabulary knowledge and verbal reasoning, which may mask the decoding problems when reading words in context? Children with this profile may survive in the early grades but often experience a great deal of difficulty in reading and writing in Grade 4 and above when curriculum requirements increase. Also, children's talents including verbal reasoning may not be recognized and nurtured if not identified.

Why is it important to understand that some children may have a problem in writing by hand that compromises their ability to communicate in written language as much as problems with speech do in communicating in oral language? These children who have typical or better intelligence may 1) fail at school, which requires successful completion of written work to pass content subjects; 2) not be promoted to the next grade level; 3) not graduate from high school; and 4) not pass high-stakes tests given in the state. Children who cannot communicate in written language are also at risk for dropping out of school altogether. All of these unfortunate outcomes may also result in emotional problems such as anxiety, work avoidance, and depression.

Why is it important to understand that dyslexia is a writing as well as reading disorder? Teaching students with dyslexia to read is necessary but not sufficient. They also need to be able to spell and complete written assignments for reasons addressed previously. Otherwise, writing quality or length of compositions may be reduced.

How do spelling problems of students with dyslexia interfere with their written composition? Inability to spell words limits word choice. Nonautomatic retrieval of word spellings slows the speed of written composition.

Why is it important to understand that some students have dysgraphia (writing problems) without reading problems or in addition to their reading problems? Just because a student has trouble producing legible letters automatically does not mean that the child is not motivated, cannot think, or lacks vocabulary knowledge or high-quality ideas. The handwriting blocks the expression of that thinking ability, knowledge, and ideas.

How do handwriting problems of students with dyslexia or dysgraphia interfere with their written composition? Students with dyslexia and/or dysgraphia may forget what they planned to write while trying to remember how to form the letters. Or, they might write the letters so slowly that they do not produce as much writing as classmates who can write letters automatically. Or, their handwriting may be so illegible that the reader cannot figure out the intended message.

QUESTIONS TO ASK WHEN REQUESTING MULTIDISCIPLINARY ASSESSMENT

Teachers who have become informed about clinically relevant research should feel empowered to ask the following questions of the psychologists and speech and language therapists to whom they refer children for assessment of reading and writing problems:

1. Does this student have absolute or relative strengths or weaknesses in verbal or nonverbal reasoning that should be recognized and nurtured?

2. Does this child have a strength or weakness compared with grade or age peers in automatic letter writing, handwriting legibility, or handwriting speed?

3. Does this child have a strength or weakness compared with grade or age peers in phonological spelling (pseudowords), orthographic spelling (equated for phonology), or orthographic/morphological spelling (real words)?

4. Does this child have a strength or weakness compared with grade or age peers in accuracy or rate of pseudoword reading? Accuracy or rate of real-word reading on a list? Accuracy or rate of real-word reading in passages?

5. Does this child have a strength or weakness compared with grade or age peers in accuracy or rate of reading comprehension?

6. Does this child have a strength or weakness compared with grade or age peers in accuracy or rate of written composition for narrative or expository genre?

7. Does this child have a strength or weakness compared with grade or age peers in accuracy or rate of the following reading- and writing-related skills:

    a. Phonological word-form storage (coding) and processing?

    b. Orthographic word-form storage (coding) and processing?

    c. Morphological word-form storage (coding) and processing?

    d. Rapid automatic naming—letters?

    e. Expressive orthographic coding—writing words and letters in them?

    f. Executive function for inhibition, rapid automatic switching, verbal fluency?

    g. Oral language syntax?

Teachers should also feel empowered to ask the professionals who provide the assessment information for problem-solving consultation in planning instructional treatment based on the assessment results. The assessment should include teacher interview and classroom observation of the student during instruction (response to the planned and implemented instructional intervention) in order to assess the curriculum as well as the students' characteristics that mediate response to instruction.

DEBUNKING ASSESSMENT MYTHS

The clinically relevant research has shown that many widely held assumptions about learning disabilities need to be reexamined.

Diagnosis Is Not the Same as Qualifying for Special Education Services

Just because the federal or state special education laws do not have a category labeled *dyslexia* for qualifying students for special education services does not mean that dyslexia does not exist. It does. Both researchers and the IDA can now define it, and schools can learn evidence-based ways to define it, diagnose it, and treat it.

Biologically Based Educational Problem

Just because a learning problem has a biological basis (see Chapter 7), it does not mean that it requires a medical treatment. Nature–nurture interactions influence learning. Dyslexia and related learning disabilities have biological bases, but instructional research has shown that individuals with such disabilities are very responsive to specialized instruction (see Chapter 9), which can be delivered in the general education classroom.

Evidence-Based Assessment Measures for Diagnosis

Research-supported diagnostic procedures exist for dyslexia, OWL LD, and dysgraphia (Berninger, 2007). This assessment–intervention system draws on different test instruments, and more than one test can be used to assess each of the components in Figure 8.3. What matters is that each of these components is assessed and, if impaired, instruction is directed to that component within a balanced instructional program that teaches all of the relevant reading and writing skills. A User Guide on CD provides tutorial assistance in translating assessment results into instructional practice.

TEACHER REFLECTIONS ABOUT CONTRIBUTIONS FROM THE CLINICAL DISCIPLINES

The distinctions between dyslexia and OWL LD are consistent with the second author's classroom experience and observations. In her experience, both students with only dyslexia and those with impaired oral language skills in addition to dyslexia showed response to instruction that included what was needed by students with dyslexia (phonology, oral reading accuracy and fluency, and written spelling) and what was needed by the language-affected students with OWL LD (morphology, syntax, and comprehension treatment for oral and written language). Many students with OWL LD who successfully decode and read do not comprehend what they have unlocked because of their oral language weaknesses. Unmet oral language needs affect both reading comprehension and the organization and complexity of written language productions. Guidance and practice in understanding and using the structure of language as a tool for reading comprehension, which is necessary for students with OWL LD, will also help students with and without dyslexia. Thus, it is worth the time and effort for teachers in general education to learn these instructional strategies.

Identification of dysgraphia helps teachers to understand why some students whose handwriting appears adequate write so little. Those students typically do not have automatic recall of letter forms and may be drawing their letters. Others write at a typical rate but with many distortions, omissions, erasures or cross outs. Finally, those students with dysgraphia may weary from the effort of putting their thoughts on paper and produce sparse, unembellished sentences that do not reflect their true abilities to generate text. An unknowing teacher will say that these students are lazy or careless. They are neither. They need instruction and daily writing practice to develop automaticity. Teacher instruction and expectations for legible handwriting will improve performance.

Distinguishing varying student needs opens the eyes of the teacher. The debate about IQ–achievement discrepancy has missed the real issue. The real contribution of IQ tests is to show students with dyslexia, OWL LD, and dysgraphia, who do not easily experience success in academic learning, that they really are intelligent!

CONCLUSION

Clinically relevant research shows the heterogeneous nature of specific learning disabilities affecting reading and writing acquisition. This kind of research has also yielded reliable and valid measures for assessing relevant individual differences that are also relevant to planning instruction. This research has also identified common profiles within this heterogeneity. Thus, the general education teacher can meet many individual needs within group instruction in the general education classroom.

CHAPTER 9

Contributions from Instructional Disciplines

Research on early intervention for reading is showing that severity of reading problems can be prevented, and research on the treatment of persisting reading problems is showing that older students also respond to specialized instruction. These findings are not surprising to teachers who have devoted their careers to teaching students with dyslexia, oral and written language learning disability (OWL LD), and dysgraphia.

Early identification and intervention are critical and effective (Vellutino et al., 1996) for children with learning disabilities. According to Torgesen (1996), for 90%–95% of poor readers, prevention and early intervention programs that combine instruction in phoneme awareness, phonics, fluency, and reading comprehension strategies and that are taught by well-trained teachers can increase reading skills to average reading levels; however, when intervention is delayed until 9 years of age, approximately 75% will continue to have difficulties learning to read throughout high school. Training fluency is important because it is a bridge to reading comprehension (Tan & Nicholson, 1997).

INSTRUCTIONAL TOOLS FROM PROGRAMMATIC RESEARCH FOR EARLY INTERVENTION

Adams, Foorman, Lundberg, and Beeler (1998) collected a variety of instructional activities based on research by Lundberg's and Foorman's groups for developing phonological awareness in kindergarten and first grade. The activities discussed in the following sections are easily implemented by kindergarten and primary-grade teachers.

Ladders to Literacy

In their research with young at-risk readers, O'Connor, Notari-Syverson, and Vadasy (2005) developed and validated activity books for teaching phonological awareness and phonological decoding. These are teacher-friendly and have been successfully implemented in many classrooms.

Road to the Code

Blachman, Ball, Black, and Tangel (2000) translated their pioneering research in kindergarten and first-grade classrooms into lesson plans for teaching children correspondences between letters and sound and their application to phonological decoding. This instructional program helps teachers connect phonological awareness, phonics, and phonological decoding.

PAL Reading and Writing Lessons

Berninger and Abbott (2003) translated published research on teaching reading and writing to all levels of language (subword, word, and text) into Tier 1 lesson plans to be used concurrently with core curriculum to prevent reading and writing problems before children have an opportunity to fail. Lesson sets 1 and 11 (first-grade reading); 2, 6, and 9 (second-grade reading); 3 (first-grade handwriting and composing); and 4 and 5 (second- and third-grade spelling and composing) can be used with young learners. A list of instructional resources with many other instructional tools for teaching beginning reading and writing is also included with the lessons.

SPECIALIZED INSTRUCTION FOR PERSISTING PROBLEMS

Many beginning reading and writing problems resolve with evidence-based early intervention, but some children require ongoing, specialized instruction in the general education program and in some cases in special education because of underlying genetic or brain variables (see Chapter 7). Accommodations may be necessary for some students with educationally disabling conditions, such as giving a student more time to complete written work. However, specialized instruction may be needed from elementary to high school (see Chapters 7 and 8). Meta-analyses support the effectiveness of explicit instruction and strategy instruction for students with learning disabilities (Swanson, 1999a). Morphological treatment for word reading and word spelling is also necessary (Carlisle, 2000; Henry & Redding, 1996; Nagy, Anderson, Schommer, Scott, & Stallman, 1989; Nagy, Osborn, Winsor, & O'Flahavan, 1994; Nunes & Bryant, 2006; Pacton, Fayol, & Perruchet, 2005; Singson, Mahony, & Mann, 2000; Tyler & Nagy, 1989, 1990). However, specialized instruction can be delivered in the less restrictive general education classroom. Special education is needed only when the student can only learn in a more restrictive environment. In fact, many students with dyslexia, OWL LD, and dysgraphia learn to benefit from the intellectual stimulation and social interaction with age peers in the general education classroom.

The following sections describe programmatic research programs on dyslexia. The first three programs are headed by Maureen Lovett, Maryanne Wolf, and Barbara Wilson and include commercially available instructional programs and training to support them. The fourth program is headed by Nicki Nelson and is unique in that it focuses on children with OWL LD and use of technology in teaching both writing and reading to them. The last section describes four University of Washington Multidisciplinary Learning Disabilities Center (UW LDC) lesson sets for students with persisting writing and reading problems, which are in the accompanying workbook, *Helping Students with Dyslexia and Dysgraphia Make Connections: Differentiated Instruction Lesson Plans in Reading and Writing* (Berninger & Wolf, 2009).

Lovett's Empower Reading

For more than 25 years, Maureen Lovett has directed the Hospital for Sick Children's Learning Disabilities Research Program in Toronto, Ontario, Canada. Empower Reading is an instructional program with 110 lessons with a variety of activities that teachers can implement in general and special education classrooms for students in Grades 2–5. The program is based on rigorous scientific research since 1980 in hospital and community classrooms in the Toronto area for teaching students with severe reading disabilities. This research has been funded by both the National Research Council in Canada and the National Institutes of Health (NIH) in the United States. The program is designed to develop accurate and efficient decoding and word recognition and strategies for applying these skills to independent reading for meaning, information, and pleasure. Children are taught five decoding strategies to use anytime they confront an unknown word: sounding out, rhyming, peeling off, vowel alert, and SPY. Children are also taught a strategy for choosing, using, and checking these five decoding strategies. Some spelling and reading comprehension activities are included. More Empower Reading programs are being developed based on ongoing research. (For more information on Empower Reading, contact the research team at ldrp@sickkids.ca or 416.813.6329.)

Wolf's RAVE-O

Maryanne Wolf, director of the Tufts Center for Reading and Language Research (CRLR) in Boston, Massachusetts has performed pioneering research funded by the NIH on the timing and fluency problems in developmental dyslexia. Wolf and Martha Denckla, a pediatric neurologist at Johns Hopkins University, have translated this research into assessment measures for rapid automatic naming (RAN) and rapid automatic switching (RAS), which are published by PRO-ED. Research in her group and many other groups around the world, including the UW LDC, have validated RAN and RAS as significant predictors of reading and writing problems and response to reading and writing instruction (see Chapters 7 and 8).

After 10 years of research, Wolf and her colleagues (Lovett and Robin Morris at Georgia State University) have also developed and validated an instructional program for treating vocabulary, reading fluency, and comprehension problems in dyslexia: Retrieval, Automaticity, Vocabulary, Engagement with Language, Orthography (RAVE-O). The program targets major linguistic components (phonological, orthographic, semantic, syntactic, and morphological) and children's engagement in written language processes. Results indicate significant gains equal to or beyond other intervention programs in each of the targeted components: decoding, fluency, and comprehension. The Tufts Literacy Corps sends undergraduate tutors who use RAVE-O to local elementary schools to teach at-risk and struggling readers. (For more information on RAVE-O or how to obtain teacher training for using it in the classroom, contact CRLR at STEPH.GOTTWALD@tufts.edu or 617-627-3815.)

Wilson's Language Training

Barbara A. Wilson, who has a wealth of experience using special methods to teach students with dyslexia, is the co-founder of the Wilson Language Training Corporation in Oxford, Massachusetts. She is also the author of three multisensory structured language programs: the Wilson Reading System, Wilson Fundations, and Wilson Fluency, which have been used in many instructional studies and found to be effective. These programs teach not only phonics but also morphology, and thus meet the evidence-based requirement that phonology, orthography, and morphology be taught. (For further information on these programs, visit http://www .wilsonlanguage.com).

Nelson's Writing Lab

This resource (Nelson, Bahr, & Van Meter, 2004), based on a research program headed by Nickola Nelson, professor of speech and language pathology at Western Michigan University, is valuable for teachers who incorporate or want to learn how to incorporate oral language, writing, and technology-assisted instruction in their classrooms. It includes many research-based activities for helping students with oral language difficulties to learn written language. It is, however, also focused on writing—all too often instructional programs focus mainly on reading for students with dyslexia. In addition, the author draws on her wealth of research experience with computers and other technology tools in describing how technology can be incorporated into written language instruction for students with oral language problems. Teachers find it a valuable resource in planning differentiated instruction as discussed in Chapters 2 and 10.

PAL Reading and Writing Lessons

Tier 3 lesson sets 11–15 are based on instructional studies for students with dyslexia in the UW LDC. Tier 2 lesson sets 7, 8, and 10 are based on instructional studies for students with dysgraphia in the UW LDC. A list of resources is provided with many other instructional tools for teaching students who continue to struggle with reading and writing (Berninger & Abbott, 2003).

GOALS OF CHAPTER 9

Chapter 9 is designed to be used in conjunction with the four sets of evidence-based reading and/or writing lessons in the accompanying workbook, *Helping Students with Dyslexia and Dysgraphia Make Connections* (Berninger & Wolf, 2009). Lessons and the related instructional materials are included for teachers to use in their own classrooms. One goal of Chapter 9 is to explain to general and special educators the rationale underlying each of the four lesson sets, which were developed and validated in the UW LDC but never published before. The UW LDC receives many requests for these lessons because of evidence from brain imaging studies that some children's brains normalized on some imaging tasks in specific brain regions or temporal connectivity after participating in these studies (see Chapter 7).

Another goal of this chapter is to illustrate the *grammar of teaching*, which is the set of general principles of instructional design underlying evidence-based, specialized instruction. An analogy between teaching and language is relevant. Language is generative: A finite number of words can be used to construct, via the syntax of language, an infinite number of sentences, and, via the discourse schema of the language, an infinite number of texts. Syntax is created through 1) rules for *or-*

dering words in sentences or oral utterances, 2) *function words* (prepositions, conjunctions, pronouns, articles) that glue together other words in the sentence (content words such as nouns, verbs, adjectives, and adverbs), and 3) *derivational suffixes* that transform the part of speech of base words. Structures that link sentences together locally and globally create discourse schema.

Like language, master teaching is generative: Knowledge of brain-based general principles of learning (Berninger & Richards, 2008b) can be used in an infinite number of ways to teach students with dyslexia, OWL LD, and/or dysgraphia effectively. Master teaching combines art as well as science. Teachers who have deep understanding of this grammar of teaching and learning can put their own creative spin on any evidence-based instructional resources they use. It is important to remember that *there is more than one way to teach and there is more than one way to learn effectively BUT not all teaching and learning are effective*. Moreover, master teaching, like discourse-schema, creates structures in the classroom both locally for individual students and globally for the whole class.

In the lesson sets discussed in the following section, the grammar of teaching reading to students with dyslexia is illustrated in the Word Detectives lesson (Unit I), the grammar of teaching writing to students with dyslexia with or without dysgraphia is illustrated in the Mark Twain Writers Workshop (Unit II), the grammar of teaching writing and reading to struggling writing-readers is illustrated in the John Muir Writing-Readers Workshop (Unit III), and the grammar of teaching reading and writing to struggling reading-writers is illustrated in the Sequoyah Reading-Writers Workshop (Unit IV) (see Berninger & Wolf, 2009). Three of the lesson sets focus on writing (although written summarization is used in the lesson set focused on reading) because writing problems of students with dyslexia are often undiagnosed and untreated especially in the upper elementary and middle school grades, and boys with dyslexia are more severely impaired in writing than girls with dyslexia (Berninger, Nielsen, Abbott, Wijsman, & Raskind, 2008a, 2008b). After discussing the rationale for each of these lesson sets, which can be used with students with and without dyslexia, a summary of the grammar of teaching reading, writing, and integrated reading-writing is provided.

FOUR UW LDC EVIDENCE-BASED LESSON SETS FOR STUDENTS WITH DYSLEXIA

Each of these lesson sets—which were used in the UW LDC instructional studies for students with persisting reading and writing problems in Grades 4–9 and can be found in the accompanying workbook, *Helping Students with Dyslexia and Dysgraphia Make Connections* (Berninger & Wolf, 2009)—contain a teacher manual that explains the conceptual rationale, research evidence, overall organization plan for the lessons, and the lessons and related instructional tools. Also included are references to the published studies that provided the behavioral and brain evidence for the effectiveness of these instructional approaches.

In the research studies, all teachers had to participate in training sessions before the instructional studies began. Teachers who use the lessons can engage in self-study to learn the conceptual framework for these lesson sets by familiarizing themselves with all of the information, lesson plans, and instructional tools in the accompanying workbook before using the lessons. To provide effective instruction and appropriate response to students' response to that instruction, teachers need to understand *why* they are teaching, *what* they are teaching, and *how* they should teach it.

Keep in mind that the general principles of the instructional design are most important. These general principles can be applied using similar instructional materials that teachers have access to in their schools or different books on the same topic. Background information about these general principles, which can be used with any reading material, is provided in the following lesson descriptions.

Word Detectives (Unit I)

As discussed throughout this book, research has shown that students with dyslexia need explicit instruction in phonological awareness and phonological decoding; they also have difficulty with automatic naming of orthographic symbols. Research evidence is also mounting that students with dyslexia and/or dysgraphia have weaknesses in orthographic awareness, and that ability to pay attention to written words and their constituent letters is critical to developing orthographic awareness and coding into working memory. Moreover, due to the problems in inhibition (focus on relevant, suppress irrelevant), switching attention, and working memory (sustaining effort for coordinating orthography and phonology over time; see Chapters 7 and 9), students with dyslexia and/or dysgraphia are likely to habituate (stop responding to instruction) sooner than children without these disorders. One way to avoid habituation is to vary activities frequently and avoid performing the same activity over and over for a long time.

Thus, the UW LDC team was not surprised to find in earlier instructional studies that students who met research criteria for dyslexia were able to recite many phonics rules but did not know how to apply them productively to sound out written words, that is, decode unknown written words. Many of the early studies with younger students were focused on developing and validating effective ways to teach orthographic and phonological awareness, automatic correspondences between graphemes (letters that are orthographic symbols) and phonemes (small sounds that are phonological units in spoken words), and transfer of this knowledge to decoding written words out of context and in context.

The resulting method uses *Talking Letters* cards that each child has in front of her or him on the desk to examine at the near point of vision (Berninger, 1998b). These cards display rows of a single grapheme (one or two letters) and an associated picture of a word that contains a phoneme that can be spelled with that grapheme. The grapheme–phoneme correspondences represent the high-frequency ones in high-frequency words in primary-grade reading material. Consonants are on one side and vowels, organized by the syllable types of English, are on the other side. Each lesson begins with a warm-up, which is designed around general principles to develop *automatic alphabetic principle knowledge*.

An effective way to develop attention to letters is to 1) point to them (to focus visual attention and touch sensation and attention), and 2) name them (to focus auditory attention and oral-motor attention). Phonological awareness is learned through saying phonemes in and out of spoken word context. Pairing two stimuli and two responses close in time creates automatic, multimodal associations. One form of effective explicit instruction is to have the teacher model and the student imitate, then switch turns rapidly.

Thus, during the warm-up, the teacher first points to, looks at, and names the one- or two-letter grapheme; names the corresponding picture; and then names the phoneme in it that goes with the grapheme. Then the child points to, looks at, and names the grapheme; the pictured word; and the corresponding phoneme. Then the teacher and child repeat the procedure with the next grapheme. This rapid turn taking continues for one grapheme–phoneme association at a time with the teacher monitoring that the child is focusing visual attention to the letter(s), touching the letter(s), and making the corresponding phoneme correctly. If a child does not, the teacher models again and asks the child to imitate. Rules are never taught or repeated during the warm-up because that would overload working memory and defeat the purpose of activities designed to create procedural rather than declarative knowledge (see Chapter 4) of automatic grapheme–phoneme correspondences in the alphabetic principle. For example, rather than verbalizing the silent *e* rule, children's visual attention is drawn to vowel, consonant neighbor, and final *e* with an X drawn over it to indicate that it is silent. This approach helps children overcome the orthographic weakness in paying attention to written words and moving attentional focus across the letters within written words (see Chapter 7).

To avoid habituation, only a few rows are introduced or practiced in any one lesson, but all are introduced early in the lesson set. Children are told that they will do a warm-up just like athletes do before a sports game with Talking Letter cards (e.g., Berninger & Abbott, 2003). Following this warm-up, they are taught strategies to transfer alphabetic principle reviewed during the warm-up to decoding words alone and in interesting stories or to spelling words alone and in their own compositions. In this way, the high-frequency correspondences for high-frequency, one- and two-syllable Anglo-Saxon words become automatic and give the reader sufficient knowledge of the alphabetic principle to decode words in text during teacher-guided instruction *and* independent, self-regulated reading. Many teachers and parents have reported they were gratified to see children choose to read on their own during free time after receiving this kind of instruction. Later in the lessons, warm-up focuses on grapheme–phoneme correspondences in longer, more complex, three- to five-syllable Latin or French words.

The lessons then proceed to activities to develop linguistic awareness of phonological, orthographic, and morphological word forms (which are represented independently of the semantic system for linking language to cognition, see Chapters 4 and 5). For the first 7 of the 14 lessons, students complete seven activities in each lesson to develop phonological awareness and links between phonological and orthographic word forms and their parts (see Chapters 7 and 8 and the Word Detectives lesson [Unit I] in the accompanying workbook [Berninger & Wolf, 2009]): Word Building, Word Generating, Unit Finding, Word Transferring, Are They Relatives?, Sorting by Sound Features, and Sorting by Word Context. Briefly, these are activities in which the children

1. Count (clap) the number of syllables in spoken pseudsowords and move colored discs for each phoneme in a spoken syllable (note the involvement of hands with touch sensation)

2. Generate spoken words from single phonemes and view the orthographic word form the teacher writes on the board for all to see (note multisensory phonological–orthographic integration)

3. Find and underline the graphemes (spelling units) in written pseudowords that correspond to phonemes (note multimodal associations for visual, orthographic, phonological, and graphomotor codes; see Chapters 4 and 5)

4. Transfer automatic correspondences between graphemes and phonemes (*Talking Letters* warm-up) to pronounce written pseudowords on a list (note multimodal associations for orthographic, phonological, and oral-motor codes)

5. Analyze graphemes in pairs of written words to decide if they stand for the same phoneme (i.e., are alternations for grapheme–phoneme correspondence; see Chapter 7)

6. Sort written words into categories of alternations for the same grapheme

7. Choose and circle which missing grapheme fits each word context to create a real, pronounceable word with meaning (note coordination of grapheme–phonological correspondence with whole orthographic and phonological word form, semantics, and graphomotor codes)

During the instructional study, students with dyslexia had extreme difficulty with the third activity. Many could not find and underline the sequential grapheme units even though they were acquiring automatic grapheme–phoneme correspondences. Based on the brain imaging study showing a visual motion impairment in an area of the brain near the fusiform gyrus where orthographic word forms are processed (Winn et al., 2006), the research team hypothesized that children were having difficulty moving their visual attention from one letter or letter group within each written word to another. Thus, an alternative to finding and underlining was introduced. Children were asked to rewrite the word grapheme by grapheme (i.e., parse the orthographic word form). They were given two pens, each with a different color ink, (purple and gold for the University of Washington colors) and asked to write sequential spelling units (one- or two-letter units that correspond to a phoneme) in alternating colors. For example, the word *chunglewums* would be written as *ch* in purple, *u* in gold, *ng* in purple, *le* in gold, *w* in purple, *u* in gold, *m* in purple, and *s* in gold. Then children blended orally the phonemes that corresponded to the color-distinct graphemes. The UW LDC has also created color coding by printing alternating graphemes in black and red ink to provide the color cuing for graphemes to use in phoneme blending.

For the second set of seven lessons, children complete seven comparable activities to develop morphological awareness and coordination of the phonological, orthographic, and morphological word forms and their parts: Word Building, Word Generating, Unit Finding, Word Transferring, Are They Relatives?, Sorting by Three Word Forms and Their Parts, and Sorting by Sentence Context.

1. Find and underline the base words and circle the prefixes and suffixes in real written words (note multimodal visual, orthographic, morphological, semantic, and graphomotor codes)

2. Build words from bases and affixes (prefixes and suffixes) on cards and write the resulting word in the response booklet (note multimodal orthographic, morphological, and graphomotor codes)

3. Generate a new written word from a single suffix or prefix and write the resulting word in the response booklet (note multimodal orthographic, morphological, semantic, and graphomotor codes)

4. Transfer morphological codes to pronounce real words with prefixes and/or suffixes on a list (note multimodal orthographic, phonological, morphological, semantic, and oral-motor codes)

5. Analyze pairs of written words to decide if common spelling units (e.g., –er) function as morphemes and thus relate the two words in a pair semantically (e.g., *build* and *builder*) or if they do not function as morphemes and do not relate the two words semantically (e.g., *corn* and *corner*) and circle response in the response booklet (note multimodal orthographic, phonological, morphological, semantic, and graphomotor codes)

6. Sort written words into categories according to whether they share spelling, sounds, and morphemes (note multimodal orthographic, phonological, morphological, semantic, and graphomotor codes)

7. Choose the word (base word plus suffix) that fits in each sentence syntax context by circling it in the response booklet (note multimodal orthographic, morphological [derivational suffixes marking part of speech], syntactic, and semantic codes)

The lessons next focus on transfer of knowledge of the alphabetic principle and the Three Word Forms and Their Parts to decoding words in passages and reading text activity with the content theme of detectives solving mysteries for pleasure. Children read stories about Sherlock Holmes and John Watson. Children use transparency overlays to select with highlighter words they cannot decode during prereading, and the group shares strategies for decoding words each child shares. One-minute oral readings are obtained and graphed for progress monitoring before and after oral rereads, written summarizations, guided silent reading comprehension strategy instruction, and related oral discussion.

Throughout these lessons there is a hope story related to Albert Einstein, whose uncle told him to be a "word detective," which is important for motivating students who have experienced considerable failure in learning to read. However, the Word Detective lessons also contain a number of teaching strategies for helping students who have difficulty paying attention to written language maintain orthographic-phonological mapping in working memory over time and self-regulate executive functions. These strategies include

- Providing constant and frequent monitoring of attention to instruction

- Providing opportunities to respond orally and in writing; balance among activities designed to develop automatic and reflective skills, including metacognitive strategies organized around the word detective theme for each kind of phonological and morphological awareness

- Rewarding on-task behaviors, accurate responding, and improvement on progress monitoring indicators included in the lessons with points, rewards, and public praise

For details on how these strategies can be applied broadly across the reading program, see Word Detectives in the accompanying workbook, which also includes 1) a student response booklet for recording written responses and a student Word Detectives Work Folder cover for this response booklet, and 2) two certificates that can be awarded to students when they master the alphabetic principle (from the "Spell-Phone Society") and the awareness and integration of the three word forms (from the "POM POM Society"). Teachers who successfully teach students with dyslexia to master the alphabetic principle and awareness and coordination of the three word forms and their parts also earn a certificate.

Mark Twain Writers' Workshop (Unit II)

The workshop begins with the story of Mark Twain, whose mother was concerned because of the many life challenges he faced in his early development. This theme of Mark Twain the writer and his life is interwoven throughout the lessons to provide 1) a model of what good writing is (and how it relates to talking), and 2) hope that one's initial writing does not necessarily predict the writer he or she will become (see Mark Twain lessons in Unit II in the accompanying workbook [Berninger & Wolf, 2009] for details of Mark Twain's life and related biography for developing this theme).

Automatic alphabetic principle and strategic knowledge of alternations in the alphabetic principle (Venezky, 1970, 1999) are necessary for skilled spelling. However, spelling is taught *from phonemes to graphemes*; that is, in the reverse direction compared with reading. As discussed in Chapter 5, these phonological-orthographic mappings in word spelling are not always identical to orthographic-phonological mappings in word reading. In this lesson set, two modifications are introduced to the warm-up. First, explicit attention is drawn to the alternations (see Chapter 5) by teaching them as *substitutions*: Children are told the same sound can be spelled with different letters or letter groups so that any one letter does not get too tired from overwork (like coaches who substitute players so no one player gets too tired; Berninger, 1998b). Second, children write by hand from memory all the substitutions for the targeted phoneme in pictured example words in *Talking Letters* that they can within 10 minutes. Then students self-monitor their written responses by reviewing a visual matrix with pictured key words containing each phoneme and the associated possible graphemes in the same row (for details, see Berninger and Abbott, 2003, Lesson Set 7 and Substitutes Chart in the Reproducibles section).

This warm-up activity combines reflection on the alphabetic principle (its alternations that can be used strategically) and automatic phoneme–grapheme correspondences. This activity also engages the hand rather than the mouth in teaching the alphabetic principle. fMRI findings point to the importance of the hand in normalizing phonological skills (Richards et al., 2007) and in differentiating good and poor writers in fifth grade (Berninger & Richards 2008a; Richards, Berninger, Stock, Altemeier, Trivedi, & Maravilla, 2008). Engaging the hand when teaching the alphabetic principle may be critical to helping students with dyslexia overcome their spelling problems. This approach to teaching the alphabetic principle normalized the temporal connectivity of the brain including working memory regions during an fMRI task that assessed application of knowledge of alternations to written words (Berninger & Richards, 2008b).

Next, explicit strategies for spelling are taught. Orthographic strategies are taught in the first seven lessons, and morphological strategies are taught in the last seven lessons. The Mark Twain lessons (Unit II in Berninger & Wolf, 2009) provide the word lists for each lesson and detailed instructions on the orthographic strategies that are first taught and then the morphological strategies that are taught next. In addition, homework activities that can be sent home or used during independent work time to develop orthographic and morphological awareness are provided.

Finally, lesson plans are provided for teaching composition. Each of these includes a planning component, a translating component, and a reviewing/revising component. These are the major cognitive processes in composing (see Chapter 5 models proposed by Hayes & colleagues). The planning component begins with oral discussion for reflection and idea generation on the writing topic for the lesson. Graphic organizers (Berninger & Abbott, 2003; see the Reproducibles section) are used for planning each composition. Explicit strategies for planning and generating different genres of writing (e.g., informational, compare and contrast, persuasive, narrative) are taught. Prompts are provided to stimulate the translation of ideas into written language on the writing topic of the lesson. Explicit strategies for report writing are taught and include graphic portrayals in the workshop lesson plans. Explicit strategies are taught for revising the compositions and for using computers in the revision process; these include keyboard fluency training.

To help students develop their executive functions for self-regulation of the writing process, in each lesson the teacher develops, in collaboration with individual students, one or two goals for improving their writing. In the next lesson, teachers and students evaluate whether they met their goals. Feedback forms are provided for this metacognitive strategy of setting and evaluating goals for writing, which was introduced by Bernice Wong at Simon Frazier University (Wong & Berninger, 2004). These forms provide a relevant kind of progress monitoring for response to composition instruction.

The goal of the Mark Twain lesson set is to provide explicit instruction in spelling and written composition to help students to begin to express ideas effectively in writing. A set of instructional resources is provided for sustaining initial successes in spelling and written expression. Teachers may draw on these as they see fit to use along with or after the remaining two lesson sets.

John Muir Writing-Readers Workshop (Unit III)

This next lesson set teaches the alphabetic principle in both the reading direction (graphemes by eye/orthography to phonemes by mouth/oral-motor codes) and the spelling direction (phonemes by mouth/ear to hand/sensory touch).

For the *reading direction*, students are given Nickname Visual Charts (Berninger & Abbott, 2003; see the Reproducibles section) with the graphemes and associated word pictures. For each grapheme (one or two letters) they produce all the sounds they remember are associated with it and then self-check their knowledge by inspecting the Nicknames visual chart that has the pictures from *Talking Letters* that have the sounds that go with that letter (see Berninger & Abbott, 2003, Reproducibles). This training makes them aware of the possible phonemes for each grapheme so if they are stuck decoding a word they can try the different options as a strategy.

For the *writing direction*, they are given Substitute Visual Charts (Berninger & Abbott, 2003; see the Reproducibles section) with pictured words taught in *Talking Letters* and are asked to write for each phoneme all the graphemes (single letters or letter groups) that can spell the target phoneme in the pictured word. Then they use the Substitute Visual Chart (Berninger & Abbott, 2003, Reproducibles) to check their work. Rules are never verbalized; rather, the goal is to make the alternations in orthographic–phonological correspondences of the alphabetic principle both automatic and available as strategies in reading or spelling words.

In addition, students work on their phonological awareness by playing syllable and phoneme games as in Word Detectives but with unfamiliar bird names rather than spoken pseudowords. Children also spell these bird names from dictation to promote transfer of the alphabetic principle to spelling. When they spell the names successfully, an electronic recording of the bird's call is sounded. Children enjoy hearing the unique bird calls. Phonological awareness training does not have to be boring.

Students have an opportunity to apply (transfer) this phonological awareness of syllables and phonemes in spoken words and the alphabetic principle in the word-reading direction through oral reading. They take turns reading aloud about John Muir, a writing scientist who led the movement to establish the National Park System in the United States. They also have an opportunity to apply (transfer) the phonological awareness and the alphabetic principle in the word-spelling direction by listening to an audiotape of the autobiography of John Muir. Children take written notes as they listen.

Teacher-guided oral reading is designed to increase awareness of the connection between the intonation of oral language and capitalization and punctuation, which are not mechanical skills. To improve students' ability to pay attention to these written turn-taking signals, children who are paying attention when a punctuation mark appears at the end of a sentence and their name is called may take a turn at oral reading. The length of any turn at oral reading, which can be hard work for students with dyslexia, is never more than one sentence. When a child cannot pronounce a word, that word is written on the board, and all students share strategies for decoding it until a group consensus emerges about the correct decoding.

Children are also taught note-taking strategies as they listen to the oral autobiography. They are encouraged to listen for the main idea and important details. Then while progress monitoring measures are collected, they write summaries of their notes from listening, and they play word and board games.

Next, students have opportunities to read science content material about nature that has been scanned into a computer. While students view the written text on the monitor, the computer program reads it orally to them. Then they reread it as often as they like while they take written notes. They are taught note-taking strategies to apply while they read and listen to the text. Then they are taught report-writing strategies to generate science reports. These integrated reading and writing activities at the text-level draw on their word-reading and word-spelling skills taught and practiced earlier in the lesson and prior lessons.

Collectively, the activities in the John Muir lessons (see Berninger & Wolf, 2009, Unit III) provide learning opportunities for integrating heard aural language through the ears, oral production of language through the mouth, visual input of written language through the eyes, and graphomotor output of written language through the hands. This mutimodal (multisensorimotor modes, not just multisensory; see Chapters 4–6) integration is needed for coordinating the four language systems (Liberman, 1999) that underlie reading comprehension, note taking, and report writing in content areas. Most school assignments in fourth grade and above require such integrated reading and writing.

Sequoyah Reading-Writers Workshop (Unit IV)

This lesson set uses the hope theme of Sequoyah, the Cherokee Native American who, despite being physically disabled and a nonreader, at age 50 created a written language for recording the oral language of the Cherokee. As a result, Cherokee is one of the only Native American languages that has been preserved through a written language system. During these lessons, students listen to the song "Talking Leaves" recorded by Johnny Cash (n.d.) about Sequoyah, who taught his people that ideas could be written down.

The warm-up for this lesson set begins with the group chanting *Talking Letters* alphabetic principle correspondences in the reading direction, as in the Word Detectives lessons. Total time for the group is recorded to monitor improved speed from one session to the next. Next, phonological awareness activities are used for counting the number of syllables and phonemes in spoken words, as used in the John Muir lessons. Then children are asked to pronounce pseudowords to apply phonological awareness and automatic letter–sound correspondences to decode them. Both accuracy and time for decoding these pseudowords are recorded on growth graphs, which are inspected from one session to the next to determine if accuracy is going up and time is going down (Berninger & Abbott, 2003, Reproducibles). Children like this visible record that they can examine as evidence that they are making progress.

Over the course of these lessons, children read two books (see the *Helping Students with Dyslexia and Dysgraphia* workbook; Berninger & Wolf, 2009). Workshop lessons specify the questions for the teacher to ask in guiding silent and oral reading in the first award-winning book about Sequoyah and his accomplishments. Note the comparable kind of explicit questioning at different levels of language in the teacher perspective sections in Chapters 3 and 4. The content of this beautifully illustrated book, which is written in English and Cherokee, provides insights into *linguistic science:* Written language is talk written down with visual symbols that stand for speech sounds. Some of the text is read in choral readings to emphasize the relationship between oral language melody and written language structures. The integration of reading and writing is taught by having children write summaries of what they read in personal journals. Strategies for finding the main idea and supporting details to include in these summaries are taught.

The second book introduces children to *cultural anthropology.* Life in an Iroquois village before the American Revolution is compared with life in contemporary America. Children read selected parts of the book that are scanned into computers and displayed on the monitor while a voice reads the text orally. Next, children practice rereading the text orally to develop oral reading fluency. Then, they apply note-taking strategies to write notes in their journal about the text. Finally, they add their own thoughts and reflections about the text they read. In later lessons they learn how to use their journal writing about the book they are reading to write a book report to share their views of the book with others. In the process they learn much about Native American culture.

GRAMMAR OF TEACHING READING, WRITING, AND INTEGRATED READING-WRITING

These lessons illustrate a grammar of teaching reading and writing that can be applied to teaching all students including those with dyslexia, OWL LD, and/or dysgraphia, because instruction takes into account all the necessary processes that the learner has to coordinate during learning.

Teaching Reading

The syntax for generating effective reading instruction across curriculum materials involves the following components:

- Automatic grapheme–phoneme correspondences in the alphabetic principle (orthographic-phonological maps)

- Reflective awareness of the alternations for different phonemes that may correspond to the same grapheme

- Attention strategies for finding grapheme units in written words that may be larger than a single letter and include nonadjacent letters as in the silent *e*

- Reflective activities that develop awareness of phonological, orthographic, and morphological word forms and their parts and coordination of these word forms and their parts (orthographic, phonological, morphological word-form maps)

- Transfer of the automatic alphabetic principle and word-form awareness and coordination to decoding unknown words alone and in text (orthographic-phonological, morphological word-form maps)

- Teacher-guided and independent, self-guided practice in reading real words in interesting, meaningful text to develop fluent oral and silent reading for meaning (integrating triple word-form maps with activated semantic information in association networks and categories in long-term memory)

- Strategies for developing reading comprehension based on 1) morphological word forms that build bridges between vocabulary meaning and syntax in text; 2) background knowledge in long-term memory; 3) stated information in text; 4) inferences that go beyond what is stated and relate that to background knowledge; 5) abstracted discourse schema for organizing content; 6) summaries of the main ideas and supporting details; and 7) generation of implications, extensions, and elaborations of text

- Reading for pleasure on one's own or as part of a reading club that reads and discusses common books

- Hope themes for students who have to exert more effort than others to learn to read

- Strategies for dealing with problems in paying attention to written language, dealing with timing issues in working memory, and impaired executive functions

Teaching Writing

The syntax for generating effective writing instruction across curriculum materials involves the following components:

- Generating ideas and planning

- Translating those ideas into language at the word level, the sentence syntax level, and the discourse-level genre (narrative, expository-informational, compare and contrast, and persuasive essays)

- Transcribing the language into writing at word level through automatic and strategic letter writing (handwriting) and word spelling

- Reviewing and revising during planning and translating

Teaching Integrated Reading-Writing

The syntax for teaching integrated reading-writing across curriculum materials involves the following components:

- Automatic application of the alphabetic principle in reading direction

- Strategic application of coordination among phonological, orthographic, and morphological word forms and their parts in reading direction

- Strategic application of internal comprehension strategies at the word level (vocabulary meaning via semantics), sentence syntax level, and discourse-level schema to link language and cognition (including background knowledge, inferences about presuppositions and implications of stated language, abstracting main ideas and supporting details, summarization, and elaboration) or *these same comprehension strategies externalized through writing*

- Generation of written text at the same levels as comprehension for varied purposes, including writing about read texts and reading written texts

Intellectual and Hands-On Engagement and Play with Language

Common syntax for teaching reading, writing, and integrated reading-writing recognizes the importance of creating lessons that keep children engaged intellectually. The content themes that pervade all of the lesson described in this chapter are designed to provide that grade-appropriate intellectual engagement. Older students with dyslexia protest if they think all they will be taught is baby phonics; they seem to sense when they have not responded to instruction that contains only phonics. Students with dyslexia also need multimodal instruction including hands-on activities; use of hands engages the frontal attentional system and may improve students' abilities to attend to written language. Moreover, no matter what aspect of language may pose challenges for individual students—phonology, morphology, syntax, semantics (word retrieval)—they benefit from word play including humor, riddles, and puns (e.g., see Berninger & Abbott, 2003, Lesson Sets 6, 7, 9, 10, 13, 14, and 15). Rules are best taught as metacognitive strategies to be applied reflectively when stuck on a word rather than as rote knowledge. Automatic alphabetic principle is best taught as procedural knowledge (through naming and writing) with options rather than as declarative, factual knowledge without options. Ultimately, effective treatment does not allow students to think they cannot learn to decode words or spell because English is hopelessly irregular.

Orchestrating Mental Processes in Reading, Writing, and Integrated Reading-Writing in Conscious Working Memory

All of these processes, which may be on their own time scales, must be orchestrated in real time (Bowers & Wolf, 1993; Breznitz, 2006; Minsky, 1986; Posner, Petersen, Fox, & Raichle, 1988; Wolf, 2001) in conscious working memory. To the extent that some of the processes are automatic (outside of conscious awareness), conscious working memory may be able to coordinate these processes in real time. However, reading, writing, and integrated reading and writing do not rely only on automatic processing. Resource-draining and capacity-limited working memory is needed to support the conscious mental activity underlying reading comprehension and written composition. These higher order, meaning-driven skills draw automatically on some mental processes but flexibly on many language, cognitive, and memory components, and speed, per se, does not differentiate what is automatic outside of conscious awareness and what is reflective in conscious awareness—strategic processing can be fast (Berninger & Nagy, 2008).

For many students, these various component processes in implicit (outside) and explicit (inside) conscious working memory are acquired with ease in response to the typical instructional and learning activities in the reading and writing program for their grade level (e.g., Connor, Morrison, & Katch, 2004). For students with disorders such as dyslexia, OWL LD, and/or dysgraphia, the language codes for orthographic, phonological, and morphological word forms and their parts, the loops for coordinating them, and/or the executive functions for orchestrating all these processes in real time may be impaired. These children can learn to read, write, and integrate reading and writing, but they are more dependent than other children on the nature of the instruction provided for facilitating self-regulation of this orchestration process through explicit, teacher-guided other-regulation. General and special education teachers who succeed in providing this kind of quality instruction, which requires coordination of many mental processes in time, and results in expected reading and writing achievement, should be as greatly valued as the maestro orchestra conductor and the NASA ground control crew for their executive functions in other-regulation.

TEACHER REFLECTIONS ON CONTRIBUTIONS OF INSTRUCTIONAL RESEARCH

It is gratifying that so much of the instructional research is confirming what really works for teachers who were effective in teaching students who do not learn to read and write as easily as their classmates. The recent work extends the earlier focus on multisensory-only to oral language (see Chapter 3) and motor output or production (see Chapters 4, 5, 6, and 7) as well. Many master teachers know that implicitly, but it is important for education professionals to become more aware of this new knowledge and discuss how they do or plan to incorporate it in their teaching practices. The notion of teaching students strategies for regulating their own independent learning when teachers are not available to guide them is an important concept that needs to be emphasized more. This notion is not the same as expecting students to self-generate their own discovery process. It requires teaching explicit strategies that they can use on their own to self-manage their attention and learning while they work independently.

Over the years, research has provided information about teaching and learning that can be applied to improve teaching. At the same time, knowledge gained from teaching experience, especially with students who find learning to read and write challenging, could be a fruitful source of new research studies. The conversation should not always be in the researcher-to-teacher direction. The teacher-to-researcher direction is equally important. Teachers might collaborate with researchers in helping to define the instructional issues that really need to be investigated and how the research questions might be conceptualized to be maximally useful to teachers. Most teachers do not want to be researchers; however, many do want to use evidence-based instructional methods. Some would also like to become collaborators with researchers by contributing to the framing of the research questions, interpreting significance of results for practice, and applying knowledge gained.

CONCLUSION

Instructional research has validated many different effective approaches for teaching students with dyslexia, OWL LD, and/or dysgraphia. Some of these are discussed in this chapter. Research about effective instruction has revealed a common theme: It is important to develop three kinds of linguistic awareness—awareness of the phonological, orthographic, and morphological properties of words. It is also important to develop syntactic and discourse awareness. Language is a complex skill that has to be understood at many different levels or units of language. In addition, because many students with reading and/or writing disabilities have weaknesses in working memory, teachers should also provide instructional activities that help them develop automatic word recognition and spelling and fluent oral reading and written composition. Accomplishing this goal requires teacher attention to not only what is taught but also how the instruction is delivered in time and the children's performance is monitored to provide daily feedback as to whether they are reaching their accuracy and time goals.

CHAPTER 10

Creating Building-Level Plans for Teaching All Students Effectively and Efficiently

This chapter provides practical recommendations for organizing instructional delivery, based on teaching and instructional research experience, which can be applied in any school or school district. The following three goals help achieve this purpose.

1. Convince general education teachers that they *can* teach students with dyslexia, oral and written language learning disability (OWL LD), and/or dysgraphia.

2. Help these students gain access to general education curriculum.

3. Create a building infrastructure to achieve the first and second goals.

In this chapter, some general issues are considered in planning to meet these goals. Then, a separate section is devoted to practical strategies that can be implemented to achieve each goal.

Explain to general education teachers how they can contribute in a positive way to the education of students with dyslexia, OWL LD, and/or dysgraphia. The educational needs of these students can often be met in the general education classroom (least restrictive environment, which should always be tried first according to IDEA) if teachers are alert to the signs of dyslexia, OWL LD, and dysgraphia; and refer students for appropriate assessment to determine if such a diagnosis is warranted. (See Chapter 8 for questions to pose to assessment specialists on the multidisciplinary team.) If a diagnosis is warranted, collaborate with members of the multidisciplinary team in planning an appropriate educational program for the student. Special education pull-out services are not always necessary to meet a student's instructional needs and should be considered a last resort. Nevertheless, diagnosis is needed if an educationally disabling condition exists so that 1) necessary instructional components in handwriting, spelling, word decoding, automatic reading, oral reading fluency, reading comprehension, and/or morphological and syntactic awareness are identified and implemented; and 2) a student qualifies for 504 accommodations, which may be needed in addition to free appropriate public education under the Individuals with Disabilities Education Act (IDEA) Amendments of 2004 (PL 108-446).

Discuss among professional staff the various options a school might consider for providing an appropriate instructional program for students with dyslexia, OWL LD, and/or dysgraphia. Chapter 2 emphasized the importance of organizing instructional groups on the basis of instructional levels. However, the nature of the specific learning disability and the student's individual profile of strengths and weaknesses should be considered in planning appropriate educational programs for students with specific learning disabilities (see Chapter 5). As many as one in five students may have or be at risk for specific learning disabilities, which comprise the highest incidence of educationally disabling conditions in school-age populations; that is, special education pull-out services are not available for that many students. Thus, program planning may need to occur at the building level as well as individual classroom level.

Consider these issues in creating a plan that will serve the needs of all students in a building, including those with specific learning disabilities affecting written language acquisition. At a building level, the goal is to optimize the learning of all students including but not restricted to those with specific learning disabilities. Such a plan may need to make wise use of both general education and special education resources, both of which are limited, in order to meet the needs of all students. However, children who are learning English as a second language or who come from homes that have not provided many literacy experiences may also benefit from the kinds of instructional experiences that help students with dyslexia, OWL LD, and/or dysgraphia. Many students may be helped by differentiated instruction, and many teachers are gratified to learn they can meet the instructional needs of students with dyslexia, OWL LD, and dysgraphia and at the same time meet the needs of all the other students in the class.

GOAL 1: CONTRIBUTION OF GENERAL EDUCATION TEACHERS

Each of the sections that follow contains additional information for addressing the three goals outlined at the beginning of this chapter.

Challenges in Meeting the Needs of Diverse Learners

In the authors' experience, educators want to teach all of the students in their classes, but educators often do not know how to deal with the individual differences among students in general. General education teachers often wonder whether devoting instructional time to those with learning differences will interfere with the teacher's ability to spend sufficient time with the other students in the class. Often they report not feeling adequately prepared by their professional training programs for the daunting task of teaching students with learning disabilities or other problems. Organizational plans are discussed later in this chapter for general educators to use in teaching reading and writing to all students in general education, including those with dyslexia, OWL LD, and/or dysgraphia.

Advantages of Having Students with
Learning Disabilities in the General Education Program

Why should general education teachers want to teach reading and writing to students with dyslexia, OWL LD, and/or dysgraphia? One reason is that these students are intelligent and can contribute to the intellectual climate of the classroom while benefiting from access to the general curriculum. They may excel in areas of the curriculum that are not as dependent on reading and writing, such as math, science, social studies, art, music, athletics, or drama. Some are even talented in written expression of ideas despite severe handwriting or spelling problems. Research on adult outcomes has shown that many individuals with dyslexia become successful adults, especially if they had family and other social supports along the way (e.g., Goldberg, Higgins, Raskind, & Herman, 2003; Raskind, Goldberg, Higgins, & Herman, 1999). Despite the success stories that often appear in the media, however, not all students with dyslexia and related learning disabilities are successful as adults. If not treated effectively, learning disabilities can compromise quality of life in adulthood. Often, having a caring teacher who tries to understand a student's struggles can make a difference in the student's ability to deal with learning challenges both during and after school (Gilger & Wilkins, 2008; Yates, Berninger, & Abbott, 1994).

Also some students are twice exceptional—they may be intellectually gifted but also have learning disabilities (Craggs, Sanchez, Kibby, Gilger, & Hynd, 2006; Gilger, Hynd, & Wilkins, 2008; Gilger, & Wilkins, 2008). They need both intellectually stimulating instruction and specialized instruction for their dyslexia, OWL LD, and/or dysgraphia in the general program.

Some researchers believe that brain differences that compromise written language learning may confer special talents in other cognitive abilities to individuals with specific learning disabilities such as dyslexia. However, the University of Washington Multidisciplinary Learning Disabilities Center's research has not supported this hypothesis. Children with and without dyslexia did not differ on visual tasks in a virtual reality, science problem-solving summer program; however, the students with dyslexia were slower than those without dyslexia in their rate of performance on these visual tasks (Winn et al., 2006). Individuals with dyslexia may indeed have special talents, but these talents are by virtue of genetic inheritance, independent of the genes for dyslexia, and environmental experiences. This is why psychologists do not refer to students with dyslexia as *dyslexics*, but rather call them *students with dyslexia*. Individuals are not defined by their disability. A student may have a disability, but it is in the context of many other dimensions of his or her personality and profile of relative strengths and weaknesses.

Access to the General Curriculum

Children with specific learning disabilities require access to the general curriculum to grow intellectually and develop in age-appropriate ways. Leaving the general program can disrupt their learning. Alternative ways exist to teach content of curriculum integrated with explicit reading, writing, and integrated reading-writing instruction. The authors hope that this book provides teachers with practical ideas for teaching not only reading and writing to students with reading and writing problems but also content subject areas of the curriculum (see Chapter 9 and the companion workbook, *Helping Students with Dyslexia and Dysgraphia Make Connections: Differentiated Instruction Lesson Plans in Reading and Writing* [Berninger & Wolf, 2009]). Reading and writing instruction can also be integrated with teaching word problems in math or drama (e.g., reading and acting out play scripts).

A fifth grader moving from a school for students with dyslexia, of which the second author was the principal, to a public school summed up his dreams this way:

What I want in my new school is good teachers that explain things and take time to help. . . that would give me support if I'm stuck on something. I hope they have someone special to help with special needs. I want classes to be fun but educational.

Despite reading and writing problems, students with learning disabilities can learn from being in the general education classroom if teachers do not rely solely on lecturing, reading assignments, and writing assessments and draw on a variety of other instructional approaches to make learning interesting and fun.

GOAL 2: MODELS FOR ORGANIZING INSTRUCTIONAL DELIVERY IN GENERAL EDUCATION

The organizational plans that follow require collaboration among educators across individual classrooms within a school building. For many of these models, students can be taught in the general instructional program.

Cross-Grade Instructional Groups During the Language Arts Block

For the "walk about," as it is often called, teachers remain in their classrooms while children walk to another classroom during the regular language arts block of the school day. This model of service delivery allows teachers across a single or multiple grades to provide reading and writing instruction at students' instructional levels more efficiently. One teacher may have only one or two students at a particular instructional level, but across classrooms within the grade or across two or three grade levels, there may be 8–10 students at that instructional level. Each teacher may be responsible for one or, at most, two instructional groups during this language arts block, which should be scheduled at the same time for all students in the general program.

This walk about model requires initial assessment to determine instructional levels at the beginning of the school year and reassessment at midyear to determine if adjustments in instructional groups are needed (see Chapter 2). Paraprofessionals and other professionals in the building (e.g., school psychologists, special education teachers, speech and language specialists) may assist classroom teachers in the initial and midyear assessment. The advantage of this approach is that more students receive reading and writing instruction at their instructional level without being stigmatized by being pulled out of the general program. All students participate and may change classrooms. They are all taught reading and writing at the same time, including those who excel at reading and writing. No stigma is attached to walking about to find one's reading or integrated reading-writing group. Although this approach requires more preplanning and cross-school collaboration, it typically makes the teaching load more manageable and allows teachers to provide instruction to more students at their appropriate instructional levels. See Chapter 2 for additional discussion of instructional levels.

Continuous Structured Language Class in General Education Grades 1–12

An innovative approach that has been adopted by a few school districts in Washington State beginning in the 1960s is based on recognition that some students, because of genetically based language learning problems, require explicit language-based instruction in all areas of the curriculum throughout the school day and throughout their public school years. At each grade level, one class is set aside in which the teacher provides highly explicit, language-based instruction across the curriculum. Parents can request that their child be assigned to this class, which is open not only to students with learning disabilities but also to other students who benefit from this kind of instruction for a variety of reasons; for example, children who come from low-literacy homes or are English language learners also benefit from explicit, hands-on, intellectually engaging instruction. The other classes at the same grade level provide traditional educational experiences. Parents and students with learning disabilities tend to like the option of choosing a class that offers structured language instruction. These students are typically bright and thrive better in these classes, but some parents and professionals are confused why this option in general education is needed. One reason is that the student can receive a structured program that teaches to all levels of language in an integrated fashion on a daily basis (see Chapter 2) in contrast to a special education pull-out program which requires that the child miss some of the regular program and offers instruction that may not be well integrated with the rest of the instructional program. Children with dyslexia, OWL LD, and/or dysgraphia often fail to respond to piecemeal, fragmented instruction that does not help them to integrate all the processes in a coordinated way. However, if the purpose was better articulated and appropriate professional development were provided for the teachers in this classroom, this approach may be an effective, resource-efficient way to provide appropriate services in grades K–12.

Four Models for Schoolwide Language Arts Instruction

Next, we discuss four models that schools might consider on a schoolwide basis to provide explicit, structured, and integrated instruction in reading, writing, and related oral language skills. These include 1) a language arts block in which all classes at one or several grade levels offer reading and writing instruction at the same time, and in which children are grouped by instructional level and taught by the teacher assigned to that instructional level (rather than to a particular classroom); 2) a special section in a required language arts course in which all students in a certain grade enroll; 3) tutoring before or after school; and 4) summer school programs. At the end of this section we consider staffing issues in implementing these models.

Language Arts Block   This model requires a team approach in which all teachers at one or several grade levels agree to teach reading and writing at the same time every day and collaborate in 1) identifying each student's instructional level, 2) forming instructional groups for students with similar instructional levels, 3) assigning these groups to specific teachers, and 4) having students leave their regular classroom and go to another classroom for reading and writing instruction unless the group to which they are assigned happens to be their regular classroom. By teaming with colleagues, teachers are able to offer differentiated instruction on a larger scale than if they attempted to do so only in their own classrooms. Students benefit because more students at a particular instructional level are likely to exist across classes than in a single class, and thus students receive instruction more closely tailored to where they are in their literacy development. This model does not preclude teachers also providing some literacy enrichment activities for all students in their class at other times of the day. For specific suggestions on identifying students' instructional levels and providing differentiated instruction to different instructional groups, see Chapter 2. This model, which seems to be growing in popularity and is used increasingly in schools where the authors live, requires enormous commitment, communication, and professional collaboration among all building staff than other models, but the payoff in terms of student learning outcomes and professional satisfaction can be great. Not only classroom teachers but also paraprofessionals and parent or grandparent volunteers may participate if supervised by an experienced, certified teacher. However, this model is generally implemented only in elementary schools and not in middle or high schools for practical reasons (e.g., scheduling).

Language Arts Section   In middle schools and high schools, students generally are required to take at least one language arts course per year. This course may cover reading and writing but also literature. Because instruction in the upper grades is delivered by multiple teachers as students switch from class to class during the day, multiple sections of language arts are typically scheduled. Not all sections for the same subject are taught at the same time, and students have to by necessity sign up for a section of a required course. In this model, one of these sections can cover the same content as the others but provide all instruction in more explicit, structured, and systematic lessons, which students with dyslexia, OWL LD, and/or dysgraphia need more than peers without these specific learning disabilities require. No stigma in attending special pull-out classes is attached for those in the more explicit language arts section. It happens during a regularly scheduled section and is equally engaging intellectually. Other students may also choose this alternative approach. Also, providing such explicit language arts instruction within the general education program is more cost effective than small group pull-outs at this age level. This model can be so popular among students, parents, and teachers that, depending on buildingwide needs, more than one section of language arts may be designated for explicit, structured, systematic, intellectually engaging language arts instruction. However, the success of this model depends on assigning to the special section(s) one or more teachers who are well trained, knowledgeable, and effective in providing this kind of language arts instruction.

Before- or After-School Tutoring   Some schools have instituted before- or after-school tutoring to assist those students who struggle more than classmates in reading or writing. In some schools, extra tutoring is provided by paraprofessionals or parent, grandparent, or community volunteers under the supervision of a general or special education teacher, reading specialist, or school psychologist. If a school is located near a college or university, tutors from the federally sponsored America Reads program may be available to provide tutoring. The America Reads program supports college students who qualify for financial assistance to earn as they learn by providing tutoring to children in local schools. The tutors are supervised and given training by a designated university official.

The biggest challenge with before- and after-school tutoring is providing transportation for students to arrive at school earlier or leave later. Sometimes the parent teacher association raises money to provide transportation for students whose families cannot afford it. Sometimes transportation is provided as part of after-school child care for working parents. After-school tutoring should be scheduled in conjunction with a student's other after-school activities (e.g., sports, scouting, community activities, playtime with friends).

Tutoring does not have to be one-to-one, with one tutor for each student. In fact, children often enjoy working in small groups more than being singled out for individual assistance. It can be reassuring to them that others need special help too. Also, children typically enjoy the social interactions with others during the learning activities. One study found that second graders who participated in after-school reading clubs did better than controls on the state standards in reading fluency (see Lesson Set 9, Berninger & Abbott, 2003), and fourth graders who participated in writing clubs did better than controls on the state's high-stakes test in writing (see Lesson Set 10, Berninger & Abbott, 2003).

Tutoring may occur at school or in other setting. Some parents, for example, choose to hire private tutors. However, asking parents to hire a private tutor is not an acceptable alternative to providing free, appropriate education for students with educationally disabling conditions under IDEA 2004. Whenever students receive instruction outside of their usual classrooms, teachers and the remediation specialists must maintain close communication to ensure understanding of specific learning needs and consistent classroom follow up.

Special Summer Programs Some school districts offer summer programs for students who are not at grade level in reading or writing. These can be as effective as extra help during the regular school year. Some children do require extra time to learn the same skills as their classmates do.

Staffing Plans Each school in the case of the first three models and the school district for the fourth model will need to decide how to allocate professional resources to implement the model chosen to serve students with specific learning disabilities affecting written language acquisition. Schools vary greatly in access to special kinds of professional expertise such as school psychology and speech-language pathology for assistance in implementing these models. Many schools have reading specialists. However, as pointed out by Barbara Efrè at the University of Padua and Verona, Italy, to the first author (B. Efrè, personal communication, September 21, 2008), although the schools she observed during her graduate student global exchange experience in the United States had reading specialists, none had writing specialists. Moreover, speech and language specialists have more training in oral language than in written language or literacy.

Another issue is that, in general, teachers are trained to teach rather than perform diagnostic or individualized assessments, and psychologists are trained to assess individuals but not usually to provide instructional interventions. As a result, links between assessment and intervention are not always clear to an interdisciplinary team. One staffing model that might facilitate a buildingwide implementation of the four models would be to create positions for more broadly prepared learning specialists to integrate assessment and instructional interventions.

Learning specialists would receive preservice training in oral and written language, psychology, and curriculum and instruction and acquire supervised experience in both assessment and teaching. They would have to demonstrate at least 5 years of successful teaching experience before being appointed as the learning specialist in a school. Both their preservice and in-service professional development would equip them with professional skills to provide group and individual assessments in oral language, reading, and writing and to plan, conduct, and evaluate individualized instruction in group settings in the same domains. Sometimes these interdisciplinary learning specialists would supervise the teachers or paraprofessionals in providing assessment and instructional services. Interdisciplinary learning specialists would also be available for ongoing consultation with any teacher for any student as learning problems in literacy (and numeracy) might arise during the school year.

Partnerships with College or University Training Programs or State-Funded Centers

If a school is located near a college or university, administrators may be able to create partnerships with universities to secure additional help in serving students with learning disabilities. For example, if a teacher training program is nearby, part of the student teaching experience could include supervised practica in local schools for teaching students with dyslexia, OWL LD, and/or dysgraphia. An experienced teacher with expertise in the kind of specialized instruction needed would supervise the practica. As a result of such partnerships, students with learning disabilities benefit from extra help while the student teachers are better prepared after graduation to teach students with learning disabilities in their own classrooms. Some states have model programs that partner special university-based centers with local schools (see Chapter 12).

GOAL 3: ISSUES TO CONSIDER

Multidisciplinary Collaboration and Planning

Serving students with written language disabilities requires the support services of an interdisciplinary team, coordination of general and special education teachers, and cooperation of building principals and district administrators. Scaling up to increasing the number of students served entails creating building- and district-level plans to serve the needs of students with dyslexia, OWL LD, and/or dysgraphia in general education. All team members should be involved in making building-level plans. Teachers in local schools as well as district-level administrators should be involved in making district-level plans (see Dunn & Miller, in press). These plans should include recommendations for mentoring administrators on recent research developments and the unmet needs, despite federal reading initiatives and special education, of many students with dyslexia, OWL LD, and/or dysgraphia. General education teachers who teach students with these specific learning disabilities require professional development support from their buildings and districts.

Contribution of Skilled Managers

The principal, department head, or curriculum coordinator at the school has knowledge of students, staff, and curriculum that allows the administrator to make developmentally appropriate decisions about literacy instruction that encompass a broad range of variables. The decisions affect scheduling, space assignments, budgeting, and placement of students with appropriate teachers. The Florida Center for Reading Research (http://www.fcrr.org) provides resources to assist administrators in making such decisions.

Implementation of building- and district-level plans requires adequate resources: staff, time, space, materials, and financial support and plans for managing these. Provision of adequate time is dependent on decisions about student, teacher, support staff, and administrative schedules and allows for team meetings, inservice training time, progress monitoring, evaluation, and record keeping. Adequate time and support allows teachers to concentrate their efforts on instruction rather than paperwork. Space or lack of it often dictates the model or plan selected. There must be space for both whole-group and small-group intervention and tutoring. If technology is part of the intervention, the space must have provision for the necessary electronic equipment. Parents and staff need space to confer and plan. Volunteers need space for materials and to carry out their work.

Class Configurations

Some students, especially those with executive function problems, need highly structured teachers, whereas other students respond more readily to an open-ended, less structured approach. Some students work well in small groups, but others do not. Matching teachers and learners on their tolerance of and need for highly structured versus open-ended learning environments can facilitate instruction and learning.

Buildingwide Commitment

Serving students with dyslexia in the general education program requires that the entire staff recognizes the individual needs of each student and provides for those students at both ends of the spectrum—both those who are advanced and those who struggle to keep up with classmates. When each staff member accepts responsibility for the success of every child and participates in planning, opportunities increase for all students to succeed.

Three-Tier Models

Many schools have begun adopting a three-tier approach to service delivery. The first two tiers are implemented within general education, and the third tier is implemented within special education.

Within tier 1, all students receive structured, sequential, multimodal instruction in the core curriculum. All students interact with each other in the general education classroom and can learn from one another. Because student strengths and weaknesses vary from one activity to another, each student has an opportunity to excel. This model requires that all staff members possess a broad range of skills in both methodology and the ability to individualize. It requires a perceptive teacher who constantly evaluates student responses and individualizes instruction accordingly within a given lesson by adjusting the difficulty of material or mode of support from one student to another. This support may be unobtrusive allowing students to find success at their own rates. No child should be at a disadvantage in this model because strong students can strengthen or extend their skills within the lesson while students with dyslexia receive the instruction they need.

Within tier 2, pull-out supplementary instruction is provided in general education. Classroom groups of at-risk students who have not responded adequately to core curriculum are given additional help. Sometimes they receive additional help with the core curriculum. Sometimes they receive instruction with programs designed for struggling readers or writers in general. Many schools attempt to keep class sizes slightly smaller for these students, as they may need more time for specialized help. In this model, students are assigned a time to work with teacher aides, paraprofessionals, or reading specialists. Whoever delivers the instruction should be well trained in the nature and methods of supplementary instruction that are likely to be effective for struggling readers and writers.

Within tier 3, which is provided only to students who fail to respond adequately to tier 2 supplementary services, comprehensive assessment is performed to evaluate why the student is not responding and determine if the student qualifies for special education services. Tier 3, in contrast to the first two tiers in general education, is special education. If a child qualifies for special education, the child receives an individualized education program, which indicates where the specialized instruction will occur—in the pull-out resource room or in the general education classroom.

The three-tier model may not meet the needs of all students. For example, a student with OWL LD who needs oral language therapy along with literacy instruction may not receive assessment that diagnoses this language learning disability until third or fourth grade, after chronic struggles for several years. An alternative approach is to screen all kindergartners and first graders for the research-supported indicators of who is at risk for dyslexia, OWL LD, and/or dysgraphia and make certain that supplementary instruction is in place from the beginning to prevent reading and writing disabilities (see Berninger, 2007).

Three-tier models are not new. Originally, many school districts adopted a preventive approach in which children were screened in kindergarten or first grade and placed with a Slingerland-trained teacher. The goal was to identify and intervene before children failed. In this model, from 25% to 30% of the students with difficulties ranging from mild to severe were placed with trained teachers. The teachers used the Slingerland teaching approach (see Chapters 3 and 4) and the district-adopted curriculum in conventional class-size groupings. The difference was in the mode of instruction. By the end of third grade, few students needed continued services, but in some cases, classes had to continue in the intermediate grades. Most of the students in these classes had more severe problems or had entered the school districts after the early grades when prevention programs were offered. With early intervention, students avoided failure and fewer students were referred for individual testing. Some districts offered summer training for teachers but left implementation to building or teacher discretion. This approach did not provide the continuity of instruction from grade to grade, but it did enrich teachers' skills and benefit the students with whom they worked. Nevertheless, schoolwide professional development of teachers may be critical to the success of any tier 1 and tier 2 prevention approach.

CONCLUSION

Providing effective education for all students requires skilled management; a buildingwide commitment to the recognition, identification, and instruction of students with dyslexia, dysgraphia, and OWL LD; building plans for teacher training, class configuration, and grouping for individual needs and instruction; and continued teacher education that includes mentoring and keeping abreast of current research in the field of oral and written language, including reading, writing, and spelling.

Professional Development for Blending Science and Educational Practice

[T]raining seems inadequate if we expect teachers to be able to. . . individualize instruction in order to optimize reading and writing achievement for all students. . . Inservice workshops provide continuing education for teachers but do not eliminate the need for better preservice education. Few of us would want to be operated on by a physician with two courses in surgery and a smattering of continuing education courses.

Reading and Writing Acquisition: A Developmental Neuropsychological Perspective (Berninger, 1994a, p. 62)

Preservice Teacher Education

Teaching is what teachers do—what they say and write verbally and communicate nonverbally and how they structure learning activities and situations for teacher-directed explicit instruction and student-guided learning and discovery. Learning is what students do in response to teaching—what they say and write verbally and communicate nonverbally or how they behave in learning activities and teacher-directed or student-guided situations. Teaching and learning are not unrelated, but they are not the same. Preservice teachers must be prepared both to teach and assess learning in response to instruction.

Effective teachers must become knowledgeable about the following during their preservice education:

- Domains of child development: cognition and memory, receptive and expressive language, gross and fine motor skills, attention and executive function, and social and emotional function

- Brain development

- Content-specific knowledge across the curriculum

- Normal sequences of skill acquisition in each of the developmental and academic learning domains

- Normal variation and developmental and learning disorders in these domains

- Research findings about effective instructional practices for typically developing students and those with learning differences in specific areas of the curriculum

Cognition involves thinking and specific intellectual abilities. Aural language through the ear requires listening (receptive language), and oral language through the mouth requires speaking (expressive language, which is not the same as speech articulation or producing sounds, and includes words, syntactic structures, and discourse organizational schemes). Gross motor skills involve the large muscles in the arms and legs, whereas fine motor skills involve the small muscles in the hands and fingers and mouth. Attention and executive functions regulate focusing (on what is relevant and suppressing what is not relevant), staying on task, switching tasks, and self-regulating observable behaviors including activity level and impulsive acts. Social function refers to interpersonal awareness and interactions. Emotional function refers to the affect that is experienced, which may range from negative affect such as fear, anxiety, and sadness to positive affect such as pleasure, joy, and happiness.

Within each of these developmental domains, students show normal variation in the stepping stones of development. Preservice education should prepare teachers to identify variation that is outside the normal range and represents learning differences or disorders. Reading and writing, like listening and speaking, are language systems. When word decoding, reading, and spelling fall outside the normal range, a student may have dyslexia. When word reading and reading comprehension fall outside the normal range, a student may have oral and written language learning disability (OWL LD). When handwriting and/or spelling skills fall outside the normal range, a student may have dysgraphia. Students with learning disabilities involving written language require modification of instruction in the reading and writing programs and sometimes in other areas of the curriculum that require reading and writing. Yet, these students are capable of learning the content and other skills in the academic domains of the curriculum. However, they may learn best in learning environments that are intellectually engaging with many opportunities for hands-on learning activities that allow them to actively manipulate objects and materials in problem solving and creative expression.

Teachers need to understand the characteristic developmental sequences, their normal as well as atypical variation, and the normal ebb and flow with periodic plateaus, regressions, and advancement. Such knowledge will allow teachers, once they are in their own classrooms, to 1) design and implement age- and grade-appropriate instruction, 2) tailor instruction to individual students' unique profiles of strengths and weaknesses across the developmental and academic domains, 3) set reasonable levels of expected achievement in these domains of development and academic learning, and 4) evaluate whether response to instruction is appropriate for age and grade. Effective teachers will begin to learn during preservice professional development how to assess individual students' response to instruction and evaluate when it is necessary to reteach and provide scaffolding over hurdles. The Chapter 11 appendix contains a list of recommended readings and instructional resources that might be used in preservice teacher education to prepare prospective teachers for teaching literacy to students who exhibit wide ranging individual differences.

Classes in teaching methods alone, however, do not prepare prospective teachers to be successful in helping all students learn; teachers also need supervised experiences in teaching and putting research into practice (Uhry & Goodman, in press). Such tailored instruction is best learned under the guidance of a mentoring supervisor during preservice practica in 1) tutoring students with learning differences, 2) small-group instruction with typically developing students and those with learning differences, and 3) student teaching in classrooms in real-world school settings.

Brain structures and functions change across infancy, early childhood, middle childhood, and adolescence. These changes may influence response to instruction and learning—interfering with or facilitating acquisition of age- and grade-appropriate knowledge and skills. The brain mediates response to instruction—what is attended, how it is processed and understood in the context of existing knowledge and skills, and whether appropriate responses can be constructed to demonstrate that learning has occurred (Berninger & Richards, 2008b). Rarely are preservice teachers given coursework on the brain, its development, and its role in learning. Berninger and Richards (2002) wrote *Brain Literacy for Educators and Psychologists*, which can be used by preservice teachers as a textbook for formal coursework on the brain or by preservice or in-service teachers as a reference book for self-study about the brain and its role in academic learning. Knowledge of the brain lays the foundation for understanding variation—no two brains are alike (see Figures 1 and 2 in Berninger & Richards, 2008a)—and learning differences such as dyslexia, OWL LD, and dysgraphia. Knowledge of the brain, coupled with the growing body of research-supported, evidence-based instruction (see McCardle & Miller, in press; Fletcher, Lyon, Fuchs, & Barnes, 2006) may also help teachers to design individualized instruction for students with learning differences in an era of educational accountability.

WHAT TEACHER SURVEYS TELL ABOUT UNMET PRESERVICE PREPARATION NEEDS

A 2006 report by the National Council on Teacher Quality (NCTQ), a nonprofit research and advocacy group dedicated to reforming the nation's teaching policies, reported that 85% of the nation's education schools were not educating future elementary teachers in the basic knowledge and skills necessary to teach children to read. The comprehensive report determined that few education schools teach prospective teachers the principles of good reading instruction. They concluded that most schools continue to teach ideas about approaches to reading instruction that years of scientific study have found to be ineffective with 40% of all children.

Education professors may be clinging to views and approaches from their own education and training, even though they are now outdated. Many are convinced that teaching the science of reading would mean having to "prescribe a single approach" to reading instruction rather than simply educating their students in the general knowledge of what alternative approaches a reading program should include. Or, the ones who have graduated more recently may believe in philosophical approaches to education that reject science and believe the role of preservice education is to prepare future educators who think deeply about issues rather than have technical expertise in implementing instructional methods. In addition, most of the available textbooks are authored by individuals who are not experts in the science of reading instruction.

As part of this study, NCTQ offered specific reform proposals in five different areas to address the lack of effective teaching for reading instruction:

1. State Governments/Departments of Education: In an effort to create more accountability for the five components of reading instruction, states should receive a mandate to develop stronger reading standards and teacher tests of knowledge of the science of reading and reading instruction.

2. Membership Organizations: Accrediting agencies such as the National Council for Accreditation of Teacher Education and the Teacher Education Accreditation Council should hold teacher education programs accountable for preparing aspiring teachers in the science of reading.

3. Textbook Publishers: Publishers should seek out experts in the science of reading to produce textbooks suitable for preparing teachers at the undergraduate levels.

4. The Federal Government: No Child Left Behind Act of 2001 (PL 107-110) reauthorizations should require states to implement a reading test requirement for

elementary teachers, in addition to the test of broad subject matter knowledge that is already required.

5. Teacher Preparation Programs: Tenured faculty who are not well versed in the science of reading should either not continue to teach reading or update their instruction accordingly.

The American Psychological Association (2006) surveyed in-service teachers nationally and asked them what they most wished their preservice training had included but did not. Responses indicated that teachers desired more preparation in teaching to individual differences and in learning the research, based on psychological science, regarding effective ways to teach. In-service teachers, who are increasingly being held accountable for student learning outcomes, were open to learning more about how science informs reading and writing acquisition.

MODEL PROGRAM FOR PRESERVICE, INTERDISCIPLINARY TRAINING IN LITERACY

Professors Diane Sawyer and Stuart Bernstein at Middle Tennessee State University have developed one of the first models of exemplary preparation for future trainers of preservice educators. As stated in the proposal for their state-approved and funded Ph.D. program in literacy studies, the purpose of this interdisciplinary program is to address one of education's most pressing needs, the shortage of scholars, practitioners, administrators, and policy-makers who can help bridge the gap between the rapidly expanding body of scientific research relevant to the development of literacy and the knowledge base on which educational practice, policy and professional preparation are based.

For further discussion of these issues of bridging the gap between research and educational practice, see Foorman and Nixon (2006). The interdisciplinary program developed by Sawyer and Bernstein (see Figure 11.1) provides a flexible framework of courses, field experiences, and opportunities for original research that will equip professionals with knowledge, insights, and skills essential to effectively address the lack of educators trained in evidence-based literacy instruction.

Experienced faculty from the College of Education and Behavioral Sciences and the College of Liberal Arts provide the coursework and supervise the research of the graduate students who take common core courses to provide a comprehensive understanding of literacy within biological, psychological, linguistic, social, developmental, learning, and motivation research. Students also take courses in one of the following four areas of specialization related to their dissertation research and electives: Literacy Instruction & Staff Development, Reading Disabilities/Dyslexia, Literacy Measurement & Analysis, and Administration/ Policy. They also participate in course-based, supervised field practica that expose them to a variety of environments in which research is put into practice. These practica often involve participation in the assessment, consultation, and intervention activities of the Tennessee Center for the Study and Treatment of Dyslexia (see Chapter 12).

This graduate training is grounded in normal and abnormal development of spoken language and how it relates to learning written language, including reading, spelling, and writing (Silliman & Wilkinson, 2004). Sanders and Rivers (1996) reported that achievement scores were 50 percentile points higher for Tennessee

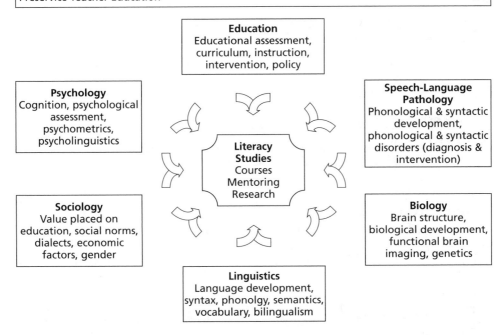

Figure 11.1. Middle Tennessee State University interdisciplinary model for preservice teacher preparation program that bridges the gap between research and educational practice. Copyright © D. Sawyer & S. Bernstein. Middle Tennessee State University, Murfreesboro, TN; reprinted by permission.

children who were taught by highly qualified, well-prepared teachers for 3 years when compared with children with the same initial score who were trained for 3 years by teachers who did not have the same kind of preparation. For further information, e-mail djsawyer@mtsu.edu (URL: http://www.mtsu.edu).

CONCLUSION

Current preservice teaching programs are not preparing teachers adequately for providing differentiated instruction in reading and writing and for learning the results of scientific research on the biological and behavioral bases of oral language, reading, and writing and effective, practical instructional practices for teaching these skills. Preservice teachers would benefit from better preparation in research knowledge and in implementing research-based knowledge into practice. The Middle Tennessee State University Preservice Teacher Training Program provides an interdisciplinary model for other teacher training programs to emulate in order to change this state of affairs.

Chapter 11 Appendix

RECOMMENDED READINGS AND/OR
IINSTRUCTIONAL RESOURCES FOR SUPERVISED
PRACTICA FOR PRESERVICE TEACHER EDUCATION

Understanding Language
Disorders, Learning Disability, and Dyslexia

Cicci, R. (1995). *What's wrong with me? Learning disabilities at home and school.* Timonium, MD: York Press.

Clark, D., & Uhry, J. (1995). *Dyslexia: Theory and practice of remedial instruction* (2nd ed.). Timonium, MD: York Press.

Nelson, N. (1998). *Childhood language disorders in context: Infancy through adolescence* (2nd ed.). Boston: Allyn & Bacon.

Wong, B. (Ed.). (2007). *Learning about learning disabilities* (4th ed.). New York: Academic Press.

Understanding the Language
Foundations Including Morphological
Awareness of Reading and Writing Instruction

Balmuth, M. (1992). *The roots of phonics: A historical introduction.* Timonium, MD: York Press.

Beeler, D. (1988). *Book of roots: A full study of our families of words.* Homewood, IL: Union Representative.

Birsh, J.R. (Ed.). (2005). *Multisensory teaching of basic language skills* (2nd ed.). Baltimore: Paul H. Brookes Publishing Co.

Carlisle, J. (1995). Morphological awareness and early reading achievement. In L. Feldman (Ed.), *Morphological aspects of language processing* (pp. 189–209). Mahwah, NJ: Lawrence Erlbaum Associates.

Carlisle, J. (2000). Awareness of the structure and meaning of morphologically complex words: Impact on reading. *Reading and Writing. An Interdisciplinary Journal, 12,* 169–190.

Carlisle, J., & Nomanbhoy, D. (1993). Phonological and morphological development. *Applied Psycholinguistics, 14,* 177–195.

Carlisle, J., & Stone, C. (2003). The effects of morphological structure on children's reading of derived words. In E. Assink & D. Sandra (Eds.), *Reading complex words: Cross-language studies* (pp. 27–52). Dordrecht, The Netherlands: Kluwer.

Fowler, A., & Liberman, I. (1995). The role of phonology and orthography in morphological awareness. In L. Feldman (Ed.), *Morphological aspects of language processing* (pp. 157–188). Mahwah, NJ: Lawrence Erlbaum Associates.

Graves, M. (2000). A vocabulary program to complement and bolster a middle-grade comprehension program. In E. Rothkopf & P. van den Brock (Eds.), *Reading for meaning: Fos-*

tering comprehension in the middle grades (pp. 116–135). New York: Teachers College, Columbia University.

Leong, C.K. (1989). Productive knowledge of derivational rules in poor readers. *Annals of Dyslexia, 39,* 94–115.

Leong, C.K. (2000). Rapid processing of base and derived forms of words and grades 4, 5, and 6 children's spelling. *Reading and Writing: An Interdisciplinary Journal, 12,* 277–302.

Mahoney, D., & Mann, V. (1992). Using children's humor to clarify the relationship between linguistic awareness and early reading ability. *Cognition, 45,* 163–186.

Mahoney, D., Singson, M., & Mann, V. (2000). Reading ability and sensitivity to morphological relations. *Reading and Writing: An Interdisciplinary Journal, 12,* 191–218.

Moats, L.C. (2000). *Speech to print: Language essentials for teachers.* Baltimore: Paul H. Brookes Publishing Co.

Nagy, W., Diakidoy, I., & Anderson, R. (1993). The acquisition of morphology: Learning the contribution of suffixes to the meaning of derivatives. *Journal of Reading Behavior, 25,* 150–170.

Nagy, W., Osborn, J., Winsor, P., & O'Flahavan, J. (1994). Structural analysis: Some guidelines for instruction. In F. Lehr & J. Osborn (Eds.), *Reading, language, and literacy* (pp. 45–58). Mahwah, NJ: Lawrence Erlbaum Associates.

Singson, M., Mahony, D., & Mann, V. (2000). The relation between reading ability and morphological skills: Evidence from derivational suffixes. *Reading and Writing: An Interdisciplinary Journal, 12,* 219–252.

Thomson, G.B., & Nicholson, T. (Eds.). (1999). *Learning to read: Beyond phonics and whole language.* Newark, DE: International Reading Association and New York: Teachers College Press.

Tyler, A., & Nagy, W. (1989). The acquisition of English derivational morphology. *Journal of Memory and Language, 28,* 649–667.

Tyler, A., & Nagy, W. (1990). Use of derivational morphology during reading. *Cognition, 36,* 17–34.

Instructional Resources for Phonological Awareness

Adams, M.J., Foorman, B.R., Lundberg, I., & Beeler, T. (1998). *Phonemic awareness in young children: A classroom curriculum.* Baltimore: Paul H. Brookes Publishing Co.

Blachman, B.A., Ball, E.W., Black, R., & Tangel, D.M. (2000). *Road to the code: A phonological awareness program for young children.* Baltimore: Paul H. Brookes Publishing Co.

Jenkins, J., Vadasy, P., Firebaugh, M., & Profilet, C. (2000). Tutoring first grade struggling readers in phonological reading skills. *Learning Disabilities: Research and Practice, 15,* 75–84. (Order Sound Phonics from Washington Research Institute, 150 Nickerson Suite 305, Seattle, WA 98109.)

O'Connor, R.E., Notari-Syverson, A., & Vadasy, P.F. (2005). *Ladders to literacy: A kindergarten activity book* (2nd ed.). Baltimore: Paul H. Brookes Publishing Co.

Instructional Resources for Developing Fluency

Cooper, T., Pikulski, J., & Au, K. (1997). *Early success: An intervention program.* Boston: Houghton Mifflin.

Ihnot, C. (1997). *Read naturally.* St. Paul, MN: Turman Publishing.

Mercer, C., & Campbell, K. (1997). *Great leaps reading.* Gainesville, FL: Author.

Instructional Resources for Integrating Phonological, Orthographic, and Morphological Awareness

Bear, D., Invernizzi, M., Templeton, S., & Johnston, F. (2000). *Words their way: Word study for phonics, vocabulary, and spelling instruction* (2nd ed.). Upper Saddle River, NJ: Prentice Hall.

Berninger, V., & Abbott, R. (2003). *Research-supported reading and writing lessons.* San Antonio, TX: Pearson Assessment. (Lesson Sets 11, 12, and 15.)

Henry, M. (1990). *Words: Integrated decoding and spelling instruction based on word origin and word structure.* Austin, TX: PRO-ED.

In-Service Teacher Education and Models for Teacher Mentoring

This chapter describes two professional development models for educators of students with written language disabilities. The first is the Tennessee Center for the Study and Treatment of Dyslexia, which was founded by Dr. Diane Sawyer and is currently directed by Dr. Stuart Bernstein. The second is a four-step model designed and implemented by Beth Slingerland, which is used in all Slingerland training courses (see Chapter 1). The authors hope that these examples will inspire others to develop such models in their states or local communities.

To reinforce the personal side of these pioneering efforts, this chapter includes information obtained from an interview with Drs. Sawyer and Bernstein. We do not reproduce the interview but highlight some of the key points they made. In addition, the second author shares relevant information from her personal professional journey from teacher to teacher educator. For other inspiring examples of evidence-based, in-service teacher education, see Wise, Rogan, and Sessions (in press) and Joshi et al. (in press). Finally, we share other inspiring examples of in-service professional development and mentoring for teachers.

Finally, this chapter describes the ongoing efforts of the International Dyslexia Association (IDA) to provide ongoing professional development for educators who work with students with dyslexia and related learning disabilities.

TENNESSEE CENTER FOR THE STUDY AND TREATMENT OF DYSLEXIA

The Tennessee Center for the Study and Treatment of Dyslexia (the Center; http://dyslexia.mtsu.edu/center/aboutcenter.html) was established by a grant from the Tennessee General Assembly in 1993 to help K–12 students with dyslexia, their teachers, and their families (Tennessee Center for the Study and Treatment of Dyslexia, n.d.). Prior to the Center being established in Tennessee, only four other states—Texas, Louisiana, California, and Mississippi—explicitly acknowledged dyslexia as an actual learning disability (Sawyer & Knight, 1997), despite the wealth of evidence worldwide confirming that dyslexia does exist.

The Center operates as a unit attached to the College of Education and Behavioral Sciences at Middle Tennessee State University (MTSU). The Center offers assessment and progress monitoring for students receiving school-based intervention following Center assessment. In addition, the Center provides preservice and in-service professional development and consultation services. Professional development, which the Center implements statewide, is multifaceted and includes workshops that teach schools how to 1) conduct assessments, 2) implement detailed guidelines for interventions, 3) administer benchmarks for response to intervention, and 4) access curriculum resources. Preservice and in-service professional development are interrelated in that preservice development often involves supervised participation in assessment and treatment, whereas in-service development may involve supervised participation in assessment, treatment, and consultation services. Consultation involves guiding and supporting school-based personnel as they begin to transition to independence in identification of individual students with dyslexia and in focused intervention planning.

Dr. Diane Sawyer, founder of the Center, should not be confused with the television journalist with the same name. In an interview for this chapter with Dr. Sawyer on December 19, 2007, she confided that she has met the television journalist. One time they both stayed at the same hotel and had many run-ins due to mix-ups with phone messages and identities. In contrast to journalist Diane Sawyer who tells the news, however, Dr. Diane Sawyer is making news in the world of dyslexia. Dr. Sawyer's audience has been the Tennessee State legislature, Tennessee educators, the state and national community of university trainers, and the IDA.

Dr. Sawyer's story begins in 1990 when she took a leave of absence from her faculty position at Syracuse University, where she was professor of reading and language arts, to become the first-ever Chair of Excellence in Dyslexic Studies at MTSU. Endowed by Katherine Davis Murfree in collaboration with MTSU and the state of Tennessee, this Chair of Excellence was the first of its kind in the nation. Dr. Sawyer agreed to assume the position for 18 months with a view toward assessing and pursuing opportunities for the enhancement of services for students with dyslexia in K–12 settings in the state. Launching the Chair of Excellence involved garnering public awareness and bringing together various interest groups that might contribute to the advancement of the goals of the Chair. A presentation to the Joint Committee on Education of the Tennessee General Assembly led to a statewide survey, commissioned by the state Board of Education, of services to students with dyslexia at that time. The report of this survey, submitted to the Joint Committee on Education, led to the call for more clearly defined and inclusive services for students with dyslexia in Tennessee schools. In response to specific requests by members of the Joint Committee on Education, the President of MTSU, Dr. James Walker, requested that Dr. Sawyer prepare a proposal to systematically address services to these students. The result was a proposal to form the Tennessee Center for the Study and Treatment of Dyslexia. This proposal was supported by members in both houses of the Tennessee General Assembly and was included in deliberations of the state budget appropriations. In May 1993, support of the Center was included as a line item in the state budget and approved by members of the full Assembly. In September 1993, the Tennessee Board of Regents approved inclusion of the Center as a service unit of MTSU to function within the administrative structure of the university. Official recognition of the Center by the Tennessee Higher Education Commission, which has oversight responsibility for all programs within institutions of higher education, was granted in December 1993.

The Center was established to 1) inform the public about dyslexia, 2) establish reliable approaches to identifying students with dyslexia, 3) educate preservice and in-service teachers in effective ways to teach literacy skills to students with dyslexia, and 4) add knowledge about the nature and effective treatment of dyslexia. The Center is unique in that its mandate is to work with teachers and schools to 1) describe students' learning problems, 2) design intervention plans, 3) educate instructional staff about dyslexia, 4) assist teachers in effective instructional methods for students with dyslexia, and 5) recommend appropriate accommodations (Tennessee Center for the Study and Treatment of Dyslexia, n.d.). Of most importance, the state legislature funded the Center as a line item in the state budget AND the university committed additional supplementary money as well.

The whole process took about 7 months, and by the end of 1993, Dr. Sawyer's part-time visit that began in 1990 turned into a permanent stay at MTSU to foster and support the development of the newly established Center for Dyslexia. The process of establishing the Center is described in detail to emphasize the various steps involved as well as the amount of time required. In other states, the process may require additional steps or time. Readers interested in establishing a state-level professional development program for dyslexia in their state might request a copy of the Tennessee legislation as a possible blueprint for similar legislation in their states. See this web site for further information: http://dyslexia.mtsu.edu/center/aboutcenter.html

Passing legislation, however, is but a first step. For the first 3 years after establishing the Center, the state budget covered all of the expenses, and the Center was given rent-free space in local schools. As the demand for Center services grew, it became necessary to rent space in a commercial facility and to add staff. It also became necessary to ask schools requesting in-service training of teachers and other professionals to cover the costs of reproducing handout materials. Over time, MTSU had to begin to supplement the state appropriation. University support is now equal to about three fourths of the Center's annual operating budget. For the most part, Center services are free of charge and accessible to anyone who needs the services. Those who request assessment services, however, are charged a processing fee to help to defray some of the costs associated with the services.

The Center's accomplishments are impressive. The direct services to children, the teacher training services, and the consultation services reach every county in the state. The research arm of the Center also has notable accomplishments. For example, Center personnel have created the Assessment of Decoding and Encoding Progress (ADEP), a tool with six forms used for progress monitoring (baseline and five repeated assessments) of the same student over a 2- to 3-year period. This assessment tool is unique in that levels within the test are organized by levels of typical developmental phases. The assessment tool pinpoints which aspects of decoding (reading), fluency (reading), and encoding (spelling) a student has mastered and not mastered, and it translates those assessment results into goals for the student's individualized education program and into instructional levels for forming instructional groups in the classroom. Note that this tool works best when used with the definition of dyslexia that is currently recommended by the IDA (see Chapter 8).

The Center's staff members also developed a tool for the early identification of children at risk of acquiring literacy skills. This 14-item questionnaire is rooted in an extensive survey of the literature on best predictors of factors that put students at risk. It is designed for parents to complete when their children enter kindergarten. It has been field-tested on a sample of nearly 2,000 children entering kindergarten, in three cohorts, whose progress in literacy acquisition has been followed through third grade. Early results indicated that this may be a very useful tool for use in schools. Norms are in the process of being developed.

As the demand for programs at the Center grew and the focus on research increased, the need for a full-time director became apparent. Dr. Stuart Bernstein (Ph.D., Cognitive Psychology) was named Center Director in 2006. Dr. Bernstein joined the University as an assistant professor in the Psychology Department in 1998. Initially he taught research methodology and statistics, but he became interested in the large database accumulating in the Center and saw its potential for his own research. He began working with the Center staff on their research on spelling and became fascinated by the kinds of spelling errors made by students with dyslexia. He also brought his research expertise in attention, word recognition, and spelling to the interdisciplinary work of the Center. His long-term association with the Center and his enthusiasm for the work of the Center made him an ideal choice for director.

For others who may wish to implement innovative in-service professional development programs, Dr. Sawyer offers this advice during the interview: First, find out what people are willing to support that may benefit professional development efforts. Second, one does not have to be political to be sensitive to the interests that exist and capitalize on those interests.

Dr. Bernstein also added this insight during the interview: Developing and implementing evidence-based professional development at the beginning of the 21st century faces many of the challenges that psychology did at the end of the 19th century when the field emerged as a wedding of philosophy (belief systems) and science (empirical studies in which beliefs, which are hypotheses, are tested with data). For many, education is still based on deeply held philosophical beliefs. The idea that education should be grounded in empirical science is still novel and not universally accepted. Much remains to be accomplished in providing ongoing, preservice education to share with teachers the ever growing body of scientific knowledge that is relevant to teaching all students, including those with dyslexia oral and written language learning disability (OWL LD), and dysgraphia.

With the Center well established and under Dr. Bernstein's direction, Dr. Sawyer turned her attention to providing more formal preparation of school personnel to address more effectively the needs of students with dyslexia. In 2003, her efforts led to the Tennessee Board of Regents approval of a Graduate Certificate in Dyslexic Studies. This 18–credit-hour program has attracted school principals, classroom teachers, speech-language pathologists, reading teachers, school psychologists, and curriculum consultants. Efforts are now being directed toward obtaining a state credential for those who complete this interdisciplinary program. To address the need for information about dyslexia among those who are not interested in or able to enroll in the certificate program, the Center has just launched an on-demand overview course for which continuing education credit is available through MTSU. For more information about the Center, the certificate program, and the on-demand course, readers are encouraged to visit the Center web site (http://dyslexia.mtsu.edu).

To have a broader impact on teacher preparation in Tennessee and beyond, Dr. Sawyer also pursued a more elusive goal—to establish an interdisciplinary

Ph.D. program in literacy studies. This dream began in 2001 with a presentation to the University president, Dr. Sydney McPhee. Preparation of the proposal involved the collaboration of faculty in the College of Education and Behavioral Science and the College of Liberal Arts. The program was approved by the Tennessee Higher Education Commission in July 2007 and admitted its first students in the fall of 2008.

The Ph.D. program in literacy studies is interdisciplinary (see References for web site, requesting brochure, submitting application), with faculty from the disciplines of cognitive psychology, human development, speech and language, neuroscience, and literacy, and representatives from these disciplines running the program.

One goal of the Ph.D. program is to train leaders for preservice and in-service professional development of teachers. Another goal is to produce a new generation of administrators who, as in the past, are instructional leaders. (The current model is to train principals who are CEOs, that is, chief operating officers, of their school buildings.) To accomplish these goals, the program teaches students to build friendships on a personal level, become comfortable working with teachers, provide coaching and mentoring for in-service teachers, and provide consultation through workshops on assessment and interventions. The new vanguard of instructional leaders is knowledgeable in implementing schoolwide, evidence-based instructional practices for differentiated instruction sensitive to individual differences. Research is pointing to the importance of supervised in-service practica experiences in in-service professional development of teachers (Uhry & Goodman, in press), as offered in this Ph.D. program, for learning to put research into practice.

Dreams can be actualized when one works with a team to bring to fruition well-designed plans to improve the education of those who teach reading and writing.

SLINGERLAND FOUR-STEP PROFESSIONAL DEVELOPMENT PROGRAM

Teacher training in the Slingerland adaptation of the Orton-Gillingham Approach was formally launched in the summer of 1960 in Renton, Washington. A group of 12 teachers attended a 21-day session and received graduate-level credit from Seattle Pacific University. The mornings were devoted to observing Beth Slingerland's demonstration of teaching techniques with students enrolled in summer school and a 1-hour practicum in which the teacher-participants tutored the students. This one-to-one instruction allowed the teachers to observe the application of the multisensory teaching approach and then practice it while Slingerland observed and gave guidance. Both teachers and students benefited. Afternoons were devoted to reviewing the morning demonstration and practicum, lectures on specific language disabilities, details and rationale for instruction, lesson planning, and preparation of materials. The enthusiasm of the teachers and the parents of the attending students led to increased interest and a greater number of students attending summer school. As local staff was trained, Slingerland was able to respond to requests for training in California and Texas. Further interest in the approach took the training to Alaska, Montana, Oregon, and Washington. By 1985, there were 45 teacher training sessions offered throughout the United States.

Evolution of Slingerland's Original In-Service Teacher Training

The Slingerland Institute for Literacy trains teachers. The Institute was founded to carry on Slingerland's work and to protect the integrity of the approach she developed. In addition to the original summer classes, teachers may now receive the full training during the school year, with the practicum taking place in their own classrooms as they work with their own students. For those teachers or schools unable or unwilling to invest the necessary time or money for full training, short courses in handwriting, written language, reading, prereading skills, or screening are also available. Many teachers across the country continue to teach Slingerland classes following the model developed in 1960.

On a personal note, the second author (Wolf) began as a demonstration teacher in the Renton summer schools. She demonstrated instructional methods with groups of 15–20 children and supervised approximately the same numbers of teachers under a director who was responsible for lectures and the overall quality of the training. After 3 years, she was sent to Olympia to direct a session for St. Martin's College. The following year she directed a session in Port Orchard with three staff teachers and 55 participants. Then she was placed in charge of the Slingerland program in Renton and took over that summer program too. The first year, she had 105 participants in seven demonstration classrooms. This proved to be too many. After that first year, she limited the sessions to eighty teachers.

Wolf left Renton in 1983 to become dean of faculty for the Slingerland Institute. She traveled and visited summer sessions and classrooms from New Hampshire to Hawaii. She spent a lot of time in Dallas, Texas while three inner-city schools implemented Slingerland's program as part of their resegregation program. Students were returned to their home schools and given enriched instruction. That project was hampered by the district requirement that all students at a grade level must be on the same page in the reading book on the same day. Lesson plans came from the central office. Needless to say, no grouping or individualization was allowed. The teachers, however, did teach handwriting and phonics and morphology using comprehension strategies.

When Wolf moved to the Hamlin Robinson School in Seattle, she started teacher training there. Classes were smaller because by then whole language was in full bloom. Fewer public school teachers attend now but many more private schools and tutors do. She taught two training classes during the school year. The advantage is that the teachers must use their whole classroom for the practicum. The downside is the intensity of the training during the busy school year.

With the advent of the whole-language approach, interest in a structured approach that incorporated handwriting, written language, and phonics declined. The Slingerland Institute for Literacy continues to train teachers, though in smaller numbers and in fewer school districts. Though many public school districts still encourage their teachers to participate in Slingerland training, focus shifted from public schools that felt their special education programs were serving their students with dyslexia to programs in private schools that see this approach as a means of reaching their struggling readers. Many parochial schools have sponsored Slingerland training programs for their teachers, and, incidentally, for their students. Some schools have adopted models similar to those originally used in Renton. Others provide services from a reading specialist who uses the Slingerland teaching approach to language arts, offer private tutoring on site for a fee, or a combination of options.

Classroom teachers continue to use the approach and adapt it to their classroom situations. Working with heterogeneous groupings, they follow the basic principles for instruction. By individualizing, the stronger students find greater success, while students with difficulties are supported by the teaching structure. The skilled teacher guides those who need additional help while enriching those who do not. Though designed for use with classroom groups, the Slingerland teaching approach is used successfully by tutors as well.

Current Four-Step Professional Development Model

The current version of Slingerland's professional development model consists of four sequential steps within a training session: 1) sharing of research-generated information on effective teaching practices; 2) modeling by a mentor teacher of these instructional strategies in teaching students with written language disability; 3) supervision by the mentor teacher who observes the participating teacher implement the same instructional strategies with the students; and finally 4) debriefing sessions in which the mentor teacher and participating teachers reflect on the process of translating research-supported strategies into practice and the mentor teacher provides constructive feedback to the teachers for improving the translation process. See sample course syllabi in the Chapter 12 appendix.

When the first author visited the Slingerland summer school at Our Lady of the Lake Parish School (Seattle, Washington), it was not only informative for her, but validating for the summer school staff and participants. The day began with a brief overview of the format and a lecture on reading from the book, followed by observation of demonstrations in both the introductory and the continuum classes. These demonstrations included both trainees observing experienced mentor teachers and mentor teachers observing trainees in implementing concepts and methods explained during the lecture. The day ended with a reflection session in which mentor teachers provided feedback to the trainees regarding putting the ideas into practice. Impressed with this teacher training model, she also asked questions and provided information about research that supports each aspect of the approach.

While visiting the school, the first author realized that both the opportunity for trainees to observe trainers and trainers to observe trainees and the feedback session are missing components in most teacher training programs. The analysis by the mentor teacher and participants during and after demonstration and in the afternoon provide a time for reflection. As participants review what happened during each part of the day, they build the skills of analysis that make them stronger, more effective teachers who self-reflect on their own teaching and continually try to improve.

EDUCATING THE EDUCATORS

The IDA was founded in honor of the work of Dr. Samuel Orton, who, with his colleagues, brought national and international attention to the educational needs of students with dyslexia, speech disabilities, and associated language disorders. IDA encourages and promotes

1. Study and research concerning the nature of such disabilities

2. Facilities for the diagnosis and treatment of such disabilities

3. Measures to prevent the academic and personality difficulties that may arise from such disabilities

4. Facilities for the training of personnel in the diagnosis and treatment of such disabilities (From the Bylaws of the Orton Society, Inc.)

In cooperation with other organizations focused on students with differing needs, over the years the IDA has provided position papers, information, and recommendations for lawmakers that have an impact on educational legislation, promote the rights of people with dyslexia, and support and value their teachers as a strong force in the educational and scientific communities. IDA provides a forum through its conferences and publications for parents, educators, and researchers to share information and heighten awareness of dyslexia, its causes, and approaches to intervention:

1. The use of comprehensive diagnostic evaluations to identify learning disabilities, particularly reading and writing disabilities

2. The importance of early intervention using evidence-based remediation and explicit reading remediation for students with reading disability

3. The need for continuing emphasis on rigorous standards for research

4. The need for increased teacher training and professional development

5. Accreditation of teacher and therapist training programs that meet criteria for appropriate instruction for students with dyslexia

OTHER INSPIRING MODELS

Barbara Wise has developed Linguistic Remedies as a professional development tool for teachers that is based on research she and Richard Olson and others have conducted at the NICHD-funded University of Colorado, Boulder Learning Disabilities Center for about three decades. See Wise, Rogan, and Sessions (in press) for detailed information about how this pioneering professional development program can be customized to bring research into the classroom and meet the needs of individual teachers in doing so.

Joanne Uhry, supported by the Hello Ennis Foundation established by Bill Cosby in memory of his son Ennis, who before he tragically was killed was devoted to helping inner city children with learning disabilities, has developed an innovative graduate level teacher education program at Fordham University in New York City that emphasizes both evidence-based instructional practices and supervision of graduate students in implementing those practices in inner city classrooms. For evidence that combining formal coursework and supervised mentoring is superior to formal coursework alone, see Uhri and Goodman (in press).

Malatesha Joshi has established a leading edge graduate level teacher education program at Texas A&M that focuses on building in-service teachers' knowledge of research on reading and related skills. He and his colleague gather evidence about how teacher knowledge changes as a function of the graduate-level professional development. For further information about evidence-based approaches to transmitting evidence-based knowledge and about the scale-up in Texas to provide continuing education professional development for all teachers, see Joshi et al. (in press), available online at www.interdys.org.

A matrix, *Framework for Informed Reading and Language Instruction* (Henry, 2005), compares similarities and differences among 12 approaches to reading and language instruction widely used in the United States. It enables teachers, school administrators, and parents to make educated choices among the various teacher training programs. The matrix is intended to help educators and parents evaluate and gain access to effective, sequential, multisensory, and structured language programs that have been successful in clinical and classroom settings. Though many programs are not included in the matrix because of space limitations, the IDA encourages use of programs that meet their listed standards. Among the program characteristics considered necessary for effective reading and language instruction are those that include training in the following:

1. Phonological awareness: the ability to segment words into their component sounds

2. Phonics: sound–symbol association

3. Decoding: practice in word attack skills for reading based on phonics and understanding of the morphology of language

4. Encoding: practice in combining sounds for spelling in association with phonics and the understanding of the morphology of language

5. Fluency: the ability to read orally with speed, accuracy, and proper expression (National Institute of Child Health and Human Development, 2000)

6. Reading comprehension: with instruction in vocabulary and the sentence and narrative levels of text

7. Written expression: including handwriting and instruction in constructing text

Teacher training should include instruction in the background and rationale for the lessons, demonstration by mentor teachers, a supervised practicum, and follow-up training. Further information is available on the IDA web site (http://www.interdys.org).

CONCLUSION

Although professional development for teachers is widely available now, primarily through workshops sponsored by local school districts, state agencies, or professional organizations, much of it does not involve the transmission of evidence-based practice. Much of what is taught is based mainly on philosophy or belief rather than ideas that have been empirically evaluated and compared with other ideas. In this chapter, innovative models are shared for transforming the nature of professional development so that evidence-based instructional practices are shared with in-service teachers.

RESOURCES

Tennessee Center for the Study and Treatment of Dyslexia. 200 N. Baird Lane, Middle Ten-
    nessee State University, Box 397, Murfreesboro, TN 37132; www.mtsu.edu~dyslexia
Brochures available upon request:
    Services for Teacher Educators
    Staff Development Opportunities for School Systems in Tennessee
    Tennessee Center for Study and Treatment of Dyslexia
    Graduate Certificate in Dyslexic Studies. Real Answers to Real Problems.
    Tennessee Ph.D. in Literacy Studies. For information www.mtsu.edu~literacy
    Request brochure: Ph.D. in Literacy Studies. College of Education and Behavioral
        Science College of Liberal Arts

Chapter 12 Appendix

REPRESENTATIVE SYLLABI FOR
PROFESSIONAL DEVELOPMENT OF EDUCATORS

Course Syllabus: Introduction to Instructional Techniques in Specific Language Disability

The Slingerland Adaptation for Classroom
Use of the Orton-Gillingham Multisensory Approach
for Children with Specific Language Disability (Dyslexia)

> **Dates:** June 22, 2004 through July 16, 2004, from 8:00 A.M. to 3:00 P.M.
>
> **Requirements:** Teaching experience or permission
>
> **Credits:** 11 credits

Course Description

This course covers a 4-week period of intensive study. It offers training in the etiology and diagnosis of specific language disability (dyslexia) and provides training in the techniques designed for a preventive and/or remedial program for classroom use. These techniques were developed by Beth H. Slingerland as an adaptation of the approach originated by Dr. Samuel T. Orton and Anna Gillingham. They are based on sound neurological principles of learning. Multisensory in their organization, these techniques give the child the tools needed to function successfully in all areas of language arts, whether reading, writing, spelling, or speaking.

Course Objectives

To provide instruction in the introductory steps of handwriting, written language, decoding, and reading comprehension

To develop understanding of the etiology of dyslexia

To introduce phonic rules and their application to encoding and decoding

To provide understanding of the neurology of language and offer means of developing oral language skills

To provide information about history, philosophy, and current research in the field of dyslexia

To guide in the understanding of relationships of curriculum and classroom organization to the language arts program

Student Expectations

Participants will

Learn the Slingerland Approach through multisensory strategies; they will see demonstrations and read their texts, hear lectures, and experience this way of teaching by practicing in class and working with children

Practice skills with other teachers in small groups

Participate in discussion of students and strategies used in the classroom

Read the text and materials chosen from the bibliography

Apply the approach to work in the practicum with children

Special Features: EDU and Special Education credits are available

Instructor: Beverly J. Wolf, M.Ed., 14702 S.E.105 Street
Renton, WA 98059-4209; 425-255-7336
bwolf2@mindspring.com

A former classroom teacher, Beverly Wolf has served as Head of Hamlin Robinson School, Dean of the Slingerland Institute, and currently as a private consultant. She is a member of the Council of Advisors of the International Dyslexia Association, author of articles and books for teachers and parents, and serves on the HRS Board of Trustees

Methods of Instruction

Each day is divided into the following components:

Observation of a group of children taught by a master teacher using Slingerland techniques

Guided practice in the use of multisensory techniques with a child or children

Lectures involving the areas listed below

Preparation of plans and materials

Individual and group conferences

Content/Topics and Outline for Each Session

The daily schedule consists of

8:00 Lecture

9:00 Assembly with children, working with oral language

9:15 Demonstration class—Slingerland techniques

10:30 Recess—observation of children in less-structured settings

10:30   Practicum—individual tutoring of one or two children

11:45   Story—observation of listening skills, further oral language experience

11:55   Prepare for lunch or dismissal

12:30   Evaluations of morning work

12:45   Lecture
        Additional explanation or practice with techniques
        Preparation, under guidance, of lesson plans

The general outline may vary slightly according to the needs of the children and the participant teachers. Lecture topics are in italics, demonstration and planning take place from day 3 to the end of the course.

Day 1 (6/22): (Teachers only) *Get acquainted, review of syllabus, oral language development; definition of dyslexia; characteristics of dyslexia; phonological awareness; organization of tutoring station; Slingerland Approach; demonstration and overview of the approach; planning for first day with children*

Day 2 (6/23): (First day with children) *Format for instruction, demonstration, understanding of and writing of lesson plans*

Day 3 (6/24): *Learning to write; demonstration, procedures for teaching new letters*

Day 4 (6/25): *Phonological awareness, auditory alphabet review and encoding*

Day 5 (6/28): *The reading process, reparation for reading*

Day 6 (6/29): *Preparation for reading, teaching the structure of language*

Day 7 (6/30): *Reading from the book step 1, relationship to language structure*

Day 8 (7/1): *Phonics*

Days 9 & 10 (7/2): *Reading from the book, steps 2 and 3*

Day 11 (7/6): *Spelling, affixes, phrases*

Day 12 (7/7): *Additional review as needed*

Day 13 (7/8): *Rules*

Day 14 (7/9): *Dictation, take home exam*

Day 15 (7/12): *Overview of screening*

Day 16 (7/13): *Preparation for conferencing, continuum of instruction, assistance in evaluating students, conferencing strategies*

Day 17 (7/14): *Questions and answers*

Day 18 (7/15): *Grade-level curriculum K–1–2, 3–4, 5–6; creative activities; working as a tutor; planning independently*

Day 19 (7/16): *Review of structure, basic principles, parent conferences*

Grading Criteria/System and Evaluation Activities

Criteria for all participants:

30%   A daily plan for work with individual pupils, to be turned in each day before leaving—plans are precise to ensure understanding and application of the Slingerland Approach. Teacher participants will be guided by staff teacher. A daily, objective running account of child's progress will include observed strengths and weaknesses and ways in which their performance will affect planning for the next day's lesson. Brief annotated notes on five books or articles related to the subject of dyslexia and/or oral or written language will include a brief synopsis and the purpose or value of the material. A summary of the conference with pupil's parents is submitted.

10%   Preparation of teaching materials and organization of space

10%   A willingness to be observed and to accept constructive criticism and guidance

35%   Participation in activities for children—use of the technique, directed play periods, story time, dismissal

15%   A test, or tests, covering demonstrations, lectures, and reading

Attendance Affects All Areas

Due Dates

Lesson plans are due each day

Annotated notes are due July 12

Take home test to be returned July 12

Parent conference report due July 16

Course Syllabus: Third-Year Continuum of Instruction in Specific Language Disability

The Slingerland Adaptation for Classroom Use of the Orton-Gillingham Multisensory Approach for Children with Specific Language Disability (Dyslexia)

Dates: June 22, 2004 through July 16, 2004, from 8:00 A.M.–3:00 P.M.

Requirements: Teaching experience, completion of the second-year course, and permission

Credits: 11 credits

Course Description

This course is designed for a limited number of participants wishing to become staff teachers in the Slingerland Summer Sessions.

Course Objectives

Under the guidance of the director and/or staff teacher, the teacher-participant will be able to

Demonstrate the use of the Slingerland Approach with a classroom group of children

Make appropriate evaluations of the participants' lesson plans, materials, and teaching stations

Make appropriate evaluations of the participants' delivery of planned lessons

Make appropriate evaluations of the participants' tests and required readings

Assist in completing forms required by the Slingerland Institute

Prepare five lectures and satisfactorily deliver two of them to the participants

Prepare an orientation about dyslexia and the Slingerland Approach

Satisfactorily complete the individualized requirements assigned by the director

Student Expectations

Participants will:

Learn the Slingerland Approach through multisensory strategies; they will observe demonstrations and read advanced materials on language and dyslexia, hear lectures, and experience this way of teaching by demonstrating and working with children and teachers.

Demonstrate practice skills for other teachers in small groups

Participate in discussion of students, teacher participants, and strategies used in the classroom

Special Features: EDU and Special Education credits are available

Instructor: Beverly J. Wolf M.Ed., 14702 S.E.105 Street
Renton, WA 98059-4209; 425-255-7336,
bwolf2@mindspring.com

A former classroom teacher, Beverly Wolf has served as Head of Hamlin Robinson School, Dean of the Slingerland Institute, and currently consults for school districts. She is a member of the Council of Advisors of the International Dyslexia Association, author of articles and books for teachers and parents, and serves on the HRS Board of Trustees

Methods of Instruction

Following the same general format as the introductory courses, each day is divided into the following components:

Daily lectures

Observation or demonstration with a group of children of these techniques, with emphasis on the recognition and use of the diagnostic and prescriptive elements embedded in the daily plan

Guided practice in observing, diagnosing, and prescribing and using multisensory techniques with children and teacher participants

Participation in individual and group conferences for teachers and children

Individual research

Content/Topics and Outline for Each Session

8:00　Lecture

9:00　Assembly with children, working with oral language

9:15　Demonstration class—Slingerland techniques

10:30　Recess—observation of children in less-structured settings

10:30　Practicum—individual tutoring of one or two children

11:45　Story—observation of listening skills, further oral language experience

11:55　Prepare for lunch or dismissal

12:30　Evaluations of morning work

12:45　Lecture
　　　　Additional explanation or practice with techniques
　　　　Preparation, under guidance, of lesson plans

2:00　Staff planning and review sessions

Grading Criteria/System and Evaluation Activities

Criteria for all third-year participants:

40%　Instruction:

- Work with staff in coordinating daily plans for children and teacher participants

- Participation in demonstration lessons

- Observe and critique individual work with children by participants

35%　Evaluation:

- Check participant's lesson plans, tests, and reading

- Participate in individual and group conferences with staff, participants, and parents

25%　Knowledge:

- Read no fewer than 15 scholarly articles or chapters on one area of interest in the fields of dyslexia or language, and write a brief summary of each. Prepare a paper suitable for presentation to a group of teachers or parents based on your research.

For a third-year participant who is not interested in or ready for consideration as a potential demonstration teacher, requirements may be individualized by the director by substituting appropriate options from the following list:

Daily individual work with a child using continually advanced techniques

Review, administer, score, and evaluate two each from any three levels of the Slingerland Screening Procedures

Compose a story for use with the Slingerland reading techniques

Prepare a weekly spelling dictation lesson, with daily lesson plans for use with the Slingerland Approach

Correlate a current textbook from any reading, spelling, or content area with the Slingerland Approach

Attendance Affects All Areas

Due Dates

Lesson plans are due each day

Annotated notes and written paper are due July 14

Classroom demonstrations completed by July 14

Parent conference report due July 16

Texts

The following Slingerland texts/materials are included in course tuition:

Slingerland, B.H. (1971). *A multisensory approach to language arts for specific language disability children (Book I).* Cambridge, MA: Educators Publishing Service.

OR

Slingerland, B.H. (1976). *Basics in scope and sequence of a multi-sensory approach to language arts for specific language disability children: A guide for primary teachers in the second year continuum* (Book 2); (Rev. ed.). Cambridge, MA: Educators Publishing Service.

Slingerland, B.H., & Murray, C. (1987). *Teacher's word lists for reference.* Cambridge, MA: Educators Publishing Service.

Teacher's hand pack for classroom use

Manuscript alphabet cards

Yellow card pack

Wall cards or chart

Phonogram Chart

Cursive wall cards (for Grades 3 and above)

Commencement

From Book Endings to New Beginnings in Teaching Students with Dyslexia, OWL LD, and Dysgraphia

May the Warm Winds of Heaven
Blow softly upon your house.
May the Great Spirit
Bless all who enter there.
May your Moccasins
Make happy tracks
in many snows,
and may the Rainbow
Always touch your shoulder.

Cherokee Prayer Blessing

Cherokee is one of the few Native American languages with a written component. Effective reading instruction can combine multiculturally sensitive curriculum and science-supported reading and writing instruction.

CHAPTER 13

Commencement

From Book Endings to New Beginnings

A major goal of this book was to share with readers the results of programmatic research funded by federal grants made possible by the Interagency Initiative of 1987 (see Berninger, 2008b, for information about this initiative). This initiative was the result of parental requests for greater support of research on more effective educational services in public schools for students with learning disabilities. Thus, research made possible by this federal initiative was discussed throughout the book so that teachers can use it to teach students with specific learning disabilities more effectively.

Federal initiatives at the beginning of the 21st century have emphasized the importance of grounding educational practice in scientific knowledge. At the same time, experienced teachers bring knowledge gained from practice in effective teaching that is also relevant to student learning outcomes. Effective teachers are scientist-practitioners—knowledgeable about the science of learning and the art of teaching.

As noted in the Introduction, the goal of this book was to share both researcher and teacher perspectives on how to teach students with specific learning disabilities affecting written language acquisition. To accomplish this goal, Chapter 1 reviewed the history of the field with a focus on the early pioneers in medicine and education who first raised awareness of children with reading and writing disabilities and began to develop educational treatments for them.

Chapter 2 dealt with the practical issues of organizing the teaching day to provide differentiated instruction for individual differences among students, some of whom have specific learning disabilities and others who do not. Chapters 3, 4, and 5 covered instructional issues and methods for teaching oral language, reading, and writing to students with dyslexia, oral and written language learning disability (OWL LD), and/or dysgraphia. Chapter 6 emphasized the importance of explicit instruction that integrates the listening, speaking, reading, and writing in learning environments that are intellectually engaging. Research findings from biological, behavioral, and linguistic scientific disciplines were reviewed in Chapter 7. Research findings relevant to clinical assessment were reviewed in Chapter 8. Research findings from instructional studies were reviewed in Chapter 9.

Chapter 10 dealt with the practical issues affecting how schools and school districts might develop programs to meet the instructional needs of all students, including those with dyslexia, OWL LD, and/or dysgraphia within the general education program. Chapters 11 and 12 discussed issues to consider in preservice and in-service professional development, respectively, , along with examples of the forms this professional development might take to prepare general educators for the challenging task of tailoring teaching to individual differences.

In this final chapter, the second author discusses how teachers mentor each other and how teaching experience informs teaching knowledge. Then the first author discusses how her thinking changed beyond what she knew from her teaching experiences after being able to conduct programmatic research for more than 25 years.

HOW TEACHING EXPERIENCE INFORMS TEACHER KNOWLEDGE

Lillian Hellman (Hellman & Feibleman, 1984) pointed out that, like children in circle dances, by holding the hand of a good dancer one dances even better. Likewise, competent, dedicated teachers and teacher educators making connections with each other contribute to children's effective learning. Anna Gillingham and Bessie Stillman taught Beth Slingerland, Sally Childs, and other pioneers (see Chapter 1) who, in turn, taught present-day teachers and teacher educators, including the second author, to teach students with dyslexia. Slingerland emphasized teachers' responsibility to teach present and future teachers. The Slingerland Approach was not a narrow method, but one that was based on teaching experience and understanding child development and the continuum of skills needed to move through the curriculum. She taught teachers that they should never stop gathering the newest information about the brain and learning. Her strategies for teaching oral language skills explicitly as part of the reading and writing program are practical and effective with students with dyslexia and OWL LD.

Leaders in the fields of speech and language complete the circle too. Katrina de Hirsh and Doris Johnson taught Jeanette Jansky and Regina Cicci who provided the second author with an understanding of the importance of oral language skills and their relationships to reading and written expressive language. Cicci's thoughtful assessment of the interconnectedness of all language skills reinforces the role of the language specialist as an integral part of the educational team.

Teachers and teacher educators learn from the teachers with whom they work. In teaching and mentoring groups, instructors lead teachers to examine their observations and refine their questions. Teachers are guided to explore the entire performance of the child, not just the result of a single task. What does the child do well? When? Teachers are led to new insights and directions for intervention that benefit the instructor as well as the teacher.

Teachers want evidence-based strategies that work well and are consistent with what they know of children's learning. They desire administrative support of quality teaching that pinpoints and addresses learning needs. Using the knowledge acquired from careful observation, study, and teaching experience, a teacher, a building, or a school district can create an effective program for all of their students (see Chapter 10). "Accomplishment begins with vision. Between its start and its outcome are accountability, leadership, courage, and performance—a freedom not merely to see the possibilities but to commit and to act, to make something happen" (Steeves, 1990).

HOW RESEARCH TRANSFORMED TEACHER KNOWLEDGE

The first author did not have a mentor teacher as did the second author. As a psychology major in undergraduate school, the first author chose electives in teaching reading and children's literature and did an honor's thesis that involved tutoring a student with reading problems. The course work was organized developmentally, with a focus on teaching phonics (and its links to speech) and decoding, oral reading accuracy and fluency, vocabulary development, and reading comprehension in the early grades, and on teaching structural analysis for longer, more complex words and silent reading along with grade-appropriate vocabulary development and reading comprehension in the upper grades. In the preparation for teaching phonics, digraphs (two letters but only one has phoneme correspondence) and diphthongs (two letters associated with one phoneme that does not correspond to either letter alone) were emphasized along with single-letter phoneme correspondence. In the structural analysis, both syllable and morpheme patterns were emphasized.

The course work also covered informal reading inventory procedures linked to basal readers for determining instructional levels and groupings at the beginning of the year and monitoring them throughout the year through unit tests that came with basal readers and informal inventories. Teachers were taught to organize instruction for three to four instructional groups formed on the basis of instructional levels (see Chapter 2).

Instructional design emphasized the Directed Reading Activity (DRA; Berninger, 1994a; Bond & Tinker, 1967) with prereading activities that included teaching decoding and vocabulary meaning for new words in the stories in graded readers, discussion of background knowledge, and purpose-setting questions. Children were first instructed to read silently to find answers to these purpose-setting questions, which served as advanced organizers; this silent prereading avoided embarrassment for children with oral-motor planning problems whose oral reading was dysfluent until they were able to decode the words. Then the teacher guided the oral reading by first asking children to read sentences that answered the purpose-setting questions and then by taking turns in reading other parts of text orally with fluency and expression. During independent seatwork while the teacher worked with one instructional group, the other children practiced previously taught skills and read independently for pleasure. The recommendations from the National Reading Panel (National Institute of Child Health and Human Development, 2000) were not a surprise—all were an integral part of the course work and related textbooks (see Chapters 2 and 7).

The first author's graduate training in the Psychology of Reading Clinic operated by the Psychology Department at Temple University during her first year of teaching reinforced her undergraduate course work. This training included practica in which in-service teachers worked with individual students under supervision to administer tests and provide individual tutoring on reading skills. The tutoring covered all of the steps of the DRA but emphasized the particular skills with which an individual student was having difficulty. Response to intervention was monitored frequently to determine when students mastered the target skills with which they had problems on the pretreatment assessment measures.

There was no clear distinction, however, between having dyslexia and having reading disability. One faculty member said that *dyslexia* was the term medical doctors used and *reading disability* was the term that educators used. The educational linguist in the program dwelled on the work of the descriptive linguists who documented the role of phonemes in linking spoken and written words. Throughout the program, the emphasis was on the relationships of reading to oral language and speech, that is, the child's first language. Learning to read was considered a matter of building bridges (maps) between reading and writing and listening and speaking.

During 9 years after the first author completed her graduate work, she had many opportunities to put her knowledge into practice as a general education teacher, a special education resource teacher, a reading specialist, and a private tutor. Although she thought she had a grasp on what reading was and how to teach it based on her teaching experience, having additional research experience deepened and in some ways changed her understanding of reading and its relationship to writing and oral language, normal variation in learning to read and write, the biological basis of reading and writing disabilities, and effective instructional treatments. In the sections that follow, she highlights some of the insights she gained from the programmatic research in which she took part—a series of studies in a line of investigation.

Multimodal, Leveled Language

As discussed in Section I of this book, many professionals in the field of dyslexia emphasize the need for multisensory methods for teaching students with dyslexia. Chapter 2 introduced the idea that what is needed probably extends beyond multi-sensory instruction. Brain, speech and language, and reading research also point to the role of motor output channels through the mouth (oral reading) and hand (writing) in learning to read and write. Thus, it is technically the case that multi-*modal* (sensorimotor) methods are needed for reading and writing instruction (see Chapters 4 and 5). In fact, based on a number of findings from the programmatic research in the University of Washington Multidisciplinary Learning Disabilities Center (UW LDC), V. Berninger generated a working hypothesis that teaching ear–hand connections (spelling) and eye–mouth connections (reading) from the beginning of formal literacy instruction may help to prevent and overcome dyslexia. Research supported this hypothesis (Berninger, 2008c; Berninger, Dunn, & Alper, 2004; Dunn & Miller, in press; Traweek & Berninger, 1997). Sensorimotor learning may be important not only in the initial stage of cognitive development, as Piaget (1952) proposed, but also throughout oral and written language learning. However, once a child enters the preoperational and concrete operational stages, the phonological loop (links between spoken words and sounds in them and the mouth) and/or the orthographic loop (links between written words and letters in them and the hand) guide the oral and/or written language learning. Further research is needed to determine if the benefits of multimodal (sensorimotor) instruction are specific to children with dyslexia or may benefit other children as well.

While working on her Ph.D. in psychology at Johns Hopkins, the first author had an opportunity to work with a developmental sociolinguist, Dr. Catherine Garvey. Dr. Garvey introduced her to the concept of analyzing levels of language, which is a basic tool of linguistics and can be applied to analyzing oral language protocols and to teaching and learning reading and writing. These levels range from sub-word units (e.g., phonemes and letters) to words to syntactic constructions to discourse schema that have local and global organization. Many of the controversies between whole language and phonics approaches to teaching reading could have been avoided if teachers and reading experts had understood that all of these levels of language contribute to reading—*subword* correspondences between letters and sounds to decoding, written and spoken *words* to oral and silent reading word identification and vocabulary meaning, and *syntax and discourse* to oral and silent reading fluency and comprehension. Reading requires both identifying words, based on their links with speech and semantics (meaning), and constructing meaning based on syntax and discourse schema.

Spoken–Written Word Connections

Levels of language also apply to the unit size of connections between spoken and written words. Connections can be made at the whole-word level, the level of graphemes (one and two letters) and phonemes, and the level of syllables (whole syllables and onsets and rimes). Many UW LDC research findings (e.g., Berninger, Abbott, et al., 2000; Berninger, Vaughan, et al., 1998) supported multiple connections contributing to word reading and word spelling. Although many children can learn the whole-word connections from one or a few exposures (referred to as "fast mapping"), children with dyslexia or OWL LD cannot (see Chapter 4).

Because they cannot rely on fast mapping, children with dyslexia must rely even more on slow mapping than do typically developing readers and spellers. Slow mapping involves subword connections such as letters and phonemes (alphabetic principle) and syllables (especially onsets and rimes). However, depending on the individual learning profile, children may have processing impairments that interfere with this slow mapping, for example, impaired phoneme awareness (of phonemes in spoken words), orthographic awareness (of letters in written words), or rapid automatic naming (RAN). RAN, which requires oral naming of written symbols or pictures, assesses speed or accuracy of cross-code connections (e.g., a pictured object and its name or a letter or orthographic code and a whole oral word name code). Thus, RAN may be a marker of both a fast mapping and slow mapping impairment that interferes with the cross-code mapping needed to learn to read and spell written words.

Working Memory

From her collaboration with H. Lee Swanson at the University of California, Riverside, the first author learned about the importance of working memory in learning to read and write. Two insights about working memory helped the research team better understand the nature of dyslexia. First, both children and their parents with dyslexia showed impairments in the components of working memory—word form storage and processing, phonological loop, and executive functions (supervisory attention)—but each of these components has a phonological component. So, dyslexia has a phonological core deficit within an impaired working memory architecture—with the phonological deficit impairing accuracy of word reading and the working memory deficit impairing fluency (Berninger, Abbott, Thomson, et al., 2006). Fluency is impaired because the orchestration of all of the components of working memory in real time is impaired if one or more of the components is impaired (see Chapters 7 and 8). Second, the widely used RAN task assesses phonological loop function in working memory for cross-code mapping; children who are fast and automatic in cross-code mapping are more likely to rely on fast mapping and learn the slow mapping at different unit sizes, as discussed previously.

These insights about working memory are relevant to how instruction should be packaged in time for students with dyslexia who have difficulty with temporal coordination of all the component processes in the functional systems (Luria, 1973) for reading and writing. In addition to the sequential, structured systematic instruction over time that students with dyslexia need (see Chapter 4), they also need a teaching approach that helps them to coordinate these multiple processes simultaneously in time in working memory. That is why the Literacy Trek Project (focused on normally developing and at-risk writers and readers) and UW LDC (focused on family genetics studies of dyslexia, OWL LD, and dysgraphia) use an instructional approach in most studies that combines subword, word, and text/discourse instruction close in time in the same lesson. Teachers need to plan instruction from the beginning to the end of each lesson as well as longitudinally throughout the week and school year (see Wong & Berninger, 2004).

The working-memory impairment in dyslexia also explains why many students with dyslexia benefit from teaching of procedural knowledge about the alphabetic principle and not just declarative knowledge about letter–sound correspondences (see Chapter 4). Because working memory capacity and resources are limited, the more that component processes such as word decoding, recognition, or spelling can be put on automatic pilot in implicit memory, the more capacity and resources are available for the strategic, nonautomatic processes required for reading comprehension and written composition.

Finally, a children's book titled *The Vicar of Nibbleswicke* (Dahl, 1991) captures research findings about the role of working memory in dyslexia. In the book, the new pastor, when given his first assignment as vicar in a village church, suffers a reoccurrence of his childhood dyslexia—he begins to say words backwards and often in hilarious ways. This symptom highlights the vulnerability of phonological working memory in individuals with dyslexia as the UW LDC family genetics phenotyping studies had found. Also, the symptoms of dyslexia surfaced when working memory capacity was exceeded, which is likely to happen in learning new job responsibilities. The cure for the vicar's adult onset of dyslexia is walking backwards—with a rear view mirror to see where he is going. Dahl was undoubtedly making fun of the widely held belief that dyslexia is a problem in reversals—writing letters or words backward. Although research has not shown that reversals cause dyslexia, this children's story made the telling point that order of language elements can be mixed up in spoken words as well as written words when working memory is taxed in individuals with dyslexia (Brooks, 2003).

Dyslexia, OWL LD, and Dysgraphia Do Exist

Having assessed or supervised assessments for many, many students referred for reading problems over the years, it is increasingly clear to the first author that dyslexia does exist and can be defined; however, not all reading problems are dyslexia. In the characteristic profile, some discrepancy between verbal comprehension and phonological decoding, word reading, and/or spelling (accuracy, rate, and fluency) are observed. The amount of discrepancy varies depending on an individual's instructional history, but what is striking in adults with a family and personal history of dyslexia is their persisting profile of impaired phonological decoding despite their reaching reading comprehension commensurate with their oral verbal comprehension. This profile is associated with impairments on measures of phonological, orthographic, and/or RAN processes. Another characteristic profile is OWL LD in which word decoding, word reading, and spelling and written composition are impaired. OWL LD profiles have associated impairments in morphological and syntactic awareness and word retrieval (oral verbal fluency) as well as those impairments affecting dyslexia (see Chapter 8). Neither dyslexia nor OWL LD are medical problems, even though they have a biological basis. They are educational problems, and more often than not, children with such disabilities respond well to educational treatment, that is, appropriate instruction (see Chapter 9).

Dysgraphia is another characteristic profile of individuals with learning disabilities. Dysgraphia is associated with impairments in attention, orthographic coding, and planning and executing serial finger movements (see Chapter 8). Some children have inordinate difficulty learning to form letters legibly, write them automatically, and write with age- or grade-appropriate handwriting speed on sustained writing tasks. Or they can spell by applying phoneme–grapheme strategies but do not form precise representations of written words in long-term memory that they can recall automatically. Children with dysgraphia also respond to appropriate instruction (see Chapter 9).

Integrating Assessment and Instruction

Assessing profiles of reading and writing skills and related processes is important because impaired processes explain why learning is different for some individuals and point to where teaching has to be tailored, based on the grammar of teaching (see Chapter 9) and learning, within comprehensive lessons. Phonological impairments call for more intensive instruction in the sound patterns in spoken words (e.g., see Unit III in the accompanying workbook, *Helping Students with Dyslexia and Dysgraphia Make Connections: Differentiated Instruction Lesson Plans in Reading and Writing* [Berninger & Wolf, 2009]). Orthographic impairments call for more instruction in 1) paying careful attention to written words—all the letters in sequential order—and remembering written words and their parts (e.g., Looking Games; Berninger & Traweek, 1991), 2) finding letter units during decoding (Unit I of the accompanying workbook, *Helping Students with Dyslexia and Dysgraphia* [Berninger & Wolf, 2009] by rewriting spelling units in words or using color coding; 3) applying strategies for storing and analyzing written words in the mind's eye (Unit II, Mark Twain Lesson Set 2 in the accompanying workbook); integrating orthographic-phonological and phonological strategies for word learning (John Muir Unit III in accompanying workbook); and adding orthographic to phonological awareness activities and then adding morphological awareness activities so that children can learn to coordinate all three kinds of linguistic awareness (Sequoyah Unit IV in accompanying workbook). Before gaining research and clinical experience, the first author was not as aware of the relationships of specific cognitive and linguistic processes to specific reading, writing, and oral language skills or the treatment implications of these relationships.

Administration and scoring of assessment of these processes is just the beginning. How do these processes affect instruction itself? Do they affect grouping, choice of materials, or time spent on various tasks? Teachers and schools need to understand that there is no one assessment or instructional tool that answers all of these questions for all students. The *teacher as detective* uncovers information about individual children and with knowledge of instruction provides the appropriate differentiated instruction.

Grammar of Teaching

Teachers who learn to plan and implement differentiated instruction in the classroom that meets the needs of students with dyslexia, OWL LD, and/or dysgraphia will not only be effective teachers but also have expertise for mentoring other teachers. In the process, they will abstract their own grammar of teaching (see Chapter 9). Although it is important to incorporate all of the necessary instructional components for teaching reading and writing, *there is room for teacher creativity in the process.* It is not necessary to teach the same way all the time. In the various randomized control studies and design experiments the UW LDC and Literacy Trek Project have conducted, the components of the grammar for teaching and learning are included but never in exactly the same way—yet the students respond to the instruction. The qualitative reports are as informative as the quantitative results. Below is one example of the many emails and letters that the UW LDC has received from parents over the years (the student's name has been changed, but the email is not edited for spelling or grammar; the WASL mentioned by the parent is the high-stakes test in Washington). These letters serve as reminders that the hope that is transmitted to students is as important as the skills that are taught.

> Hi,
> I had to drop you an email to let you know how well Stephanie is doing in school now. She participated in your Dyslexic research project last year. She averaged a C to C+ in 7th grade (last year) which was good for her at that time. She really struggled and let her frustrations get to her. But this year she is maintaining a strong B–B+ and she is shooting for honor roll. It seems like what she learned through the program has finally clicked.
>
> She still has some of the worst spelling (other then mine) which isn't the end of the world and her teachers can read it fine and don't count it against her. And when she has to do a final report or project she will use the computer and uses spell check, which is great but she has faced the wrath of "no suggestions" like I do on occasions. Both her mom and dad feel it was such a great program and was so worth all those nights of driving to the U.W. for about two hours and fighting traffic and weather to get there every Tuesday and Thursday night. She so wants to try and get an A in each of her classes and she is darn close to it. I never thought I would see her get a B let alone an A out of her History or Language class. She only had one class on her progress report that she didn't have an A and she said it would go up to an A because she re-took one of her tests after school and it would put it at an A. Her teachers have been great with working with her and me; it has really giving her new drive to succeeding. Most of her teachers she's had year after year, in fact her teachers made sure she was in there classes the following year. Her WASL testing this last year were the closest she has come to "at grade level" ever. She is within 2 or 10 points of hitting them, as compared to last year being way below grade level, even her reading has come up significantly. But what I see the most is how much more she comprehends what she reads and is learning. That has really improved and seems to have made such a difference.

As her parents we thought we should let you know who well she is doing and see if there was anything new going on with your research there at the U.W. There is nothing greater then see your child go from feeling like the dumbest kid in the world to feeling pride in all her work. And truly we owe a lot of that to your program and all the great research that the Professor's are exploring.

Finally, the grammar of teaching and learning is not restricted to reading and writing skills. Rich classroom environments that integrate music, science, social studies, or math with language instruction make learning exciting and meaningful. By incorporating a variety of subject areas into language instruction, teachers can capture student interest and help them understand the value of learning. One of the saddest stories the first author encountered was a boy referred for severe reading problems whose teacher threatened him if he could not pass the state high-stakes test. The teacher's goal was to be the first in the state to have all children in her class pass all the sections of the test. Assessment showed that the boy had superior intelligence, severe dyslexia, and talent in science. At age 8 he was already collecting rare biological specimens and knew more about the phyla of the plant world than the psychologists assessing him. Moreover, he loved science. When he was asked what the class was learning in science, he replied that they did not have time to ever do science. They spent all their time practicing for the test so that everyone could pass and not let the teacher down. Readers can form their own conclusion about what is wrong with this learning environment and why it was not appropriate for this boy with an educationally disabling condition. Above all else, what any teacher can give to a student with educational disabling conditions is compassionitivity—the art of compassion or deep caring about another human being whether or not the teacher possesses full scientific understanding of the basis for the educational disabling condition. (See Berninger & Richards, 2002, for further discussion of the concept of *compassionitivity*, which combines morphological awareness with the need for teachers to bring heart as well as mind to their teaching; caring goes a long way for students who struggle).

Although some teachers may feel they are not equipped to teach reading and writing to students with dyslexia, OWL LD, and/or dysgraphia, they are probably very capable of providing intellectual engagement and joy in learning, which are equally important. In this grammar of teaching and learning, critical components include the following: 1) at the end of the school day each student—with or without a specific learning disability—knows something he or she did not know when school started that day, 2) each student experiences success in at least one activity each day, and 3) each student believes that the teacher cares about her or him as a learner.

Teachers who desire to learn more about the research on teaching reading and writing to students with and without dyslexia, OWL LD, and/or dysgraphia can contact the nearest college or university offering graduate courses on relevant topics or a systematic program in science-based literacy preparation (see Chapter 12) or their alma mater. One principal, in frustration, suggested that teachers whose students did not pass high-stakes tests should sue their alma mater for not preparing them for the realities of teaching in the real world. The authors propose that instead they consider contributing to the fundraising efforts of the institution IF it offers appropriate, science- and practitioner-based preservice and in-service education that prepares teachers to serve all students, including those with dyslexia, OWL LD, and/or dysgraphia. Increasingly, institutions of higher education are responsive to the interests and concerns of alumni and others who contribute to their fundraising efforts.

Biological Basis

Just because a child has a learning disorder with a genetic or biological basis, it does not mean that the child cannot learn. Although not all developmental and learning disorders are equally responsive to teaching, research on dyslexia, OWL LD, and dysgraphia to date shows that children with such disabilities do respond to teaching (see four lesson sets for workshops in associated book and Chapters 4, 5, and 7 in this book). They can learn, but they typically must work harder than classmates to do so, and teachers must work harder to teach them in specialized ways. The rewards for both students and teachers, however, can be enormous.

Compensation Versus Normalization

When teaching in the public schools or tutoring privately, the first author observed that most students responded to instruction and appeared to overcome their problems at a behavioral level. Just because a student responds to instruction, it does not mean, however, that they do not have a learning disability or have completely overcome their biologically based learning disorder. Their brains may use alternate pathways, or all of the relevant brain regions may not be fully normalized or synchronized in time. If the genetic or neural vulnerability is present, students may overcome problems at one stage of schooling only to confront new challenges as the nature of the curriculum and curriculum requirements change. Students with dyslexia, OWL LD, and/or dysgraphia should not be dismissed from special education and denied individualized education programs as soon as they learn to read reasonably well. They need continued explicit instruction in writing and integrated reading-writing.

Reflections on Scientist-Practitioner Career

Many researchers are seeking the single variable that explains causality and treatment of dyslexia. Teachers know, in contrast, that teaching and learning are complex and involve many variables. In addition to the components of effective instruction identified by the National Reading Panel (NICHD, 2000), research by the UW LDC (family genetics and treatment of persisting reading and writing disabilities) and Literacy Trek Project (normal writing and reading development and intervention for at-risk students) and other research groups has shown that two additional linguistic awareness components are essential for learning to read and write—orthographic and morphological awareness. In addition, writing—handwriting, spelling, and composition—influences reading acquisition, and successful school performance requires integrated reading-writing. Finally, executive functions (strategies for paying attention—focusing, staying on task, and switching tasks—and self-regulation of reading and writing processes) are critical. Learning to read and write involves many processes that have to be orchestrated in time in functional systems to achieve literacy goals. Individual differences in learners and their response to instruction across the life span are facts of life.

Finally, 40 years after she first tutored a boy with reading disability, the first author learned that the Scottish Rite organization provides free assessment and treatment services for children with dyslexia in some states but in many states, provides free assessment and treatment for oral language disability (in children ages 2–8). Because oral language disability typically leads to OWL LD if not treated, this latter service is a wonderful free resource. Individuals with language learning disabilities may have exceptional talents in nonverbal expression of ideas by hand; thus teachers should strive to create learning environments in schools that are nurturing of hands-on learning and not just verbal learning.

CLOSING COMMENTS FOR NEW BEGINNINGS

Former Washington State Governor Dan Evans was noted previously in this book for his comment that what research shows is effective instruction for students with dyslexia may work well for all students. Certainly many of the approaches described in this book could be used with other students in general education, including English language learners and students from low-literacy home environments or culturally different backgrounds. All of these students are likely to benefit from sequential, structured, systematic reading and writing instruction that teaches to all levels of language close in time. Teachers should assess all students' response to instruction and decide if whatever program is in place is working for each student. If the program is not working for all students, teachers should modify it for individuals, assess response to the modification, and revaluate. Therefore, the teaching strategies covered in this book should have high utility for teaching a diverse student body in general education. At the same time, the authors caution that not all students struggle in learning to read and write and need this kind of specialized instruction. However, all students may benefit from some common core activities such as word study (vocabulary development geared to morphological awareness and word origins) and word play (creating humor through language).

Another motivation for writing this book was the concern of both authors that not all parents can afford to pay for private tutoring or private schools for their children with special learning needs. Their children may succeed only if public schools offer instructional programs geared to their instructional needs. Furthermore, the federal law guaranteeing free appropriate education in public schools to all students with educational disabling conditions applies independent of parental level of income. Both authors are committed to making the knowledge of effective instruction for students with dyslexia, OWL LD, and/or dysgraphia available to all children, especially those attending public schools whose parents cannot afford private tutoring or private schools. Often their learning needs require more than pull-out services two or three times per week. They need specialized learning environments throughout the school day every day, but it is possible to create such learning environments within general education classrooms if teachers are taught why and how.

According to Faust (2007), "Education is the engine that makes American democracy work. And it has to work, and that means people have to have access." Slingerland had an understanding of private and public education. Her work at Punahou School in Hawaii had shown her excellence in the private sector. However, she understood that her true calling was working with students and teachers in public schools. In adapting the Orton-Gillingham Approach to the classroom, she was motivated by the need to help as many children as possible. A United Nations (1959) resolution says, "Mankind owes to the child the best it has to give." Schools owe children the same. An adequate education is not enough when the knowledge exists to provide the best education possible. This knowledge stems from 1) classroom experience in teaching students who differ in the ease of learning to read and write, *and* 2) research on how students learn to read and write and effective teaching methods for students with diverse learning profiles and instructional needs.

In closing, we emphasize that we are all connected. The second author had the benefit of close personal mentoring from Beth Slingerland and has over a 40-year career done the same for countless other teachers and teacher educators in Washington and other states. She has also been nurtured by many connections over the years with other professionals and parents in the International Dyslexia Association (IDA). The first author's connections to the second author stem from their meeting at a local media event to promote awareness of learning disabilities. At this event, it was painfully evident that the various stakeholders were not talking about the same population of students. The authors joked about the fact that no one could define what it was that they are really talking about. The second author made the astute observation that the controversies about IQ–achievement discrepancy were missing the real issue that individuals with specific learning disabilities such as dyslexia need constant reassurance that they really are bright when they struggle so much more than others in the two tasks expected of school-age children—learning to read and write. That fortuitous meeting was the beginning of a collaboration for more than a decade in which the second author helped the UW LDC find and work with families with multigenerational histories of dyslexia, OWL LD, and/or dysgraphia.

The first author's connections to Beth Slingerland are not as strong as for the second author but are there nonetheless. When she was hired as a special education resource teacher during a pilot phase before the Education for All Handicapped Children Act of 1975 (PL 94-142) went into effect, she was given the book Beth Slingerland wrote on teaching children with language learning disabilities (see Chapter 2) and the screening test for children most at risk. There were no guidelines for either identifying or teaching children in the resource room. She used the screening tool along with other measures and observed many children who had difficulty with analyzing letters in written words and remembering written words they saw briefly but had to analyze from memory. That was the beginning of her interest in orthographic processing, which is not the same as visual perception (see Chapters 4, 5, and 8). She had the opportunity to meet Beth Slingerland once when Slingerland gave a presentation at a lunch sponsored by the Baltimore branch of IDA (then, the Orton Society). In her enthusiasm to share with the audience, Slingerland inadvertently fell off the stage and was rushed to the hospital. Out of deep respect and concern, the audience remained for more than 3 hours until she returned to finish her presentation. The talk was well received, and the audience sensed that Beth Slingerland was truly remarkable and committed to the education of children.

Connections to Marcia Henry, whom the first author met for the first time when seated beside her at a National Institutes of Health workshop on research on instruction, have also played an important role in the first author's research. For the first time she learned about the role of word origin in the phonology, orthography, and morphology of word decoding (see Chapter 4). That knowledge played a pivotal role in the first UW LDC study showing that the brain normalized after comprehensive, explicit reading and writing instruction and science problem solving for intellectual engagement (see Chapter 7) and in Sylvia Abbott's dissertation showing that it is never too late to remediate (Abbott & Berninger, 1999).

The authors hope that the message of this book has been clear. On the one hand, the increasing recognition of the importance of grounding educational practice in science and research is a good trend. On the other hand, researchers alone cannot generate all the knowledge necessary for effective teaching of students with dyslexia, OWL LD, and/or dysgraphia. Teachers learn valuable knowledge from teaching experience that is also relevant. The relationship between researchers and teachers is bidirectional—contributions can go in both directions. Teachers' daily observations of student performance provide background and generate questions of value to the researchers. Teacher interaction with students exhibiting a broad spectrum of strengths and weaknesses provides a perspective that places the information gained from research into the framework of the classroom. Both science and teaching benefit from close connections and collaborations between researchers and teachers. A majority of students with specific learning disabilities can benefit from these researcher–teacher connections.

References

Abbott, R., Berninger, V., & Fayol, M. (2008). *Longitudinal structural equation modeling of development of writing-writing and writing-reading connections at the letter, word and text levels in grades 1 to 7.* Manuscript submitted for publication.

Abbott, S., & Berninger, V.W. (1999). It's never too late to remediate: A developmental approach to teaching word recognition. *Annals of Dyslexia, 49,* 223–250.

Adams, M.J. (1990). *Beginning to read: Thinking and learning about print.* Cambridge, MA: The MIT Press.

Adams, M.J., Foorman, B.R., Lundberg, I., & Beeler, T. (1998). *Phonemic awareness in young children: A classroom curriculum.* Baltimore: Paul H. Brookes Publishing Co.

Altemeier, L., Abbott, R., & Berninger, V.W. (2008). Executive functions for reading and writing in typical literacy development and dyslexia. *Journal of Clinical and Experimental Neuropsychology, 30,* 588–606.

Altemeier, L., Jones, J., Abbott, R., & Berninger, V.W. (2006). Executive factors in becoming writing-readers and reading-writers: Note-taking and report writing in third and fifth graders. *Developmental Neuropsychology, 29,* 161–173.

American Psychological Association. (2006, September 15). APA Coalition for Psychology in Schools and Education survey of teacher needs. Retrieved September 8, 2008, from http://www.apa.org/releases/teacher needs.html

Amtmann, D., Abbott, R., & Berninger, V.W. (2007). Mixture growth models for RAN and RAS row by row: Insight into the reading system at work over time. *Reading and Writing: An Interdisciplinary Journal, 20,* 785–813.

Amtmann, D., Abbott, R., & Berninger, V.W. (2008). Identifying and predicting classes of response to explicit, phonological spelling instruction during independent composing. *Journal of Learning Disabilities, 41,* 218–234.

Anderson, J.R. (1993). *Rules of the mind.* Mahwah, NJ: Lawrence Erlbaum Associates.

Anderson, J.R., & Bower, G.R. (1973). *Human associative memory.* Washington, DC: Winston & Sons.

Apel, K., Oster, J., & Masterson, J. (2006). Effects of phonotactic and orthotactic probabilities during fast-mapping on five year-olds' learning to spell. *Developmental Neuropsychology, 29,* 21–42.

Aram, D., Ekelman, B., & Nation, J. (1984). Preschoolers with language disorders: 10 years later. *Journal of Speech and Hearing Research, 27,* 232–244.

Arieti, S. (1976). *Creativity the magic synthesis.* New York: Basic Books.

Auman, M. (2003). *Step up to writing* (2nd ed.). Longmont, CO: Sopris West Educational Services.

Aylward, E., Richards, T., Berninger, V., Nagy, W., Field, K., Grimme, A., Richards, A., Thomson, J., & Cramer, S. (2003). Instructional treatment associated with changes in brain activation in children with dyslexia. *Neurology, 61,* 212–219.

Baddeley, A., & Hitch, G. (1974). Working memory. In G.A. Bower (Ed.), *Recent advances in learning and motivation* (pp. 47–90). New York: Academic Press.

Badian, N.A. (1998). A validation of the role of preschool phonological and orthographic skills in the prediction of reading. *Journal of Learning Disabilities, 31,* 472–481.

Balmuth, M. (1992). *The roots of phonics: A historical introduction.* Timonium, MD: York Press.

Bear, D., Invernizzi, M., Templeton, S., & Johnston, F. (2000). *Words their way: Word study for phonics, vocabulary, and spelling instruction* (2nd ed.). Upper Saddle River, NJ: Prentice Hall.

Beck, I.L., & McKeown, M.G. (2001). Text talk: Capturing the benefits of reading aloud for young children. *The Reading Teacher, 55*(1), 10–19.

Beck, I.L., & McKeown, M.G. (2007). Increasing young low income children's oral vocabulary repertoires through rich and focused instruction *Elementary School Journal, 107*(3), 251–271.

Beeler, D. (1988). *Book of roots: A full study of our family of words.* Self-published. Union Representative. 2202 Cedar Rd., Homewood, IL 60430. ISBN 0-91-8515-00-9.

Beery, K. (1982). *Administration, scoring, and teaching manual for the Developmental Test of Visual–Motor Integration* (Rev. ed.). Cleveland, OH: Modern Curriculum Press.

Benbow, M. (1990). *Loops and groups: A kinesthetic writing system.* San Antonio, TX: Therapy Skill Builders.

Berninger, V.W. (1994a). *Reading and writing acquisition: A developmental neuropsychological perspective.* Madison, WI: WCB Brown & Benchmark Publishing. Reprinted 1996, Westview Press, Boulder, CO. Distributed by Pearson Assessment (orig. Psychological Corporation)

Berninger, V.W. (Ed.). (1994b). *The varieties of orthographic knowledge I: Theoretical and developmental issues.* Dordrecht, The Netherlands: Kluwer Academic Press.

Berninger, V.W. (Ed.). (1995). *The varieties of orthographic knowledge II: Their relation to phonology, reading, and writing.* Dordrecht, The Netherlands: Kluwer Academic Press.

Berninger, V.W. (1998a). *Handwriting program.* San Antonio, TX: Pearson Assessment.

Berninger, V.W. (1998b). *Process Assessment of the Learner (PAL): Guides for intervention—Reading and writing.* San Antonio, TX: Pearson Assessment.

Berninger, V.W. (2000). Dyslexia an invisible, treatable disorder: The story of Einstein's ninja turtles. *Learning Disability Quarterly, 23,* 175–195.

Berninger, V.W. (2001). Understanding the "lexia" in dyslexia. *Annals of Dyslexia, 51,* 23–48.

Berninger, V.W. (2004a). The reading brain in children and youth: A systems approach. In B. Wong (Ed.), *Learning about learning disabilities* (3rd ed., pp. 197–248). New York: Academic Press.

Berninger, V.W. (2004b). Understanding the graphia in dysgraphia. In D. Dewey & D. Tupper (Eds.), *Developmental motor disorders: A neuropsychological perspective* (pp. 328–350). New York: Guilford Press.

Berninger, V.W. (2006). A developmental approach to learning disabilities. In I. Siegel & A. Renninger (Eds.), *Handbook of child psychology, Vol. IV: Child psychology and practice* (pp. 420–452). New York: Wiley.

Berninger, V.W. (2007). *Process Assessment of the Learner, second edition (PAL-II): Diagnostic for reading and writing* (PAL-II Reading and Writing). San Antonio, TX: Pearson Assessment. (Contains Diagnostic Test Kit with *PAL-II User Guide* on CD by the same author; explains how to do evidence-based Tier 1, Tier 2, and Tier 3 assessment-intervention.)

Berninger, V.W. (2008a). Defining and differentiating dyslexia, dysgraphia, and language learning disability within a working memory model. In M. Mody & E.R. Silliman (Eds.), *Challenges in language and literacy: Brain, behavior, and learning in language and reading disorders* (pp. 103–134). New York: Guilford Press.

Berninger, V.W. (2008b). Listening to parents of children with learning disabilities: Lessons from the University of Washington Multidisciplinary Learning Disabilities Center. In *Perspectives on language and literacy* (pp. 22–30). Towson, MD: International Dyslexia Association.

Berninger, V.W. (2008c, September 3–5). *Writing first: Teaching children to write at the beginning of schooling facilitates reading and writing development.* Agence National de la Recherche research project on development of written and spoken expression in French monolingual low SES children and adolescents. University of Lyon, Lyon, France.

Berninger, V.W., & Abbott, S. (2003). *PAL research-supported reading and writing lessons and Reproducibles.* San Antonio, TX: Pearson Assessment.

Berninger, V.W., & Abbott, R. (2008). *Developmental changes in predicting writing outcomes from listening, speaking, and reading in grades 1, 3, 5, and 7.* Manuscript submitted for publication.

Berninger, V.W., Abbott, R., Abbott, S., Graham, S., & Richards, T. (2002). Writing and reading: Connections between language by hand and language by eye. *Journal of Learning Disabilities, 35,* 39–56.

Berninger, V., Abbott, R., Augsburger, A., & Garcia, N. (2008). *Comparison of pen and keyboard transcription modes in children with and without learning disabilities affecting transcription.* Manuscript submitted for publication.

Berninger, V.W., Abbott, R., Brooksher, R., Lemos, Z., Ogier, S., Zook, D., et al. (2000). A connectionist approach to making the predictability of English orthography explicit to at-risk beginning readers: Evidence for alternative, effective strategies. *Developmental Neuropsychology, 17,* 241–271.

Berninger, V.W., Abbott, R., Jones, J., Wolf, B., Gould, L., Anderson-Youngstrom, M., et al. (2006). Early development of language by hand: Composing, reading, listening, and speaking connections; three letter-writing modes; and fast mapping in spelling. *Developmental Neuropsychology, 29,* 61–92.

Berninger, V.W., Abbott, R., Thomson, J., & Raskind, W. (2001). Language phenotype for reading and writing disability: A family approach. *Scientific Studies in Reading, 5,* 59–105.

Berninger, V.W., Abbott, R., Thomson, J., Wagner, R., Swanson, H.L., Wijsman, E., et al. (2006). Modeling developmental phonological core deficits within a working-memory architecture in children and adults with developmental dyslexia. *Scientific Studies in Reading, 10,* 165–198.

Berninger, V.W., Abbott, R., Vermeulen, K., & Fulton, C. (2006). Paths to reading comprehension in at-risk second grade readers. *Journal of Learning Disabilities, 39,* 334–351.

Berninger, V.W., Abbott, R., Whitaker, D., Sylvester, L., & Nolen, S. (1995). Integrating low-level skills and high-level skills in treatment protocols for writing disabilities. *Learning Disability Quarterly, 18,* 293–309.

Berninger, V.W., & Amtmann, D. (2003). Preventing written expression disabilities through early and continuing assessment and intervention for handwriting and/or spelling problems: Research into practice. In H.L. Swanson, K.R. Harris, & S. Graham (Eds.), *Handbook of research on learning disabilities* (pp. 345–363). New York: Guilford Press.

Berninger, V.W., Dunn, A., & Alper, T. (2004). Integrated models for branching assessment, instructional assessment, and profile assessment. In A. Prifitera, D. Saklofske, L. Weiss, & E. Rolfhus (Eds.), *WISC-IV: Clinical use and interpretation* (pp. 151–185). San Diego: Academic Press.

Berninger, V.W., & Fayol, M. (2008). Why spelling is important and how to teach it effectively. *Encyclopedia of language and literacy development* (pp. 1–13). London, ON: Canadian Language and Literacy Research Network. Retrieved September 8, 2008, from http://www.literacyencyclopedia.ca/pdfs/topic.php?topId=234

Berninger, V.W., & Hidi, S. (2006). Mark Twain's writers' workshop: A nature–nurture perspective in motivating students with learning disabilities to compose. In S. Hidi, & P. Boscolo (Eds.), *Motivation in writing* (pp. 159–179). Amsterdam: Elsevier.

Berninger, V.W., & Holdnack, J. (2008). Neuroscientific and clinical perspectives on the RTI initiative in learning disabilities diagnosis and intervention: Response to questions begging answers that see the forest and the trees. In C. Reynolds & E. Fletcher-Janzen (Eds.), *Neuroscientific and clinical perspectives on the RTI initiative in learning disabilities diagnosis and intervention* (pp. 66–81). New York: Wiley.

Berninger, V.W., & Nagy, W. (2008). Flexibility in word reading: Multiple levels of representations, complex mappings, partial similarities, and cross-modality connections. In K. Cartwright (Ed.), *Flexibility in literacy processes and instructional practice: Implications of developing representational ability for literacy teaching and learning* (pp. 114–139). New York: Guilford Press.

Berninger, V.W., Nagy, W., Carlisle, J., Thomson, J., Hoffer, D., Abbott, S. et al. (2003). Effective treatment for dyslexics in grades 4 to 6. In B. Foorman (Ed.), *Preventing and remediating reading difficulties: Bringing science to scale* (pp. 382–417). Timonium, MD: York Press.

Berninger, V.W., Nielsen, K., Abbott, R., Wijsman, E., & Raskind, W. (2008a). Gender differences in severity of writing and reading disabilities. *Journal of School Psychology, 46,* 151–172.

Berninger, V.W., Nielsen, K., Abbott, R., Wijsman, E., & Raskind, W. (2008b). Writing problems in developmental dyslexia: Under-recognized and under-treated. *Journal of School Psychology, 46,* 1–21.

Berninger, V.W., O'Donnell, L., & Holdnack, J. (2008). Research-supported differential diagnosis of specific learning disabilities and implications for instruction and response to instruction (RTI). In A. Prifitera, D. Saklofske, & L. Weiss (Eds.), *WISC-IV clinical assessment and intervention, second edition* (pp. 69–108). San Diego: Academic Press.

Berninger, V.W., Raskind, W., Richards, T., Abbott, R., & Stock, P. (2008). A multidisciplinary approach to understanding developmental dyslexia within working-memory architecture: Genotypes, phenotypes, brain, and instruction. *Developmental Neuropsychology, 33,* 707–744.

Berninger, V.W., & Richards, T. (2002). *Brain literacy for educators and psychologists.* New York: Academic Press.

Berninger, V. , & Richards, T. (2008a, February 9). *Brain differences of 5th graders with and without writing disabilities on fMRI handwriting, orthographic coding, and finger succession tasks.* In S. Hooper (Organizer, Symposium). The neuropsychological basis of written language in children. International Neuropsychology Association, Hawaii.

Berninger, V.W., & Richards, T. (2008b). How brain research informs reading, writing, and math instruction and learning. In E. Anderman, L. Anderman, C. Chinn, T. Murcock, & H.L. Swanson (Eds.), *Psychology of classroom learning: An encyclopedia* (pp. XX–XX). Farmington Hills, MI: The Gale Group.

Berninger, V.W., Richards, T., Stock, P., Trivedi, P., & Altemeier, L. (2007, June 28). *From idea generation to idea expression in language by hand in good and poor writers.* Keynote presentation in Learning and Teaching Writing: *British Journal of Educational Psychology* Psychological Aspects of Education Current Trends Conference. Oxford Brookes University.

Berninger, V.W., Rutberg, J., Abbott, R., Garcia, N., Anderson-Youngstrom, M., Brooks, A., et al. (2006). Tier 1 and Tier 2 early intervention for handwriting and composing. *Journal of School Psychology, 44,* 3–30.

Berninger, V.W., Stock, P., Lee, Y., Abbott, R., & Breznitz, Z. (2007, July). *Working memory enhancement through accelerated reading training.* Presentation at the symposium on Can the Dyslexic Brain Do Better? Prague, Czech Republic.

Berninger, V.W., & Traweek, D. (1991). Effects of two-phase reading intervention on three orthographic phonological code connections. *Learning and Individual Differences, 3,* 323–338.

Berninger, V.W., Vaughan, K., Abbott, R., Abbott, S., Brooks, A., Rogan, L., et al. (1997). Treatment of handwriting fluency problems in beginning writing: Transfer from handwriting to composition. *Journal of Educational Psychology, 89,* 652–666.

Berninger, V.W., Vaughan, K., Abbott, R., Begay, K., Byrd, K., Curtin, G., et al. (2002). Teaching spelling and composition alone and together: Implications for the simple view of writing. *Journal of Educational Psychology, 94,* 291–304.

Berninger, V.W., Vaughan, K., Abbott, R., Brooks, A., Abbott, S., Reed, E., et al. (1998). Early intervention for spelling problems: Teaching spelling units of varying size within a multiple connections framework. *Journal of Educational Psychology, 90,* 587–605.

Berninger, V.W., Vaughan, K., Abbott, R., Brooks, A., Begay, K., Curtin, G., et al. (2000). Language-based spelling instruction: Teaching children to make multiple connections between spoken and written words. *Learning Disability Quarterly, 23,* 117–135.

Berninger, V.W., Winn, W., Stock, P., Abbott, R., Eschen, K., Lin, C., et al. (2008). Tier 3 specialized writing instruction for students with dyslexia. *Reading and Writing: An Interdisciplinary Journal, 21,* 95–129.

Berninger, V.W., & Wolf, B. (2009). *Helping students with dyslexia and dysgraphia make connections: Differentiated instruction lesson plans in reading and writing.* Baltimore: Paul H. Brookes Publishing Co.

Berninger, V.W., Yates, C., & Lester, K. (1991). Multiple orthographic codes in acquisition of reading and writing skills. *Reading and Writing: An Interdisciplinary Journal, 3,* 115–149.

Biemiller, A. (1977–1978). Relationship between oral reading rates for letters, words, and simple text in the development of reading achievement. *Reading Research Quarterly, 13,* 223–253.

Biemiller, A., & Siegel, L. (1997). A longitudinal study of the effects of the Bridge Reading Program for children at-risk for reading failure. *Learning Disability Quarterly, 20,* 83–92.

Birsh, J.R. (Ed.). (2005). *Multisensory teaching of basic language skills* (2nd ed.). Baltimore: Paul H. Brookes Publishing Co.

Birsh, J. (2006). What is multisensory structured language? *Perspectives, 32*(2), 15–20.

Bishop, D.V.M., & Adams, C. (1990). A prospective study of the relationship between specific language impairment, phonological disorders and reading retardation. *Journal of Child Psychology and Psychiatry, 31,* 1027–1050.

Blachman, B.A., Ball, E.W., Black, R., & Tangel, D.M. (2000). *Road to the code. A phonological awareness program for young children.* Baltimore: Paul H. Brookes Publishing Co.

Bond, G., & Tinker, T. (1967). *Reading difficulties: Their diagnosis and correction.* New York: Appleton-Century-Crofts.

Bowers, P., & Wolf, M. (1993). Theoretical links between naming speed, precise timing mechanisms, and orthographic skill in dyslexia. *Reading and Writing: An Interdisciplinary Journal, 5,* 69–85.

Bradley, L., & Bryant, P. (1983). Categorizing sounds and learning to read: A causal connection. *Nature, 303,* 419–421.

Bradley, R., Danielson, L., & Hallahan, D. (2002). *Identification of learning disabilities: Research to practice.* Mahwah, NJ: Lawrence Erlbaum Associates.

Brady, S., Fowler, A., Stone, B., & Winebury, N. (1994). Training in phonological awareness: A study with inner city kindergarten children, *Annals of Dyslexia, 34,* 26–59.

Breznitz, Z. (1997). The effect of accelerated reading rate on memory for text among dyslexic readers. *Journal of Educational Psychology, 89,* 287–299.

Breznitz, Z. (2006). *Fluency in reading: Synchronization of processes.* Mahwah, NJ: Lawrence Erlbaum Associates.

Brkanac, Z., Chapman, N., Matsushita, M., Chun, L., Nielsen, K., Cochrane, E., et al. (2007). Evaluation of candidate genes for DYX1 and DYX2 in families with dyslexia. *American Journal of Medical Genetics Part B: Neuropsychiatric Genetics, 144B,* 556–560.

Brooks, A.D. (2003). Neuropsychological processes related to persisting reversal errors in dyslexia and dysgraphia. *Dissertation Abstracts International, 63*(11-A), 3850.

Bruce, D.J. (1964). The analysis of word sounds. *British Journal of Educational Psychology, 34,* 158–170.

Bruck, M. (1993). Component spelling skills of college students with childhood diagnoses of dyslexia. *Learning Disability Quarterly, 16,* 171–184.

Bryant, P., Nunes, T., & Bindman, M. (1997). Children's understanding of the connection between grammar and spelling. In B. Blachman (Ed.), *Foundations of reading acquisition and dyslexia* (pp. 219–240). Mahwah, NJ: Lawrence Erlbaum Associates.

Cain, K., & Oakhill, J. (2007). *Children's comprehension problems in oral and written language: A cognitive perspective.* New York: Guilford Press.

Cardon, L., Smith, S., Fulker, D., Kimberling, W., Pennington, B., & DeFries, J. (1995). Quantitative trait locus for reading disability on chromosome 6. *Science, 266,* 276–279.

Carlisle, J. (1994). Morphological awareness, spelling, and story writing: Possible relationships for elementary-age children with and without learning disabilities. In N.C. Jordan & J. Goldsmith-Phillips (Eds.), *Learning disabilities: New directions for assessment and intervention* (pp. 123–145). Boston: Allyn & Bacon.

Carlisle, J. (1995). Morphological awareness and early reading achievement. In L. Feldman (Ed.), *Morphological aspects of language processing* (pp. 189–209). Mahwah, NJ: Lawrence Erlbaum Associates.

Carlisle, J. (1996). *Models for writing, levels A, B, and C.* Novato, CA: Academic Therapy Publications.

Carlisle, J. (2000). Awareness of the structure and meaning of morphologically complex words: Impact on reading. *Reading and Writing: An Interdisciplinary Journal, 12,* 169–190.

Carlisle, J. (2004). Morphological processes that influence learning to read. In A. Stone, E. Silliman, B. Ehren, & K. Apel (Eds.), *Handbook of language and literacy: Development and disorders* (pp. 318–339). New York: Guilford Press.

Carlisle, J.F., & Fleming, J. (2003). Lexical processing of morphologically complex words in the elementary years. *Scientific Studies of Reading, 7,* 239–253.

Carlisle, J., & Nomanbhoy, D. (1993). Phonological and morphological development. *Applied Psycholinguistics, 14,* 177–195.

Carlisle, J., & Rice, M. (2002). *Improving reading comprehension: Research-based principles and practices.* Timonium, MD: York Press.

Carlisle, J.F., Stone, C.A., & Katz, L.A. (2001). The effects of phonological transparency in reading derived words. *Annals of Dyslexia, 51,* 249–274.

Carreker, S. (2006). The parts of speech: Foundation of writing. *Perspectives, 32*(2), 31–34. Baltimore: The International Dyslexia Association.

Carter, F. (1990). *The education of Little Tree.* Albuquerque: The University of New Mexico Press.

Cash, J. (n.d.). *Bitter tears: Ballads of the American Indian.* New York: Columbia Records.

Catts, H., Fey, M., Zhang, X., & Tomblin, B. (1999). Language basis of reading and reading disability: Evidence from a longitudinal investigation. *Scientific Studies in Reading, 3,* 331–361.

Catts, H., Fey, M., Zhang, X., & Tomblin, B. (2001). Estimating the risk of future reading difficulties in kindergarten children: A research-based model and its clinical implication. *Language, Speech, and Hearing Services in Schools, 32,* 38–50.

Catts, H., Hogan, T., & Adloff, S. (2005). Developmental changes in reading and reading disabilities. In H. Catts & A. Kamhi (Eds.), *The connections between language and reading disabilities* (pp. 25–40). Mahwah, NJ: Lawrence Erlbaum Associates.

Chapman, N., Igo, R., Thomson, J., Matsushita, M., Brkanac, Z., Hotzman, T., et al. (2004). Linkage analyses of four regions previously implicated in dyslexia: Confirmation of a locus on chromosome 15q. *American Journal of Medical Genetics/Neuropsychiatric Genetics. 131B,* 67–75.

Charles, R. (2004). *All about chocolate: Level U quick reader.* Retrieved September 8, 2008, from http://www.readinga-z.com/newfiles/levels/u/chocolateu.html

Chenault, B., Thomson, J., Abbott, R., & Berninger, V.W. (2006). Effects of prior attention training on child dyslexics' response to composition instruction. *Developmental Neuropsychology, 29,* 243–260.

Childs, S. (1962). *Sound phonics.* Cambridge, MA: Educators Publishing Service.

Childs, S. (1968). *A biographical sketch: Education and specific language disability: The papers of Anna Gillingham, M.A.* Pomfret, CT: The Orton Society.

Columbia University Health Sciences Library. (n.d.). Personal papers and manuscripts: Samuel Torrey Orton, 1879–1948, and June Lyday Orton, 1898–1977. Retrieved September

8, 2008, from http://library.cpmc.columbia.edu/hsl/archives/findingaids/ortoncasefiles.html

Connelly, V., Campbell, S., MacLean, M., & Barnes, J. (2006). Contribution of lower-order skills to the written composition of college students with and without dyslexia. *Developmental Neuropsychology, 29,* 175–196.

Connor, C., Morrison, F., & Katch, L. (2004). Beyond the reading wars: Exploring the effect of child-instruction interactions on growth in early reading. *Scientific Studies of Reading, 8,* 305–336.

Cox, A.R. (1992). *Foundations for literacy: Structures and techniques for multisensory teaching of basic written English language skills.* Cambridge, MA: Educators Publishing Service.

Craggs, J., Sanchez, J., Kibby, M., Gilger, J., & Hynd, G. (2006). Brain morphological neuropsychological profiles of a family displaying superior nonverbal intelligence and dyslexia. *Cortex, 42,* 1107–1118.

Culham, R. (2003). *6 + 1 traits of writing; The complete guide.* Teaching Resources. *Traits of good writing* (grades 1–2, 3–4, or 5–6) distributed by Scottsdale, AZ: Remedia 1-800-826-4740.

Dahl, R. (1991). *The vicar of Nibbleswicke.* London, England: Random Century Group.

Deák, G.O. (2001). The development of cognitive flexibility and language abilities. *Advances in Child Development and Behavior, 31,* 271–327.

DeFries, J., & Fulker, D. (1985). Multiple regression analysis of twin data. *Behavior Genetics, 15,* 467–473.

de Hirsch, K., & Jansky, J. (1972). *Preventing reading failure.* New York: Harper & Row, Publishers.

de Hirsch, K., Jansky, J., & Langford, W. (1966). *Predicting reading failure.* New York: Harper & Row.

Delisle, J. (Ed.). (1984). *Gifted children speak out.* New York: Walker & Company.

Derwing, B.L. (1976). Morpheme recognition and the learning of rules for derivational morphology. *Canadian Journal of Linguistics, 21,* 38–66.

Derwing, B.L., Smith, M.L., & Wiebe, G.E. (1995). On the role of spelling in morpheme recognition: Experimental studies with children and adults. In L. Feldman (Ed.), *Morphological aspects of language processing* (pp. 3–27). Mahwah, NJ: Lawrence Erlbaum Associates.

Dickinson, D., & McCabe, A. (1991). The acquisition and development of language: A social interaction account of language and literacy development. In J. Kavanagh (Ed.), *The language continuum* (pp. 1–40). Timonium, MD: York Press.

Dixon, R.C., & Engelmann, S. (2001). *Spelling through morphographs: Teacher's guide.* Columbus, OH: SRA/McGraw-Hill.

Dowhower, S. (1987). Effects of repeated reading on second-grade transitional readers' fluency and comprehension. *Reading Research Quarterly, 22,* 389–406.

Dreyer, L., Luke, S., & Melican, E. (1995). Children's acquisition and retention of word spellings. In V.W. Berninger (Ed.), *The varieties of orthographic knowledge II: Relationships to phonology, reading, and writing* (pp. 291–320). Dordrecht, The Netherlands: Kluwer Academic Publishers.

Dunn, A., & Miller, D. (in press). Who can speak for the children? Implementing research-based practices in an urban school district. In S. Rosenfield & V.W. Berninger (Eds.), *Implementing evidence-based interventions in school settings.* New York: Oxford University Press.

Eckert, M., Leonard, C., Richards, T., Aylward, E., Thomson, J., & Berninger, V.W. (2003). Anatomical correlates of dyslexia: Frontal and cerebellar findings. *Brain, 126*(2), 482–494.

Eckert, M., Leonard, C., Wilke, M., Eckert, M., Richards, T., Richards, A., et al. (2005). Anatomical signature of dyslexia in children: Unique information from manual-based and voxel-based morphometry brain measures. *Cortex, 41,* 304–315.

Eden, G., VanMeter, J., Rumsey, J., Maisog, J., Woods, R., & Zeffiro, T. (1996). Abnormal processing of visual motion in dyslexia revealed by functional brain imaging [see comments]. *Nature, 382,* 66–69.

Education for All Handicapped Children Act of 1975, PL 94-142, 20 U.S.C. 3801 §§ *et seq.*

Ehri, L. (1992). Reconceptualizing the development of sight word reading and its relationship to recoding. In P. Gough, L. Ehri, & R. Treiman (Eds.), *Reading acquisition* (pp. 107–144). Mahwah, NJ: Lawrence Erlbaum Associates.

Ehri, L., Nunes, S., Stahl, S., & Willows, D. (2001). Systematic phonics instruction helps students learn to read: Evidence from the National Reading Panel's meta-analysis. *Review of Educational Research, 71,* 393–447.

Faust, D.G. (2007, December 24). Notebook: Verbatim. *Time, 170*(26); retrieved November 11, 2008, from http://www.time.com/time/magazine/article/0,9171,1694451,00.html

Fayol, M., Zorman, M., & Lété, B. (in press). Associations and dissociations in reading and spelling French: Unexpectedly poor and good spellers. *British Journal of Educational Psychology Monograph.*

Fernald, G. (1943). *Remedial techniques in basic school subjects.* New York: McGraw Hill.

Fey, M., Catts, H., Proctor-Williams, K., Tomblin, B., & Zhang, X. (2004). Oral and written story composition skills of children with language impairment. *Journal of Speech, Language, and Hearing Research, 47,* 1301–1318.

Fletcher, J., Lyon, G.R., Fuchs, L., & Barnes, M. (2006). *Learning disabilities: From identification to intervention.* New York: Guilford Press.

Foorman, B., Francis, D., Fletcher, J., Schatschneider, C., & Mehta, P. (1998). The role of instruction in learning to read: Preventing reading failure in at-risk children. *Journal of Educational Psychology, 90,* 37–55.

Foorman, B., & Nixon, S. (2006). The influence of public policy on reading research and practice. *Topics in Language Disorders, 26*(2), 157–171.

Fry, E. (1993). *Computer keyboarding for beginners.* Westminister, CA. Teachers Created Materials.

Fry, E. (1996). *Spelling book: Level 1–6: Words most needed plus phonics.* Westminster, CA: Teacher Created Materials.

Garcia, N. (2007). *Phonological, orthographic, and morphological contributions to the spelling development of good, average, and poor spellers.* Unpublished Ph.D. dissertation, University of Washington, Seattle.

Gates, A. (1947). *The improvement of reading* (3rd ed.). New York: Macmillan.

Gentry, J. (2004). *The science of spelling: The explicit specifics that make great readers and writers (and spellers!).* Portsmouth, NH: Heinemann.

Geschwind, N. (1982). Why Orton was right. *Annals of Dyslexia, 32,* 13–30.

Gilger, J., Hynd, G., & Wilkins, M. (2008). *Neurodevelopmental variation as a framework for thinking about the twice exceptional.* Manuscript submitted for publication.

Gilger, J., & Wilkins, M. (2008). Atypical neurodevelopmental variation as basis for learning disorders. In M. Mody & E. Silliman (Eds.), *Language impairment and reading disability: Interactions among brain, behavior, and experience* (pp. 7–40). New York: Guilford Press.

Gillingham, A., & Stillman, B. (1956 and 1960). *Remedial training for children with specific disability in reading, spelling, and penmanship.* Cambridge, MA: Educators Publishing Service.

Goldberg, R., Higgins, E., Raskind, M., & Herman, K. (2003). Predictors of success in individuals with learning disabilities: A qualitative analysis of a 20-year longitudinal study. *Learning Disabilities Research & Practice, 18,* 222–236.

Graham, S. (1997). Executive control in the revising of students with learning and writing difficulties. *Journal of Educational Psychology, 89,* 223–234.

Graham, S., Berninger, V.W., Abbott, R., Abbott, S., & Whitaker, D. (1997). The role of mechanics in composing of elementary school students: A new methodological approach. *Journal of Educational Psychology, 89*(1), 170–182.

Graham, S., Berninger, V.W., & Weintraub, N. (1998). But they use both manuscript and cursive letters—A study of the relationship of handwriting style with speed and quality. *Journal of Educational Psychology, 91,* 290–296.

Graham, S., & Harris, K.R. (1994). Implications of constructivism for teaching writing to students with special needs. *Journal of Special Education, 28,* 275–289.

Graham, S., & Harris, K.R. (2005). *Writing better: Effective strategies for teaching students with learning difficulties.* Baltimore: Paul H. Brookes Publishing, Co.

Graham, S., Harris, K.R., & Fink, B. (2000). Is handwriting causally related to learning to write? Treatment of handwriting problems in beginning writers. *Journal of Educational Psychology, 92,* 620–633.

Graham, S., Harris, K.R., & Loynachan, C. (1994). The spelling for writing list. *Journal of Learning Disabilities, 27,* 210–214.

Graham, S., & Perin, D. (2007a). A meta-analysis of writing instruction for adolescent students. *Journal of Educational Psychology, 99,* 445–476.

Graham, S., & D. Perin. (2007b). *Writing next: Effective strategies to improve writing of adolescents in middle and high schools—A report to Carnegie Corporation of New York.* Washington, DC: Alliance for Excellent Education.

Graham, S., & Weintraub, N. (1996). A review of handwriting research: Progress and prospects from 1980 to 1994. *Educational Psychology Review, 8,* 7–87.

Gray, W. (1956). *The teaching of reading and writing.* Chicago: Scott Foresman.

Green, L., McCutchen, D., Schweibert, C., Quinlan, T., Eva-Wood, A., & Juelis, J. (2003). Morphological development in children's writing. *Journal of Educational Psychology, 95,* 752–761.

Greenblatt, E., Mattis, S., & Trad, P. (1990). Nature and prevalence of learning disabilities in a child psychiatric population. *Developmental Neuropsychology, 6,* 71–83.

Grigorenko, E., Wood, F., Meyer, M., Pauls, J., Hart, A., & Pauls, D. (2001). Linkage studies suggest a possible locus for developmental dyslexia on chromosomes 6 and 15. *American Journal of Human Genetics, 105,* 120–129.

Gwynne, F. (1976). *Chocolate moose for dinner.* New York: Simon & Schuster.

Hall, S., & Moats, L. (2001). *Straight talk about reading and helping the struggling reader.* Chicago: Contemporary Books.

Hart, T., Berninger, V.W., & Abbott, R. (1997). Comparison of teaching single or multiple orthographic-phonological connections for word recognition and spelling: Implications for instructional consultation. *School Psychology Review, 26,* 279–297.

Hayes, J.R., & Berninger, V.W. (in press). Relationships between idea generation and transcription: How act of writing shapes what children write. In C. Braverman, R. Krut, K. Lunsford, S. McLeod, S. Null, P. Rogers, & A. Stansell (Eds.), *Traditions of writing research.* New York: Routledge.

Hayes, J.R., & Flowers, L. (1980). Identifying the organization of the writing process. In L.W. Gregg & E.R. Sternberg (Eds.), *Cognitive processes in writing* (pp. 3–30). Mahwah, NJ: Lawrence Erlbaum Associates.

Haynes C., & Jennings, T. (2006). Listening and speaking: Essential ingredients for teaching struggling writers. *Perspectives, 32*(2), 12–16.

Hellman, L., & Feibleman, P. (1984). *Eating together.* Boston: Little, Brown.

Henry, M.K. (1988). Beyond phonics: Integrated decoding and spelling instruction based on word origin and structure. *Annals of Dyslexia, 38,* 259–275.

Henry, M.K. (1989). Children's word structure knowledge: Implications for decoding and spelling instruction. *Reading and Writing: An Interdisciplinary Journal, 2,* 135–152.

Henry, M. (1990). *Words: Integrated decoding and spelling instruction based on word origin and word structure.* Austin, TX: PRO-ED.

Henry, M.K. (1993). Morphological structure: Latin and Greek roots and affixes as upper grade code strategies. *Reading and Writing: An Interdisciplinary Journal, 5,* 227–241.

Henry, M. (1999). *Dyslexia: Samuel T. Orton and his legacy.* Baltimore: The International Dyslexia Association.

Henry, M.K. (2003). *Unlocking literacy: Effective decoding and spelling instruction.* Baltimore: Paul H. Brookes Publishing Co.

Henry, M. (2005). *Framework for informed reading and language instruction.* Baltimore: The International Dyslexia Association.

Henry, M., & Hook, P. (2006). Multisensory instruction: Then and now. *Perspectives, 32*(2), 9–11.

Henry, M.K., & Redding, N.C. (1996). *Patterns for success in reading and spelling: A multisensory approach to teaching phonics and word analysis.* Austin, TX: PRO-ED.

Honig, B. (1996). *How should we teach our children to read?* Thousand Oaks, CA: Corwin Press.

Hook, P., & Johnson, D. (1978). Metalinguistic awareness and reading strategies. *Bulletin of the Orton Society, 28,* 62–78.

Hooper, S., Knuth, S., Yerby, D., Anderson, K., & Moore, C. (in press). Review of science-supported writing instruction with implementation in mind. In S. Rosenfield & V.W. Berninger (Eds.), *Handbook on implementing evidence-based academic interventions.* New York: Oxford University Press.

Hooper, S.R., Swartz, C.W., Wakely, M.B., de Kruif, R.E.L., & Montgomery, J.W. (2002). Executive functions in elementary school children with and without problems in written expression. *Journal of Learning Disabilities, 35,* 37–68.

Hooper, S.R., Wakely, M.B., de Kruif, R.E.L., & Swartz, C.W. (2006). Aptitude-treatment interactions revisited: Effect of metacognitive intervention on subtypes of written expression in elementary school students. *Developmental Neuropsychology, 29,* 217–241.

Hsu, L., Wijsman, E., Berninger, V.W., Thomson, J., & Raskind, W. (2002). Familial aggregation of dyslexia phenotypes: Paired correlated measures. *American Journal of Medical Genetics/Neuropsychiatric Genetics, 114,* 471–478.

Huey, E.B. (1968). *The psychology and pedagogy of reading.* Cambridge, MA: The MIT Press. (Original work published 1908.)

Igo, R., Chapman, N., Berninger, V.W., Matsushita, M., Brkanac, Z., Rothstein, J., et al. (2006). Genomewide scan for real-word reading subphenotypes of dyslexia: Novel chromosome 13 locus and genetic complexity. *American Journal of Medical Genetics/Neuropsychiatric Genetics, 141B,* 15–27.

Individuals with Disabilities Education Improvement Act (IDEA) of 2004, PL 108-446, 20 U.S.C. §§ 1400 *et seq.*

Jansky, J., & de Hirsch, K. (1966). *Predicting reading failure.* New York: Harper Row Publishers.

Johnson, D. (1991). Written language. In J. Kavanagh (Ed.), *The language continuum from infancy to literacy* (pp. 147–165). Timonium, MD: York Press.

Johnson, D. (2006). *Geschwind lecture.* Baltimore: International Dyslexia Association.

Johnson, D., & Myklebust, H. (1967). *Learning disabilities.* New York: Grune & Stratton.

Johnson, N. (1986). On looking at letters within words: Do we "see" them in memory? *Journal of Memory and Language, 25,* 558–570.

Jones, D. (2004). *Automaticity of the transcription process in the production of written text.* Unpublished Doctor of Philosophy thesis, Graduate School of Education, University of Queensland, Australia.

Joshi, R.M., Binks, E., Hougen, M., Dean, E., Graham, L., & Smith, D. (in press). The role of teacher education programs in preparing teachers for implementing evidence-based reading practices. In S. Rosenfield & V.W. Berninger (Eds.), *Handbook on implementing evidence-based academic interventions.* New York: Oxford University Press.

Juel, C. (1994). *Learning to read and write in one elementary school.* New York: Springer Verlag.

Kaufman, L. (1995, November). *Phonological awareness training and Orton-Gillingham.* Presentation, International Dyslexia Association. Houston, TX.

Kerns, K.A., Eso, K., & Thomson, J. (1999). Investigation of a direct intervention for improving attention in young children. *Developmental Neuropsychology, 16*(2), 273–295.

King, D. (2005). *Keyboarding skills* (Rev. ed.). Cambridge, MA: Educators Publishing Service.

Kirk, S., & Kirk, D. (1971). *Psycholinguistic learning disabilities: Diagnosis and remediation.* Chicago: University of Chicago Press.

Kovas, Y., Haworth, C., Dale, P., & Plomin, R. (2007). The genetic and environmental origins of learning abilities and disabilities in the early school years. *Monographs of the Society for Research in Child Development, 72*(3).

Kuhn, M., & Stahl, S. (2003). Fluency: A review of developmental and remedial practices. *Journal of Educational Psychology, 95,* 3–21.

Lefly, D., & Pennington, B. (1991). Spelling errors and reading fluency in dyslexics. *Annals of Dyslexia, 41,* 143–162.

Leslie, L., & Caldwell, J. (2005). *Qualitative Reading Inventory* (4th ed.; QRI 4). Boston: Addison Wesley.

Levine, M. (1987). *Developmental variation and learning disorders.* Cambridge, MA: Educators Publishing Service.

Levy, B., Abello, B., & Lysynchuk, L. (1997). Transfer from word training to reading in context: Gains in reading fluency and comprehension. *Learning Disability Quarterly, 20,* 173–188.

Liberman, A. (1999). The reading researcher and the reading teacher need the right theory of speech. *Scientific Studies of Reading, 3,* 95–111.

Liberman, I., Shankweiler, D., Fischer, F., & Carter, B. (1974). Explicit syllable and phoneme segmentation in the young child. *Journal of Experimental Child Psychology, 18,* 201–212.

Logan, R. (1986). *The alphabet effect.* New York: William Morrow and Company.

Lovett, M. (1987). A developmental perspective on reading dysfunction: Accuracy and speed criteria of normal and deficient reading skill. *Child Development, 58,* 234–260.

Lovett, M.W., Lacerenza, L., & Borden, S.L. (2000). Putting struggling readers on the PHAST track: A program to integrate phonological and strategy-based remedial reading instruction and maximize outcomes. *Journal of Learning Disabilities, 33,* 458–476.

Luria, A.R. (1973). *The working brain.* New York: Basic Books.

Lyon, G.R., & Krasnegor, N.A. (Eds.). (1996). *Attention, memory, and executive function.* Baltimore: Paul H. Brookes Publishing Co.

Lyon, G.R., Shaywitz, S., & Shaywitz, B. (2003). A definition of dyslexia. *Annals of Dyslexia, 53,* 1–14.

Mahony, D., Singson, M., & Mann, V. (2000). Reading ability and sensitivity to morphological relations. *Reading and Writing: An Interdisciplinary Journal, 12,* 191–218.

Manis, F., & Keating, P. (2005). Speech perception in dyslexic children with and without language impairments. In H. Catts & A. Kamhi (Eds.), *The connections between language and reading disabilities* (pp. 77–99). Mahwah, NJ: Lawrence Erlbaum Associates.

Manis, F., McBride-Chang, C., Seidenberg, M., Keating, P., Doi., M., & Petersen, A. (1997). Are speech perception deficits associated with developmental dyslexia? *Journal of Experimental Child Psychology, 66,* 211–235.

Martin, J. (1998). *Snowflake Bently.* Boston: Houghton Mifflin.

Masland, R. (1979). Subgroups in dyslexia: Issues of definition. *Bulletin of the Orton Society,* 23–30.

Masterson, J., Apel, K., & Wasowicz, J. (2002). SPELL: Spelling Performance Evaluation for Language and Literacy (spelling assessment software for Grade 2 through adult.) Also, SPELL-Links to Reading & Writing—A Word Study Program for K-Adult (assessment linked to instruction.) Available from http://www.learningbydesign.com

Mattingly, I. (1972). Reading, the linguistic process, and linguistic awareness. In J. Kavanagh & I. Mattingly (Eds.), *Language by ear and by eye: The relationships between speech and reading* (pp. 133–147). Cambridge, MA: The MIT Press.

Mayer, R. (2004). Should there be a three-strikes rule against pure discovery learning? *American Psychologist, 59,* 14–19.

McCardle, P., & Chhabra, V. (Eds.). (2004). *The voice of evidence in reading research.* Baltimore: Paul H. Brookes Publishing Co.

McCardle, P., & Miller, B. (in press). Review of science supported reading instruction (SSI) and policy implications. In S. Rosenfield & V.W. Berninger (Eds.), *Handbook on implementing evidence based academic interventions.* New York: Oxford University Press.

McGregor, K.K. (2004). Developmental dependencies between lexical semantics and reading. In C.A. Stone, E. Silliman, B. Ehren, & K. Apel (Eds.), *Handbook of language literacy: Development and disorders* (pp. 302–317). New York: Guilford Press.

Meyer, M., & Felton, R. (1999). Repeated reading to enhance fluency: Old approaches and new directions. *Annals of Dyslexia, 49,* 283–306.

Minsky, M. (1986). *Society of mind.* New York: Simon & Schuster.

Moats, L.C. (2000). *Speech to print: Language essentials for teachers.* Baltimore: Paul H. Brookes Publishing Co.

Monroe, M. (1936). *Reading aptitude tests.* New York: Houghton Mifflin.

Morgan, W.P. (1896, Nov. 7). "Congenital" word blindness. *The British Medical Journal,* 1378.

Morris, B. (2002, May 13). Overcoming dyslexia. *Fortune,* 54–70.

Morris, R., Stuebing, K., Fletcher, J., Shaywitz, S., Lyon, G.R., Shakweiler, D., et al. (1998). Subtypes of reading disability: Variability around a phonological core. *Journal of Educational Psychology, 90,* 347–373.

Nagy, W. (2007). Metalinguistic awareness and the vocabulary-comprehension connection. In R.K. Wagner, A. Muse, & K. Tannenbaum (Eds.), *Vocabulary acquisition and its implications for reading comprehension* (pp. 52–77). New York: Guilford Press.

Nagy, W., & Anderson, R.C. (1999). Metalinguistic awareness and literacy acquisition in different languages. In D. Wagner, B. Street, & R. Venezky (Eds.), *Literacy: An international handbook* (pp. 155–160). New York: Garland Publishing.

Nagy, W.E., Anderson, R.C., Schommer, M., Scott, J., & Stallman, A. (1989). Morphological families and word recognition. *Reading Research Quarterly, 24,* 262–282.

Nagy, W., Berninger, V.W., & Abbott, R. (2006). Contributions of morphology beyond phonology to literacy outcomes of upper elementary and middle school students. *Journal of Educational Psychology, 98,* 134–147.

Nagy, W., Berninger, V.W., Abbott, R., Vaughan, K., & Vermeulen, K. (2003). Relationship of morphology and other language skills to literacy skills in at-risk second graders and at-risk fourth grade writers. *Journal of Educational Psychology, 95,* 730–742.

Nagy, W., Osborn, J., Winsor, P., & O'Flahavan, J. (1994). Structural analysis: Some guidelines for instruction. In F. Lehr & J. Osborn (Eds.), *Reading, language, and literacy* (pp. 45–58). Mahwah, NJ: Lawrence Erlbaum Associates.

National Institute of Child Health and Human Development. (2000). Report of the National Reading Panel. *Teaching children to read: An evidence-based assessment of the scientific research literature on reading and its implications for reading instruction—Reports of the subgroups* (NIH Publication No. 00-4754). Washington, DC: U.S. Government Printing Office.

National Council on Teacher Quality. (2006). *What education schools aren't teaching about reading and what elementary teachers aren't learning: Executive summary.* Washington, DC: Author. (Full study is available online at http://www.nctq.org)

Nelson, N.W., Bahr, C., & Van Meter, A. (2004). *The Writing Lab approach to language instruction and intervention.* Baltimore: Paul H. Brookes Publishing, Co.

Neuhaus, G. (2002). What does it take to read a letter? *Perspectives, 28*(1), 6–8.

Nunes, T., & Bryant, P. (2006). *Improving literacy by teaching morphemes (Improving Learning Series).* New York: Routledge.

Nussbaum, E.M. (2002). Appropriate appropriation: Functionality of student arguments and support requests during small-group classroom discussions. *Journal of Literacy Research, 34,* 501–544.

O'Connor, R.E., Notari-Syverson, A., & Vadasy, P.F. (2005). *Ladders to literacy: A kindergarten activity book* (2nd ed.). Baltimore: Paul H. Brookes Publishing Co.

Oliphant, G. (1976). The lens of language. *Bulletin of the Orton Society,* 49–62.

Olsen, J. (2004). *Handwriting without tears.* Cabin John, MD: Author.

Olson, R., Forsberg, H., & Wise, B. (1994). Genes, environment, and the development of orthographic skills. In V.W. Berninger (Ed.), *The varieties of orthographic knowledge I: Theoret-*

ical and developmental issues (pp. 27–71). Dordrecht, The Netherlands: Kluwer Academic Publishers.

Olson, R., Forsberg, H., Wise, B., & Rack, J. (1994). Measurement of word recognition, orthographic, and phonological skills. In G.R. Lyon (Ed.), *Frames of reference for the assessment of learning disabilities: New views on measurement issues* (pp. 243–277). Baltimore: Paul H. Brookes Publishing Co.

Olson, R., Wise, B., Connors, F., Rack, J., & Fulker, D. (1989). Specific deficits in component reading and language skills: Genetic and environmental influences. *Journal of Learning Disabilities, 22,* 339–348.

Orton, J. (1964). *A guide to teaching phonics.* Winston Salem, NC: Orton Reading Center.

Orton, S. (1989). *Reading, writing, and speech problems in children and selected papers.* Austin, TX: PRO-ED.

Pacton, S., Fayol, M., & Perruchet, P. (2005). Children's implicit learning of graphotactic and morphological regularities. *Child Development, 76,* 324–329.

Pacton, S., Perruchet, P., Fayol, M., & Cleeremans, A. (2001). Implicit learning in real world context: The case of orthographic regularities. *Journal of Experimental Psychology: General, 130,* 401–426.

Pennington, B., & Lefly, D. (2001). Early reading development in children at family risk for dyslexia. *Child Development, 72,* 816–833.

Phelps, J., & Stempel, L. (1987). CHES's handwriting improvement program (CHIP). Dallas: CHES. (Available from the publisher, P.O. Box 25254, Dallas, TX 75225).

Piaget, J. (1952). *The origins of intelligence in children.* New York: International Universities Press.

Polacco, P. (1994). *Pink and say.* New York: Philomel.

Posner, M., Petersen, S., Fox, P., & Raichle, M. (1988). Localization of cognitive operations in the human brain. *Science, 240,* 1627–1631.

Pugh, K., Shaywitz, B., Shaywitz, S., Constable, T., Skudlarski, P., Fullbright, R., et al. (1996). Cerebral organization of component processes in reading. *Brain, 119,* 1221–1238.

Rack, J., Snowling, M., & Olson, R. (1992). The nonword reading deficit in developmental dyslexia: A review. *Reading Research Quarterly, 27,* 28–53.

Raskind, W. (2001). Current understanding of the genetic basis of reading and spelling disability. *Learning Disability Quarterly, 24,* 141–157.

Raskind, M., Goldberg, R., Higgins, E., & Herman, K. (1999). Patterns of change and predictors of success in individuals with learning disabilities: Results from a twenty-year longitudinal study. *Learning Disabilities Research & Practice, 14,* 35–49.

Raskind, W., Hsu, L., Thomson, J., Berninger, V.W., & Wijsman, E. (2000). Familial aggregation of phenotypic subtypes in dyslexia. *Behavior Genetics, 30,* 385–396.

Raskind, W., Igo, R., Chapman, N., Berninger, V.W., Thomson, J., Matsushita, M., et al. (2005). A genome scan in multigenerational families with dyslexia: Identification of a novel locus on chromosome 2q that contributes to phonological decoding efficiency. *Molecular Psychiatry, 10*(7), 699–711.

Rawson, M. (1973). Semantics—diagnostic categories: Their use and misuse. *Bulletin of the Orton Society,* 143–144.

Rayner, K. (1984). Eye movements, perceptual span, and reading disability. *Annals of Dyslexia, 33,* 163–173.

Rayner, K., Foorman, B., Perfetti, C., Pesetsky, D., & Seidenberg, M. (2001). How psychological science informs the teaching of reading. *Psychological Science in the Public Interest, 2,* 31–74.

Reynolds, M. (1974). *If you love me.* Berkeley, CA: Schroder Music Company.

Reznitskaya, A., Anderson, R., McNurlen, B., Nguyen-Jahiel, K., Archodidou, A., & Kim, S. (2001). Influence of oral discussion on written argument. *Discourse Processes, 32,* 155–175.

Rice, J.M. (1897). The futility of the spelling grind. *Forum, 23,* 163–172, 409–419.

Richards, T., Aylward, E., Berninger, V.W., Field, K., Parsons, A., Richards, A., et al. (2006). Individual fMRI activation in orthographic mapping and morpheme mapping after orthographic or morphological spelling treatment in child dyslexics. *Journal of Neurolinguistics, 19,* 56–86.

Richards, T., Aylward, E., Raskind, W., Abbott, R., Field, K., Parsons, A., et al. (2006). Converging evidence for triple word form theory in child dyslexics. *Developmental Neuropsychology, 30,* 547–589.

Richards, T., & Berninger, V.W. (2007). Abnormal fMRI connectivity in children with dyslexia during a phoneme task: Before but not after treatment. *Journal of Neurolinguistics, 21,* 294–304.

Richards, T., Berninger, V.W., Aylward, E., Richards, A., Thomson, J., Nagy, W., et al. (2002). Reproducibility of proton MR spectroscopic imaging (PEPSI): Comparison of dyslexic and normal reading children and effects of treatment on brain lactate levels during language tasks. *American Journal of Neuroradiology, 23,* 1678–1685.

Richards, T., Berninger, V.W., Nagy, W., Parsons, A., Field, K., & Richards, A. (2005). Dynamic assessment of child dyslexics' brain response to alternative spelling treatments. *Educational and Child Psychology, 22*(2), 62–80.

Richards, T., Berninger, V., Stock, P., Altemeier, L., Trivedi, P., & Maravilla, K. (2008). fMRI sequential-finger movement activation differentiating good and poor writers. Manuscript submitted for publication.

Richards, T., Berninger, V.W., Winn, W., Stock, P., Wagner, R., Muse, A., et al. (2007). fMRI activation in children with dyslexia during pseudoword aural repeat and visual decode: Before and after instruction. *Neuropsychology, 21,* 732–747.

Richards, T., Berninger, V., Winn, W., Swanson, H.L., Stock, P., Lang, O., & Abbott, R. (in press). Differences between children with and without spelling disability in brain activation on n-back fMRI working memory task. *Journal of Writing Research.*

Richards, T., Stevenson, J., Crouch, J., Johnson, L.C., Maravilla, K., Stock, P., et al. (2008). Tract-based spatial statistics of diffusion tensor imaging in adults with dyslexia. *American Journal of Neuroradiology, 29,* 1134–1139.

Richardson, S. (1989). Specific developmental dyslexia: Retrospective and prospective views. *Annals of Dyslexia, 39,* 3–24.

Rosch, E. (1978). Principles of categorization. In E. Rosch & B.B. Lloyd (Eds.), *Cognition and categorization* (pp. 27–48). Mahwah, NJ: Lawrence Erlbaum Associates.

Rosch, E., & Mervis, C.B. (1975). Family resemblances: Studies in the internal structure of categories. *Cognitive Psychology, 7,* 573–605.

Rosner J. (1974). *Helping children overcome learning difficulties.* New York: Walker & Co.

Rubel, B. (1995). *Big strokes for little folks.* Tucson, AZ: Therapy Skill Builders.

Rubin, H. (1988). Morphological knowledge and early writing ability. *Language & Speech 31,* 337–355.

Rumford, J. (2004). *Sequoyah: The Cherokee man who gave his people writing.* Boston: Houghton Mifflin.

Samuels, S. (1985). Automaticity and repeated reading. In J. Osborn, P. Wilson, & R. Anderson (Eds.), *Reading education: Foundations for a literate America* (pp. 215–230). Lexington, MA: Lexington Books.

Sanders, W., & Rivers, J. (1996, November). *Cumulative and residual effects of teachers on future student academic achievement.* University of Tennessee Value-Added Research and Assessment Center, Middle Tennessee State University, Murfreesboro, TN.

Sanderson, C. (1988). *Hands on phonics, book II.* Edmonds, WA: CLS Enterprises.

Sanderson, C. (1989). *Hands on phonics, book I.* Edmonds, WA: CLS Enterprises.

Sawyer, D. (2007, November). Symposium on closing the achievement gap: The roles of orthography, morphology AND phonology in reading and spelling. International Dyslexia Association Annual Meeting, Dallas, TX.

Sawyer, D., & Knight, D. (1997, Spring). Tennessee meets the challenge of dyslexia. *Perspectives*. Towson, MD: International Dyslexia Association.

Scarborough, H. (1991). Antecedents to reading disability: Preschool language development and literacy experiences of children form dyslexic families. *Reading and Writing: An Interdisciplinary Journal, 3,* 219–233.

Schneider, W., & Chein, J. (2003). Controlled & automatic processing: Behavior, theory, and biological mechanisms. *Cognitive Science, 27,* 525–559.

Schneider, W., & R.M. Shiffrin. (1977). Controlled and automatic human information processing: 1. Detection, search, and attention. *Psychological Review, 84,* 1–66.

Scott, C. (2004). Syntactic contributions to literacy learning. In C.A. Stone, E.R. Silliman, B.J. Ehren, & K. Apel (Eds.), *Handbook of language and literacy: Development and disorders* (pp. 340–362). New York: Guilford Press.

Scott, C., & Winsor, J. (2000). General language performance measures in spoken and written narrative and expository discourse of school-age children with language learning disabilities. *Journal of Speech, Language, and Hearing Research, 43,* 324–339.

Share, D.L. (2008). Orthographic learning, phonology, and the self-teaching hypothesis. In R.V. Kail (Ed.), *Advances in child development and behavior* (Vol. 36, pp. 31–82). Amsterdam: Elsevier.

Shaywitz, S. (2003). *Overcoming dyslexia.* New York: Alfred A. Knopf.

Shaywitz, S., Shaywitz, B., Fulbright, R., Skudlarski, P., Mencl, W., Constable, R., et al. (2003). Neural systems for compensation and persistence: Young adult outcome of childhood reading disability. *Biological Psychiatry, 54,* 25–33.

Shiffrin, R., & Schneider, W. (1977). Controlled and automatic human information processing II: Perceptual learning, automatic attending, and a general theory. *Psychological Review, 84,* 127–190.

Siegel, L. (1994). Working memory and reading: A life span perspective. *International Journal of Behavioral Development, 17,* 109–124.

Silliman, E.R., Bahr, R.H., & Peters, M.L. (2006). Spelling patterns in preadolescents with atypical language skills: Phonological, morphological, and orthographic factors. *Developmental Neuropsychology, 20,* 93–123.

Silliman, E., & Scott, C. (in press). Research-based oral language intervention routes to the academic language of literacy: Finding the right road. In S. Rosenfield & V.W. Berninger (Eds.), *Handbook on implementing evidence-based academic interventions.* New York: Oxford University Press.

Silliman, E., & Wilkinson, C. (2004). Collaboration for language and literacy learning: Three challenges. In E.R. Silliman & L.C. Wilkinson (Eds.), *Language and literacy learning in the schools* (pp. 3–38). New York: Guilford Press.

Singson, M., Mahony, D., & Mann, V. (2000). The relation between reading ability and morphological skills: Evidence from derivational suffixes. *Reading and Writing: An Interdisciplinary Journal, 12,* 219–252.

Slavin, R., Madden, N., Dolan, L., & Wasik, B. (1996). *Every child every school: Success for all.* Thousand Oaks, CA: Corwin Press.

Slingerland, B. (1967). *Training in some prerequisites for beginning reading.* Cambridge, MA: Educators Publishing Service.

Slingerland, B. (1971). *A multisensory approach to language arts for specific language disability children: A guide for primary teachers.* Cambridge, MA: Educators Publishing Service.

Slingerland, B. (1976). *Basics in scope and sequence of a multisensory approach to language arts for specific language disability children.* Cambridge, MA: Educators Publishing Service.

Slingerland, B. (1977). *Prereading screening procedures.* Cambridge, MA: Educators Publishing Service.

Slingerland, B. (1980). Unpublished personal papers.

Slingerland, B. (1987). *Teacher's word list.* Cambridge, MA: Educators Publishing Service.

Slingerland, B., & Murray, C. (2008). *Revised teacher word lists for reference.* Bellevue, WA: Slingerland Institute for Literacy.

Smith, S., Kimberling, W., Pennington, B., & Lubs, H. (1983). Specific reading disability: Identification of an inherited form through linkage analysis. *Science, 219,* 1345–1347.

Snowling, M. (1980). The development of grapheme-phoneme correspondence in normal and dyslexic readers. *Journal of Experimental Child Psychology, 29,* 294–305.

Stahl, S., & Heubach, K. (2005). Fluency-oriented reading instruction. *Journal of Literacy Research, 37*(1), 25–60.

Stahl, S., Heubach, K., & Crammond, B. (1997, Winter). *Fluency-oriented reading instruction.* Reading Research Report No. 79, National Reading Research Center Project of the University of Georgia and University of Maryland.

Stahl, S., & Nagy, W. (2005). *Teaching word meaning.* Mahwah, NJ: Lawrence Erlbaum Associates.

Stanberry, L., Richards, T., Berninger, V.W., Nandy, R., Aylward, E., Maravilla, K., et al. (2006). Low frequency signal changes reflect differences in functional connectivity between good readers and dyslexics during continuous phoneme mapping. *Magnetic Resonance Imaging, 24,* 217–229.

Stanovich, K. (1986). Matthew effects in reading: Some consequences of individual differences in the acquisition of literacy. *Reading Research Quarterly, 21,* 360–407.

Stanovich, K.E., & Siegel, L.S. (1994). Phenotypic performance profile of children with reading disabilities: A regression-based test of the phonological-core variable-difference model. *Journal of Educational Psychology, 86,* 24–53.

Steeves, J. (1990). Here's to the future. *Annals of Dyslexia, 40*(1), 39–50.

Steffler, D., Varnhagen, C., Friesen, C., & Trieman, R. (1998). There's more to children's spelling than the errors they make: Strategic and automatic processes for one-syllable words. *Journal of Educational Psychology, 90,* 492–505.

Steinbeck, J. (1976). *The acts of King Arthur and his noble knights.* New York: Farrar, Straus and Giroux.

Stolz, J.A., & Feldman, L.B. (1995). The role of orthographic and semantic transparency of the base morpheme in morphological processing. In L.B. Feldman (Ed.), *Morphological aspects of language processing* (pp. 109–129). Mahwah, NJ: Lawrence Erlbaum Associates.

Swanson, H.L. (1999a). *Interventions for students with learning disabilities: A meta-analysis of treatment outcomes.* New York: Guilford Press.

Swanson, H.L. (1999b). Reading comprehension and working memory in learning disabled readers: Is the phonological loop more important than the executive system? *Journal of Experimental Child Psychology, 72,* 1–31.

Swanson, H.L. (1999c). What develops in working memory? A life span perspective. *Developmental Psychology, 35,* 986–1000.

Swanson, H.L. (2006). Working memory and reading disabilities: Both phonological and executive processing deficits are important. In T. Alloway & S. Gathercole (Eds.), *Working memory and neurodevelopmental conditions* (pp. 59–88). London: Psychology Press.

Swanson, H.L., & Ashbaker, M. (2000). Working memory, short-term memory, speech rate, word recognition, and reading comprehension in learning disabled readers: Does the executive system have a role? *Intelligence, 28,* 1–30.

Swanson, H.L., & Berninger, V.W. (1995). The role of working memory in skilled and less skilled readers' comprehension. *Intelligence, 21,* 83–108.

Swanson, H.L., & Berninger, V.W. (1996). Individual differences in children's working memory and writing skill. *Journal of Experimental Child Psychology, 63,* 358–385.

Tan, A., & Nicholson, T. (1997). Flashcards revisited: Training poor readers to read words faster improves their comprehension of text. *Journal of Educational Psychology, 89,* 276–288.

Templeton, S., & Bear, D. (1992). *Development of orthographic knowledge and the foundations of literacy: A memorial Feltschrift for Edmund Henderson.* Mahwah, NJ: Lawrence Erlbaum Associates.

The Tennessee Center for the Study and Treatment of Dyslexia. (n.d.). *About the center*. Retrieved August 27, 2008, from http://dyslexia.mtsu.edu/center/aboutcenter.html

Texas Scottish Rite Hospital for Children, Child Development Division. (1990). Dyslexia training program developed in the Dyslexia Laboratory, Texas Scottish Rite Hospital [Videotape]. Cambridge, MA: Educators Publishing Service.

Texas Scottish Rite Hospital for Children, Child Development Division. (1996). Teaching cursive writing [Brochure]. Dallas: Author.

Thomson, J., Chenault, B., Abbott, R., Raskind, W., Richards, T., Aylward, E., et al. (2005). Converging evidence for attentional influences on the orthographic word form in child dyslexics. *Journal of Neurolinguistics, 18,* 93–126.

Thomson, J., & Raskind, W. (2004). Genetic influences on reading and writing disabilities. In H.L. Swanson, K.R. Harris, & S. Graham (Eds.), *Handbook of learning disabilities* (pp. 256–270). New York: Guilford Press.

Torgesen, J.K. (1996). *Phonological awareness: A critical factor in dyslexia*. Baltimore: The International Dyslexia Association.

Torgesen, J.K. (2004). Learning disabilities: An historical and conceptual overview. In B. Wong (Ed.), *Learning about learning disabilities* (3rd ed., pp. 3–40). San Diego: Academic Press.

Torgesen, J.K., Alexander, A., Wagner, R., Rashotte, C., Voeller, K., Conway, T., et al. (2001). Intensive remedial instruction for children with severe reading disabilities: Immediate and long-term outcomes from two instructional approaches. *Journal of Learning Disabilities, 34,* 33–58.

Torrance, E. (1963). *Education and the creative potential*. Minneapolis: University of Minnesota Press.

Traweek, D., & Berninger, V. W. (1997). Comparison of beginning literacy programs: Alternative paths to the same learning outcome. *Learning Disability Quarterly, 20,* 160–168.

Treiman, R. (1985). Onsets and rimes as units of spoken syllables: Evidence from children. *Journal of Experimental Child Psychology, 39,* 161–181.

Trieman, R. (1993). *Beginning to spell: A study of first grade children*. New York: Oxford University Press.

Treiman, R., Kessler, B., Knewasser, S., Tincoff, R., & Bowman, M. (2000). English speakers' sensitivity to phonotactic patterns. In M.B. Broe & J.B. Pierrehumbert (Eds.), *Papers in laboratory phonology V: Acquisition and the lexicon* (pp. 269–282). Cambridge, England: Cambridge University Press.

Tulving, E. (2002). Episodic memory: From mind to brain. *Annual Review of Psychology, 53,* 1–25.

Tyler, A., & Nagy, W. (1989). The acquisition of English derivational morphology. *Journal of Memory and Language, 28,* 649–667.

Tyler, A., & Nagy, W. (1990). Use of derivational morphology during reading. *Cognition, 36,* 17–34.

Uhry, J., & Goodman, N. (in press). University-school partnerships in urban classrooms: Professional development in applying reading research to practice. In S. Rosenfield & V.W. Berninger (Eds.), *Handbook on implementing evidence based academic interventions*. New York: Oxford University Press.

United Nations. (1959). *Declaration of the rights of the child*. Proclaimed by General Assembly resolution 1386(XIV) of 20 November, 1959. Retrieved November 11, 2008, from http://www.unhchr.ch/html/menu3/b/25.htm

Vaughn, S., Moody, S., & Schumm, J. (1998). Broken promises: Reading instruction in the resource room. *Exceptional Children, 64,* 211–225.

Vellutino, F. (1979). *Dyslexia, theory, and research*. Cambridge, MA: The MIT Press.

Vellutino, F., Scanlon, D., Sipay, E., Small, S., Pratt, A., Chen, R., et al. (1996). Cognitive profiles of difficult-to-remediate and readily remediated poor readers: Early intervention as a vehicle for distinguishing between cognitive and experiential deficits as basic causes of specific reading disability. *Journal of Educational Psychology, 88,* 601–638.

Vellutino, F., Scanlon, D., & Tanzman, M. (1991). Bridging the gap between cognitive and neuropsychological conceptualizations of reading disability. *Learning and Individual Differences, 3,* 181–203.

Venezky, R. (1970). *The structure of English orthography.* The Hague: Mouton.

Venezky, R. (1999). *The American way of spelling.* New York: Guilford Press.

Wadsworth, S., Olson, R., Pennington, B., & DeFries, J. (2000). Differential genetic etiology of reading disability as a function of IQ. *Journal of Learning Disabilities, 33,* 192–199.

Wagner, R.K., Torgesen, J.K., & Rashotte, C.A. (1999). *The Comprehensive Test of Phonological Processing.* Austin, TX: PRO-ED.

Wagner, R., & Torgesen, J. (1987). The nature of phonological processing and its causal role in the acquisition of reading skills. *Psychological Bulletin, 101,* 192–212.

Wijsman, E., Peterson, D., Leutennegger, A., Thomson, J., Goddard, K., Hsu, L., et al. (2000). Segregation analysis of phenotypic components of learning disabilities I: Nonword memory and digit span. *American Journal of Human Genetics, 67,* 631–646.

White, T., Power, M., & White, S. (1989). Morphological analysis: Implications for teaching and understanding vocabulary growth in diverse elementary schools: Decoding and word meaning. *Journal of Educational Psychology, 82,* 283–304.

Whitehurst, G., Falco, F., Lonigan, C., Fischel, J., DeBaryshe, B. , Valdez,-Menchaca, M., & Caulfied, M. (1988). Accelerating language development through picture book reading. *Developmental Psychology, 24,* 552–559.

Wilkinson, C., Bahr, R., Silliman, E., & Berninger, V.W. (2007, August). *Spelling patterns from grades 1–9: Implications for vocabulary development.* Presented at the 15th European Conference on Reading, Berlin, Germany.

Willcutt, E., Pennington, B., & DeFries, J. (2000). Twin study of the etiology and comorbidity between reading disability and attention deficit/hyperactivity disorder. *American Journal of Medical Genetics, 54,* 122–131.

Winn, W., Berninger, V.W., Richards, T., Aylward, E., Stock, P., Lee, Y., et al. (2006). Effects of nonverbal problem solving treatment on skills for externalizing visual representation in upper elementary grade students with and without dyslexia. *Journal of Educational Computing Research, 34,* 395–418.

Wise, B., Ring, J., & Olson, R. (1999). Training phonological awareness with and without explicit attention to articulation. *Journal of Experimental Child Psychology, 72,* 271–304.

Wise, B., Rogan, L., & Sessions, L. (in press). Training teachers in evidence-based intervention: The story of linguistic remedies. In S. Rosenfield & V.W. Berninger (Eds.), *Handbook on implementing evidence based academic interventions.* New York: Oxford University Press.

Wolf, M. (Ed.). (2001). *Dyslexia, fluency, and the brain.* Timonium, MD: York Press.

Wong, B., & Berninger, V.W. (2004). Cognitive processes of teachers in implementing composition research in elementary, middle, and high school classrooms. In B. Shulman, K. Apel, B. Ehren, E. Silliman, & A. Stone (Eds.), *Handbook of language and literacy: Development and disorders* (pp. 600–624). New York: Guilford Press.

Wood, F.B., Flowers, L., & Grigorenko, E. (2001). *On the functional neuroanatomy of fluency or why walking is just as important to reading as talking is.* In M. Wolf (Ed.), *Dyslexia, fluency and the brain* (pp. 235–244). Timonium, MD: York Press.

Yates, C., Berninger, V.W., & Abbott, R. (1994). Writing problems in intellectually gifted children. *Journal for the Education of the Gifted, 18,* 131–155.

Index

Page references followed by a *t* indicate tables and those followed by an *f* indicate figures.

Abbott, Sylvia, 213
Acquired dyslexia, 116
Activities
　abstract concept, 39–41
　composition, 151
　decoding, 55–56
　fluency, 61–62
　independent work, 63–64, 91–92
　intellectual engagement, 111–112
　oral language development, 35–38, 108
　phonological awareness, 52
　phrase recognition, 60–61
　reading, 57, 57*f*, 58
　spelling, 99
　to teach across the curriculum, 106–108
　writing, 64, 108, 108*t*
　　see also Hands-on learning; *Helping
　　Students with Dyslexia and Dysgraphia
　　Make Connections*; Strategies
Affixes, 54, 90, 102, 145, 148–149
Alphabet, 40–41, 84–87, 92
Alphabetic Phonics Approach, 8, 20*t*, 29, 86
Alphabetic principle
　automation of, 71, 146–147, 156, 206
　for reading instruction, 51, 53–56
　slow mapping, 68, 99
　in spelling, 89, 96–97, 100, 133–134
American Psychological Association, 176
American Reads program, 164
Anderson, Wilson, 8
Assessment
　diagnosis and, 136–137, 138
　evidence-based, 135–136, 139
　integrating with instruction, 207–208
　multidisciplinary, 137–138
　of multiple learning issues, 168
　of student learning, 16, 17–18, 174, 211
　through independent work, 25–26
　tools for, 183
　"walk about" model and, 162
　writing demands during, 110
Assessment of Decoding and Encoding
　　Progress (ADEP), 183
Association Method, 20*t*, 29
Attention
　components of, 27
　instructional strategies for, 28
　maintaining with eye contact, 34
　as part of developmental domain, 173
　self-managing, 157
　of students with dyslexia, 112, 122, 146
　during writing instruction, 96
　see also Motivation

Attention deficit disorder (ADD), 96
Auditory issues, 32, 33*t*
Automatic retrieval
　alphabetic principle and, 70–71, 146–147, 206
　of sight words, 124
　in spelling, 98
　working memory and, 156
　for writing, 95, 139

Basal readers, 23, 51
Base words, 53
Behavior, 17–18, 23
Behavioral markers, *see* Phenotypes
Bender, Lauretta, 5
Berninger, Virginia, 6–7, 203–204
Bernstein, Stuart, 176, 184
Biologically based learning disorder, 3, 11,
　　117, 123, 138–139, 210
Birsh, Judith, 8
Blending, 52
Blood oxygen level dependent (BOLD), 117,
　　120
Books, 42, 46–47, 50, 178–180
Bowman Gray School of Medicine, 5
Brain studies
　genes and, 116–117
　historical, 4–5
　multimodal instruction and, 64–65, 109–110
　neuroscience research in, 117–120
　teacher knowledge of, 174–175
　on visual attention, 112, 148
Broca, Paul, 4

Calendar concepts, practice in, 40, 47
Categorization, 52
Cherokee language, 153
Child development, 173–174, 202
Childs, Sally, 6, 202
Choral reading, 62
Chromosomes, 115–116, 116*f*
Cicci, Regina, 202
Classroom, 18, 22–23, 167
　see also Learning environment
Classroom strategies, *see* Strategies
Cognitive representations, 71–73
Cognitive science, 122–123
Collaboration
　of the learning processes, 128
　in mainstream education, 9, 27, 159–160,
　　163–164
　multidisciplinary, 166, 168
　between professionals, 6, 137–138, 157,
　　212–213

Compensation, 120, 210
Composition
   activities for, 151
   dysgraphia and, 133–134
   dyslexia and, 132, 137
   explicit instruction in, 90–92, 102–103, 134
   high-frequency words in, 100
   keyboarding and, 133
   lesson plans for, 151
   spelling and, 99
   student readiness for, 79
   warming up for, 86
   see also Writing
Comprehension, *see* Reading comprehension
Computers, 24, 71, 92, 95–96, 103
Concepts, student understanding of, 38–41,
   72–73, 75
Connectivity studies, 118
Consonants, 53–54, 56, 88, 89
Content areas, 24, 69, 109, 153
Controlled (strategic) spelling, 97–98
Controversies in teaching reading, 72, 73, 205
Cosby, Bill, 188
Council for Exceptional Children, 9
Cox, Aylett, 8
Cross-word form mapping, 68–69
Curriculum
   for early intervention, 141–142
   increasing complexity of, 123
   integrated, 105–106
   in the learning triangle, 128
   multimodal, 107–109
   for persistent problems, 142–145
   reading across the, 154–155
   student access to, 161–162
   writing across the, 110, 155
   see also Instructional components
Cursive, 80, 83, 85*f*, 87, 95

De Hirsch, Katrina, 7, 202
Declarative knowledge, 72
Decoding
   activities for, 55–56, 107–108, 107*t*
   dyslexia and, 24, 66, 124, 146
   fluency and, 61
   materials for, 51
   phonics and, 53–56
   phonological awareness and, 51–53
   strategies for, 121, 143, 151–152
   teacher modeling, 73
   team approach to, 19, 22
   word origin and, 69–70
Denckla, Martha, 143
Developmental domains, 173–174
Diagnosis
   distinguishing from assessment, 136–137,
      138
   establishing need for, 159
   evidence-based, 135–136, 139
   federal legislation and, 136

instructional implications of, 131–132
   of learning disabilities, 127–128, 133*f*,
      206–207
Dictionaries, 89
Differentiated instruction, 17–18, 50–51, 66,
   163–164
   see also General education classroom;
      Individual instruction
Dillon, Sandra, 8
Directed Reading Activity (DRA), 202
Discourse structure, 49, 65
Durbrow, Helene, 8
Dysgraphia
   combined with other disabilities, 136–137
   computer use and, 92, 95–96, 103
   defined, 93–94, 130–131
   existence of, 206–207
   phenotypes of, 128
   teaching students with, 84, 133–134
   word-form deficits and, 133*f*
Dyslexia
   adult quality of life and, 161
   attention and, 112, 122
   compensation and, 120, 210
   computer use and, 92, 103
   decoding and, 54, 124
   defined, 93, 129
   early manifestation of, 123
   existence of, 11, 206–207
   genetics research and, 115–117, 116*f*, 118*f*
   history of, 3–12, 64–65, 66
   linguistics research and, 121–122
   neuroscience research and, 117–120
   oral language and, 32–33
   other disabilities and, 130, 136–137
   phenotypes of, 115, 127, 134
   recommended reading for, 178–179
   teaching students with, 56–57, 71, 132, 146
   word-form deficits and, 133*f*

Early intervention, 141–142, 168, 183–184
Education for All Handicapped Children Act
   of 1975 (PL 94-142), 10, 11
Efré, Barbara, 165
Eligibility, for services, 10, 127, 136
Emotional climate, 19
Emotional problems, 17–18, 131, 137
Encoding, 22, 88, 121
End organs (sensory and motor systems), 109,
   111
Enfield, Mary Lee, 8
English as Second Language (ESL), 103, 160,
   163
Episodic memory, 72
Evaluation, *see* Assessment
Evans, Dan, 211
Evidence-based assessment, 135–136, 139
Evidence-based lessons, *see* Helping Students
   with Dyslexia and Dysgraphia Make Connec-
   tions

Executive functions
    developing, 151
    genetics research and, 116, 119, 127
    in Mark Twain writer's workshop, 151
    students with impaired, 26–28, 122, 134,
        135f
Explicit instruction
    in composition, 90–92, 102–103, 134
    in handwriting, 79, 84, 133–134
    integrating with intellectual engagement,
        111
    need for, 66
    in reading, 49–50
    in spelling, 99
    for writing, 93, 94–95, 123
    see also Instruction
Explicit memory, 156
Explicit phonics, 53
Expressive language, 32–33
Eye span, 57

Fast mapping, 68, 99, 205
Faust, D. G., 211
Federal initiatives, 19, 166, 201
Federal legislation, 10–11, 130–131, 136, 138
Fernald, Grace M., 7
Florida Center for Reading Research, 167
Fluency
    activities for, 61–62
    automatic retrieval and, 70–71
    executive function and, 134
    in hand writing, 80
    impaired by working memory issues,
        205–206
    recommended reading, 179
    strategies for, 60, 61–62
Free appropriate public education, 10, 136,
    159, 211
Free association, 72
Freud, Sigmund, 50
Function words, 69, 145
Functional magnetic resonance imaging
    (fMRI), 117–118, 118f, 119f, 120

Garvey, Catherine, 204–205
Gender, 94, 132
General education classroom
    advantages of keeping students in, 27
    collaboration in, 159, 166
    models for, 162–166, 167–168
    specialized learning environments in, 11,
        15, 160–162, 211–212
    striving to give the best education possible,
        212
    see also Differentiated instruction; Main-
        stream education
Genetics research, 115–117, 127
Geschwind, Norman, 5
Gillingham, Anna, 6, 7, 202
Grade-level guidelines, 16, 23–24

Grammar of teaching, 144–145, 154–155,
    208–210
Grapheme-phoneme correspondence, 147–148
Graphemes, 120, 146–148
Greene, Tori, 8
Grouping
    to accommodate learning differences, 27,
        28, 93–94
    classroom organization for, 22–23
    for individualized instruction, 18, 50–51
    by instructional level, 202
Guided reading, 60–61
Gwynne, Fred, 41

Habituation, 28, 146, 147
Hand preference, 81
Hands-on learning, 111–112, 150, 155–156
Handwriting
    automatic retrieval and, 139
    cursive, 88f, 95
    developmental sequence in, 83–84
    explicit instruction in, 133–134
    implements for, 82
    importance of repetition in, 84
    instruction in, 79
    manuscript print, 94–95
    paper position, 83
    paper sizes and, 83f
    student hand preference and grip, 80–82,
        83
    style of, 80, 83, 85f, 87
    teaching new letters, 84–87
    using keyboards for, 92, 95–96, 133
    see also Writing
Hellman, Lillian, 202
Hello Ennis Foundation, 188
Helping Students with Dyslexia and Dysgraphia
        Make Connections: Differentiated Instruction
        Lesson Plans in Reading and Writing
        (Berninger & Wolf, 2009)
    goals of, 144–145
    hope themes in, 111
    instructional approaches of, 27
    instructional strategies of, 28, 102
    John Muir Writing Reader Workshop, 111,
        151–153
    Mark Twain Writers Workshop, 102, 111,
        118, 150–151
    Sequoyah Reading Writer Workshop, 111,
        153–154
    Word Detectives (Unit I), 111, 146–150
    see also Activities; Strategies
Henry, Marcia K., 8, 212
Hinshelwood, James, 4
Hope themes
    Albert Einstein, 149
    for intellectual engagement, 111
    John Muir, 152
    Mark Twain, 150–151
    Sequoyah, 153–154

Hospital for Sick Children's Learning Disabilities Research Program, 143
Human Genome Project, 117
Humor, 41, 101

Implicit memory, 65, 156
Independent work
    activities for, 63–64, 91–92
    designing, 25–26
    in oral language skills, 38
    in reading, 63–64
    transfer to from teacher-led work, 124
Individual instruction, 16–17, 18, 23–24, 54–55
    see also Differentiated instruction
Individuals with Disabilities Education Improvement Act of 2004 (PL 108-446), 11, 136, 159
Inflectional endings, 57
Instruction
    clinical research in, 136–137
    diagnosis implications to, 131–132
    Directed Reading Activity (DRA), 202
    diverse learners and, 160–162
    integrating with assessment, 207–208
    issues in, 166–168
    leading, 73
    learning triangle of, 128f
    neuroscience research on, 117–120
    organization of, 162–166
    see also Explicit instruction
Instructional components
    across the language systems, 105–107
    choosing, 19
    for reading instruction, 19, 20–21t, 23–24, 50–51
    for students with dyslexia, 20–21t, 29, 160
    see also Curriculum
Intellectual engagement
    across the curriculum, 107–109
    grammar of teaching, 155
    of students with learning disabilities, 105–106
    through hands-on activities, 111–112
    through themes, 111
Intensive instruction, 72
Interagency Initiative of 1987, 201
International Dyslexia Association (IDA), 6, 9, 60, 109, 129, 187–188
International Reading Association, 9
IQ scores, 129, 132, 135, 139

Jansky, Jeanette, 7, 202
Jansky Kindergarten Index, 81
John Muir Writing-Readers Workshop, 111, 151–153
Johnson, Doris, 202
Joshi, Malatesha, 188–189

Karnes, Lucia, 8
Keyboarding, 92, 95–96, 133

Kinesthetic learner, 105
Kirk, Samuel, 10

Ladders to Literacy, 141
Langford, William, 7
Language
    see also Oral language
Language!, 20t, 29
Language
    creating, 144–145
    different levels of, 205
    disorders in, 134–135, 178–179
    multimodal teaming of, 109–110
    playing with, 41, 101, 155–156
    predictability of, 67, 120–121
    students unlocking, 90, 139
    system of, 105–112
Language arts
    block approach, 163–164
    groups during, 162–164
    Orton-Gillingham Approach and, 8
    section approach to, 164
    specialized learning environments in, 27
    tutoring in, 164–165
Learning disabilities
    compensation and, 210
    defined, 129–131
    emergence of field of, 9–11
    history of, 4–5
    multiple, 135, 136–137
    recommended reading for, 178–179
    school recognition of, 11, 138–139
Learning Disabilities Association of America, 9
Learning environment
    differentiated instruction, 17–18, 50–51
    independent work in, 25–26
    lesson pacing and, 24–25
    organizing, 15–17, 26
    positive, 19, 209
    researcher contributions to, 26–28
    students' instructional level and, 23–24
    see also Classroom
Learning mechanisms, 71–73
Learning triangle, 128f
Least restrictive environment, see General education classroom
Left-handed students, 23
Legislation, 10–11, 19, 182–183
Liberman, Alvin, 109
Lindamood-Bell, 20t, 29
Linguistic awareness, 51–52, 65–68, 157
Linguistic Remedies, 188
Linguistic research, 120–122
Literacy
    early intervention and, 141–142
    multimodal approach to, 110
    in the student's home, 73, 160
    teacher training in, 176–177
Literacy Trek Project, 206

Lovett, Maureen, 142, 143
Lovett's Empower Reading, 143
Lyday, June (Orton), 5–6

Mainstream education, 9, 110
    see also General education classroom
Maladroit pencil grip, 81–82
Manuscript print, 80, 83, 85f, 94–95, 96
Mapping, 68–69, 99, 205
Mark Twain Writer's Workshop, 102, 111, 118,
    150–151
McPhee, Sydney, 185
Mentor teachers, 187, 202, 208
Metalinguistic awareness, 56, 64
Meyer, Bonnie, 60–61
Middle Tennessee State University, 176–177,
    181–182
Monitored reading, 62
Monroe, Marion, 6
Morgan, W. Pringle, 4
Morphological awareness
    activities for, 148–149
    learning disabilities and, 133f, 207
    neuroscience research in, 117–120, 119f
    for reading, 65
    recommended reading in, 178–179, 180
    spelling and, 97–98, 102
    for students with dyslexia, 121
    studies in, 67, 68
Morphology
    receptive language and, 32
    recommended reading in, 178–179, 180
    spelling and, 87, 89–90
Motivation, 16, 25, 131
    see also Attention
Motor skills, 94, 173
Motor Theory of Speech Perception, 109
Multidisciplinary team approach, 10, 137–138,
    166
Multimodal instruction
    across the language systems, 107–109
    benefits of, 204–205
    need for, 64–65
    in oral language, 110
Multisensory teaching
    to enhance the learning process, 105–107
    spelling instruction and, 87–88
    visual, auditory, kinesthetic, tactile (VAKT)
        approach to, 7
    for writing, 79
Murfree, Katherine Davis, 182
Muscle memory, 80, 82–83, 86, 94
Myelination, 117

National Center for Learning Disabilities, 9
National Council for Accreditation of Teacher
    Education, 175
National Council on Teacher Quality (NCTQ),
    175

National Institute of Child Health and
    Human Development (NICHD), 115
National Institutes of Health (NIH), 129,
    143
National Reading Panel, 19, 67, 71, 122–123
National Research Council, 143
Nature-nurture, 3, 4–5
N-back test, 119–120
Nelson, Nickola, 142, 144
Nelson's Writing Lab, 144
Neuroscience research, 4, 117–120, 174
No Child Left Behind Act of 2001 (PL 107-
    110), 175–176
Normalization, 150, 210
Note-taking, 33, 152

Onset rimes, 67, 97
Oral and written language learning disability
    (OWL LD)
    combined with other disabilities, 136–137
    computer use and, 103
    defined, 130
    existence of, 206–207
    guided reading for, 60
Oral and written language learning disability
    (OWL LD)—continued
    multimodal instruction and, 64–65
    phenotypes of, 127, 130
    reading comprehension and, 71
    teaching students with, 132–133
    word-form deficits and, 133f
Oral language
    abstract temporal concepts in, 38–41
    activities for, 35–38, 108
    auditory issues and, 33t
    building phrases in, 39t
    connection to written language, 16, 31–33,
        57, 60, 86, 205
    importance of to reading instruction, 41–42,
        43, 64, 110, 139
    playing with, 101
    recommended reading in, 46
    strategies for, 33–38
    word origin and, 69
    see also Language
Organizational awareness, 23, 32–33, 35
Orthographic awareness
    dysgraphia and, 130
    dyslexia and, 132
    fluency and, 61
    learning disabilities and, 133f, 207
    neuroscience research in, 117–120, 119f
    for reading, 65
    recommended reading, 180
    spelling and, 98, 102
    studies in, 67
    teaching, 51–52
Orthotactic sensitivity, 99
Orton, June Lyday, 5–6
Orton, Samuel T., 4–5, 187

Orton-Gillingham Approach, 6, 7–8, 20*t*, 29, 86, 185
OWL LD, *see* Oral and written language learning disability

Pacing, 24–25, 26
PAL Reading and Writing Lessons, 142, 144
Paragraphs, 91
Parents, 9–10, 23, 124
Partner reading, 62
Pedagogy, 128, 128*f*
Peers, 22, 26, 55
Pencil grip, 80–82
Phenotypes, 127, 128, 130, 132, 134, 135*f*
Phoneme manipulation, 52
Phonemic awareness, 19, 101
Phonics
    application of, 146
    as part of reading instruction, 19, 51, 53–56, 205
    spelling and, 88–89
    studies in, 67–68
Phonics readers, 51
Phonological, orthographic, and morphological awareness (POM), 70
Phonological awareness
    activities for, 146–147
    application of, 152
    dyslexia and, 132
    fluency and, 61
    learning disabilities and, 133*f*, 207
    neuroscience research in, 117–120, 119*f*
    in primary grades, 141
    for reading, 49, 65
    receptive language and, 32
    recommended reading, 179, 180
    spelling and, 98
    studies in, 67
    teaching, 51–52
Phonotactic sensitivity, 99
Phrase awareness, 57, 58–59, 58*t*, 59*t*, 60–61
Physical climate, *see* Classroom
PL 107-110 (No Child Left Behind Act of 2001), 175–176
PL 108-446 (Individuals with Disabilities Education Improvement Act), 11, 136, 159
PL 94-142 (Education for All Handicapped Children Act), 10, 11
Plan, Write, Review, Revise (PWRR), 102
Planning, 24–25
Polacco, Patricia, 42
Polysemy, 121
Pragmatics, 49
Predictive Index, 7
Prefixes, *see* Affixes
Private schools, 27, 210
Problem solving, 17, 136–138
Procedural knowledge, 72
Professional development, *see* Teacher Education

Project Read, 21*t*, 29
Pseudowords, 115, 129
Psychology, of reading, 8–9
Public school, *see* Mainstream education
Pull-out services, 27, 159, 163, 168
    see also Special education
Punctuation, 61

Questioning for reading comprehension, 62
Questions of the day, 35–36, 44–45, 91

Rapid automatic naming (RAN), 143, 205, 206
Rapid automatic switching (RAS), 143
Rawson, Margaret, 8
Readers theater, 62
Reading
    critical components of, 19, 122
    decoding and, 53–56
    direction of, 151
    fluency in, 61–62, 70–71
    grammar of teaching and, 154–155, 208–209
    guided oral and silent, 60–61
    important words in, 75–77
    independent work in, 63–64
    linguistic awareness and, 51–52, 65–66, 157
    mapping and, 68–69
    materials for, 19, 20–21*t*, 23–24, 50–51
    multimodal instruction in, 64–65
    oral language development and, 41–42, 43, 64, 110, 139
    preparation for, 56–59
    process of, 49
    spelling and, 96–97
    word origin and, 69–70
Reading comprehension
    activities for, 57, 57*f*, 58
    cognitive representations and, 71–75
    concept words in, 75
    fluency and, 61
    oral language development and, 33, 36, 43, 139
    OWL LD and, 130–131
    strategies for, 62–63, 154
    vocabulary and, 71
    working memory and, 206
Reading inventories, 18, 50, 202
Reading psychology, *see* Psychology, of reading
Receptive language, 32
Recommended reading, 46, 178–180
Repeated reading, 61, 62
Repetition, 17, 25, 63, 84–85, 87–88
Researcher contributions, in
    the classroom environment, 26–28
    cognitive science, 122–123
    composition, 102–103
    genetics, 115–117
    language disorders, 4–5
    linguistics, 120–122
    neuroscience, 117–120

oral language development, 43
reading instruction, 64–73
spelling, 96–102
teacher knowledge of learning disabilities,
    203–204, 213
teaching across the language systems,
    109–112
writing, 93–96
Retrieval, Automaticity, Vocabulary, Engage-
    ment with Language, Orthography
    (RAVE-O), 143
Rhyming, 52
Rhythm, 60
Road to the Code, 142
Routine, 23, 24–25, 28
Rules, applying, 72, 146–147, 152, 156

Sawyer, Diane, 176, 182–183
Schwa, 53–54, 56, 69, 89, 120, 124
Scottish Rite organization, 211
Seating, *see* Grouping
Self-esteem, 17, 19, 22, 131, 209
Semantics, 49, 68
Sentence building, 36–38, 90
Sentence completion, 61
Sequoyah Reading-Writers Workshop, 111,
    153–154
Shaw, George Bernard, 120
Sight words
    automatic retrieval of, 124
    Dick and Jane books, 7
    fast mapping and, 68
    fluency and, 61, 70
    Orton-Gillingham Approach and, 8
Silent reading, 60–61
Skills, 25, 27, 42, 70
Slingerland, Beth H., 7–8, 31, 185, 202, 212
Slingerland Classroom Approach, 21t, 29,
    86–87, 202
Slingerland Four-Step Professional Develop-
    ment Program, 185–187
Slingerland Institute for Literacy, 186
Slow mapping, 68, 99, 205
Social interaction, 33, 173
Sonday, Arlene, 8
Sonday System, 21t, 29
Spalding Method, 21t, 29
Special education
    categories in, 131, 132–133, 136
    continuation of, 210
    determining need for, 142
    qualifying for, 10–11, 136, 138
    three-tier approach, 168
    see also Pull-out services
Specialized instruction, 142–144
Speech, 33, 47, 51, 59, 109
Spelling
    components of, 124
    computers and, 103
    dysgraphia and, 93

instruction in, 87–90, 100–102, 133–134
language processes in, 97–98
linguistic research and, 120–121
mapping in, 99
models for, 150–151
relationship to reading, 96–97
rules in, 90
writing and, 99
Spoken-written word connections, 205
Staffing plans, 165–166
Stillman, Bessie, 6, 7, 202
Strategies
    active listening, 34
    decoding, 143, 151–152
    evidence-based, 202
    fluency, 60
Strategies—*continued*
    handwriting, 133–134
    independent learning, 157
    new skills, 70
    oral language, 33–38
    question of the day, 35, 44–45
    reading comprehension, 62–63, 154
    to show the predictability of English, 121
    spelling, 100–102, 133–134
    to teach students how to learn, 17
    using Orton-Gillingham principles, 7–8
    writing instruction, 82–83, 94–95
    see also Activities; *Helping Students with
        Dyslexia and Dysgraphia Make Connections*
Students
    ability to learn, 210
    hope of, 208–209
    independent work and, 26
    individuality of, 11, 17–18, 110
    instructional levels of, 23–24, 50–51
    left-handed, 23
    motivating, 16
    self-esteem of, 17, 19, 22, 131
    teacher compassion for, 209
Suffixes, *see* Affixes
Summarization, 63
Summer programs, 165
Syllables
    decoding, 55–56, 56t
    identification of, 52
    spelling and, 89, 101
    types of, 53–54
    word origins and, 69
Syntax
    creating, 144–145
    of oral language, 32
    for reading, 49, 65
    teacher modeling of, 34, 35

Teacher contributions, to
    assessment of student needs, 23–26, 50–51
    choosing instructional components, 19, 51
    classroom strategies, 33–41
    compassion for students, 209

Teacher contributions, to—*continued*
  computer use, 92
  creating a positive environment, 19, 22–23
  decoding, 53–56
  differentiated instruction, 17–18
  dyslexia studies, 5–8
  fluency, 61–62
  guided reading, 60–61
  handwriting instruction, 79–87
  importance of modeling, 34, 35, 73
  importance of oral language, 31–33, 41–42
  independent work, 63–64
  intellectual engagement, 105–109
  meeting diverse learner needs, 160–162
  organizing the learning environment, 15–17
  other teacher's knowledge, 202–203, 213
  phonological and orthographic awareness,
    51–52
  prepare for reading, 56–59
  reading comprehension, 62–63
  spelling instruction, 87–90
  writing instruction, 90–92
Teacher education
  diverse learners and, 160
  interdisciplinary model, 176–177, 177*f*
  models in, 181–189
  in the Orton-Gillingham approach, 7–8
  preservice, 173–177
  as a reading specialist, 9, 165
  sample syllabi in, 191–197
  to teach children with learning disabilities, 11
  through student teaching, 166, 174
Teacher Education Accreditation Council, 175
Teacher reflections, 124–125, 139, 156–157
Technology, 24, 92–93, 95–96
Temporal activity, 206
Temporal connectivity, 150
Tennessee Center for the Study and Treatment
    of Dyslexia, 181–185
Themes, *see* Hope themes
Three-tier approach, 167–168
Time, practice in, 39
Transcription disability (TD), 130
Tufts Center for Reading and Language
    Research (CRLR), 143
Tutoring, 164–165, 174

Uhry, Joanne, 188
University of Washington Multidisciplinary
    Learning Disabilities Center (UW LDC)
  creation of, 115
  dyslexia studies of, 129
  genetics studies of, 127
  lesson sets from, 142–144, 145–154
  OWL LD studies of, 130
  phenotyping studies of, 132, 134, 135*f*
  spoken-written word connection studies of,
    206
U.S. Department of Education, 10, 11

Venezky, R., 120
Verbal mediation, 94
Visual, auditory, kinesthetic, tactile (VAKT)
    approach, 7
Vocabulary
  building through speech instruction, 59
  determining student understanding of,
    63
  importance of, 19
  reading comprehension and, 71
  reflecting on variable meanings of, 121
  student confidence with, 58
Vowels, 53–54, 55*t*, 88, 89

"Walk about" model, 162
Walker, James, 182
Websites, 24, 60, 103, 107, 167, 181
Wernicke, Paul, 4
White, Nancy Cushen, 8
Whole-language approach, 7, 93, 186, 205
Wilson, Barbara, 8, 142, 143–144
Wilson Reading, 21*t*, 29
Wilson's Language Training, 143–144
Wise, Barbara, 188
Wolf, Beverly, 8, 186
Wolf, Maryanne, 142, 143
Word blindness, 4
Word Detectives (Unit I), 111, 146–150
Word families, 67
Word origin, 69–70, 87, 89, 98–99, 102
Word segmentation, 52
Word-form storage, 119–120
Words
  concept, 75–77
  creating syntax with, 144–145
  decoding, 107*t*, 124
  high-frequency, 147
  for spelling instruction, 88–89, 100
Working memory, 65–66, 134, 150, 156,
    205–206
Writing
  across-the-curriculum movement, 110,
    155
  activities for, 64, 108
  attention during, 96
  computers and, 92
  connection to oral language, 16, 31–33, 57,
    60, 86, 205
  defined, 93
  direction of, 152
  English is the second language and, 103
  executive function and, 134
  expressive, 90–92
  grammar of teaching, 155, 208–209
  instruction in, 123, 142
  reading and, 178–179
  spelling and, 87–90, 99
  strategies for, 82–83, 94–95
  see also Composition; Handwriting